BRIA
&
ROSE MA

Conq
and reconquests
of Menorca

Micaela Mata

Traslated by *Bruce Laurie*

Cover design: *Vilaseca/Altarriba Associats*

Grafics courtesy: *Edicions 62*

First edition: April 1984

© Micaela Mata

ISBN: 84-398-1387-2
Depósito legal: B. 14397-1984

Printed in Spain

Imprenta Juvenil, S. A.
Maracaibo, 11 - Barcelona-30

Contents

Part III: 18th CENTURY

Due to Menorca's geographical position, the saga of the conquests and reconquests of the island is a history of its own, separate to a large extent from that of the Iberian peninsula, though naturally very much influenced by it. Although closer to the coasts of Europe, both to the north and east, Menorca was nevertheless, politically and socially, the most isolated of all the Balearic Islands and the last of these islands to be wrested from Arab * rule by the Crown of Aragon at the end of the thirteenth century. But Catalan colonisation, although exterminating many of the inhabitants and implanting its own race and religion, did not destroy the Arab architecture or place-names. In the sixteenth century, deprived of the protection of the House of Austria in Spain, Menorca had to undergo the brutal punishment of constant attack by Mediterranean pirates, becoming — on account of her strategic position — both the refuge and the victim of the corsairs. Early in the eighteenth century, the arrival of the Bourbons in Spain confirmed the Menorcans in their Catalan and insular patriotism, and they took up arms on behalf of the Austrian pretender to the Spanish throne, Charles III; but later, disillusioned by his neglect of their interests, they became Anglophobes during the first English occupation which followed their uprising, and fiercely defended their traditional Catholicism. Caught up in the turbulence of European politics of the day, they were obliged to accept a short French occupation in 1756, their main concern being to protect their own autonomy as far as possible. This

* The rulers of Menorca from about 950 to 1287 A.D. were Arabic in culture and language, Moorish by race and Moslem within the Islamic faith, and thus — or as Saracens — are they variously referred to in this work. In popular usage the word Moors described almost any foreigner from Mediterranean lands, including the Turks.

occupation, like the English one which preceded it, brought some benefits to the island, but the Menorcans remained in their hearts attached to their past independence. The second English occupation gave way in 1782 to a Spanish government which had little sympathy with Menorca's insular individuality, and when English troops arrived for the third time, the islanders, tossed hither and thither for almost a century by the various European powers, welcomed them meekly. Menorca's unusual international history ended with the Peace of Amiens in 1802, when the island was finally incorporated under the Crown of Spain.

These complex events, far from destroying Menorca's unique personality, served rather to strengthen its very substance. The wells, architectural styles and names left by the Arabs; the civic sense transmitted to the people by the religion, language and laws of the Catalans; the awareness of external danger aroused in them by the Spanish; the culture and refinement they perceived in the French; the respect for liberty and prosperity brought in by the English; all this forms an indelible part of Menorca, even though it may not have been part of the inherent nature of her people. Simple and reactionary, the Menorcans opposed innovation; sober and hard-working, they put aside privileges; cut off and threatened, they isolated themselves and took no part in public affairs. Like her rough and over-worked land enclosed by ancient dry-stone walls, like her tangled Mediterranean woods surrounded by pastures, her rocky cliffs and hidden beaches, Menorca in her history is austere, inviolable and secret.

Part I

13th CENTURY

THE CONQUEST OF MENORCA BY THE KINGDOM OF CATALONIA AND ARAGON

Historical appraisal

Catalonia achieved its identity and became part of European international history at the beginning of the Middle Ages, since when it took an active part in the diplomatic and territorial struggle of the kingdoms which fought to achieve political preponderance in the Mediterranean. Although its natural wealth and military strength were well below those of its adversaries, its dynamic drive both in commerce and war led it to play a leading part in the scenario of Mediterranean history during the Early Middle Ages. During this period, the Catalan-Aragonese Confederation carried on religious wars against the Muslims overseas, repelled frontier attacks by the French, intervened directly in the dynastic struggle of the House of Anjou in the south of Italy, and defended itself against unjust Papal discrimination, developing at the same time a progressive political structure in consonance with its commercial and expansionary needs.

The history of Catalonia's territorial conquests had as its basis the creation of a naval power which grew naturally and gradually from the time of the expulsion of the Moors onwards. By the eleventh century Catalonia possessed a navy sufficient not only to defend its coasts but also to protect the nascent maritime trade with the republics and kingdoms of the western shores of the Mediterranean.

Its kings were quick to recognise the importance of the sea in the life of the country and identified themselves with a naval support policy which was to become closely linked with its commercial development. Orders favouring the navy had been promulgated since the middle of the eleventh century when the Count of Barcelona, Ramón Berenguer II, proclaimed the right of naval protection and safe-conduct by establishing the custom of *Omnes Quippe Naves*: «All ships which arrive at or depart from Barcelona, by night or by day, shall be in a state of peace and truce, under the defence of the Prince of Barcelona, from Cape Creus to Salou». For his part, Jaime the Conqueror ordered that trade with Egypt, Ceuta and other Arab countries should be carried out preferably by Catalan ships; journeys to Levant waters became so numerous that the King bestowed on Barcelona the right to appoint Consuls in the more important foreign ports for the protection of sailors and traders. By 1258 the Board of Officials of the Port of Barcelona had drawn up regulations covering procedures for maritime trade.

The natural consequence of these developments in the merchant navy and of the burgeoning prosperity of this fleet was the enlargement of the royal navy, which was to bring about the victorious military actions of Jaime I and his successors. The kingdoms of Majorca, Sicily and Sardinia were the trophies won by Catalan ships; Catalan admirals, crews, citizens and traders formed one of the principal elements which initiated the tough struggle for Catalonia's expansion outside the Peninsula. Roger de Lauria, Ramón Marquet, Berenguer Mallol, and many other fervent figures made possible not only the conquest of the Balearic Islands, Tarifa and Gibraltar but also the warlike incursions into Greece, the Nile delta and the Syrian coast. These brilliant maritime expeditions were to continue for several centuries and would provide the foundation for the strength of Catalonia and Aragon against the Mediterranean powers of the Middle Ages, as well as forming the basis for the political development of Spain itself in the history of Europe in the Modern Age.

During the first part of the twelfth century, Jaime the Conqueror began his Mediterranean expansion with the conquest of the independent political nucleus which the Arabs had established centuries ago in the Balearic Islands. The Conqueror, always uneasy about Muslem power, all too close to Catalan shores, which was endangering the development of Christian shipping and trade, set sale from Salou to fight the Arabs on 5th November 1229 with a large squadron composed of 150 vessels. In his *Llibre dels Feits* (Book of Actions) the King excitedly describes the scene: «*E feia bell veer, que tota la mar semblava blanca de velas, tant era gran l'estol.*» «It was a beautiful sight: the whole sea seemed white with sails, so vast was our fleet.»

The Catalan King sought political expansion in the Mediterranean and at the same time security on the sea itself. This ambitious programme was carried out with the backing of the Catalan nobility and incipient bourgeoisie, eager to safeguard the route to the Levant so essential for its markets. Joint support of the two kingdoms, Catalonia and Aragon, was however indispensable if these territorial aspirations were to be realised. Jaime I therefore directed his attention to the Aragonese, a people more interested in their internal problems than in the country's external policy, threatening them that if they did not collaborate «not only would Catalonia lose its Empire and the ascendancy it has over the seas, to the complete advantage of its navigation and trade, but Aragon would again become the victim of Moorish invasions».

Once the Arab danger on the seas had been removed and the kingdoms of Valencia and Murcia conquered, Catalonia left to Castile responsibility for the territorial struggle against the Moslems in the Peninsula. This enabled the King to concentrate on the creation of his future empire, thus initiating the Italian policy which, after the conquest of Mallorca, was his second objective in the Mediterranean struggle. He fortified this policy by marrying his son, Pedro, to Constanza, heiress to the King of Sicily.

The result of this marriage was to be a long war, destined to last for several generations, against the House of Anjou which, following a Mediterranean policy parallel to that of the Catalans, was attempting to take possession of Sicily; it was this which led to the frontier conflicts between Catalonia and France, the latter being allied to the Angevins. Pedro III followed the steps taken by his father, the Conqueror, towards the integration of Catalonia and Aragon in the thirteenth century. He opposed every threat to his expansionist policy, tenaciously defending his rights to the Sicilian crown. Anxious, moreover, to achieve greater power and unity in his kingdoms, he organised an invasion of Mallorca whose King, Jaime II, was his

11

brother, who had inherited the whole of the Balearics through the lamentable distribution of his lands made by Jaime I. When he died, Pedro the Great left in the hands of his son, the *Infante* Alfonso, the expedition which once again set sail for Mallorca from the naval base at Salou in November 1286.

Alfonso, now crowned king of Catalonia, Aragon, Mallorca and Valencia, continued the Mediterranean policy of his predecessors and the struggle for territorial expansion. Aware of the responsibility he had inherited, he defended indirectly the independence of Sicily and achieved the conquest of Mallorca.

The strategic position of Menorca exposed the island to serious risk of attack by the enemies of the King of Catalonia-Aragon, whose maritime route to Sicily would thus be cut. A further aggravating feature was that, although this island paid tribute to the kingdom of Mallorca, its government was in the hands of an Arab chieftain of dubious fidelity to the Crown and virtually autonomous.

A few months after coming to the throne, Alfonso the Liberal, as he was called, mustered a considerable expeditionary force in Salou and set off with his fleet to conquer Menorca on 22nd November 1286. This conquest was to incorporate the destiny of the Menorcan people into the history of Catalonia.

I. Alfonso the Liberal,
II of Catalonia and III of Aragon

—

I

The *Infante* Don Pedro found himself at the height of his campaign against the Moors in Murcia when his wife, Constanza of Sicily, was delivered of his first-born son, Alfonso, on 4th November 1265, in the episcopal palace of Valencia.

The future Alfonso the Liberal (or *el Franco*) II of Catalonia and III of Aragon, was descended in direct line from the post powerful royalty of his time: Jaime I of Aragon and Manfred of Sicily were his grandfathers; Louis VII of France, Andrew II of Hungary and the Emperor Frederick II his great-grandparents. His closest relatives were the kings of Portugal and Castile. A magnificent concentration of royal blood and of hereditary potential, combined with abundant qualities of command, dash and courage, which were to make of the young prince yet another of those vital Catalan monarchs of the Middle Ages.

Be that as it may, the child Alfonso began his life in conventional manner beside his mother, an exceptional woman if we are to believe the chronicler of the day, Muntaner, who, with his usual tenderness for the royal house, considered that Constanza was «the most beautiful and intelligent creature, and the purest that had been born since the Holy Virgin Mary». «The Madonna Queen», as Manfred's daughter was respectfully known after her marriage to the *Infante* Don Pedro, was considered heiress to the kingdom of Sicily and future queen of Catalonia and Aragon. She devoted herself scrupulously to looking after her son and her palace, assisted by two nurses, Doña Sancha de Luna and Doña Sancha Tovia. Don Alfonso must have been a lively child to judge by the large quantity of shoes he destroyed. His footwear was of canvas, but he needed a new pair every ten days, as was diligently noted down by the «Madonna Queen», with the price (six *dineros* for the usual shoes and double that amount for gilded ones for dress occasions), in the «Book of the Court». Among the many entries of daily household expenditure appear also the two *dineros* spent on rue and chestnuts which the future King Alfonso had to take at the age of little more than a year when he felt indisposed. Apart from treating him with the dubious remedies of the day, his mother took care that he should eat his proper ration of sugar, spices and bread soup, and from the age of two she fed him a substantial amount of meat. All this was set out in her complete dietary, under the headings «Bread in Court» and «Meat in Court».

Life at the court of the *Infantes* Don Pedro and Doña Constanza was austere, well ordered and of only relative abundance (the royal family was not rich and the modest allowance of 100 silver marks paid by the King, Don Jaime, had of necessity to be augmented by voluntary donations, together with some tributary payments and debts) and palace manners were so coarse that Queen Helen of Sicily, Constanza's step-mother, was shocked by the vulgarity and ill-breeding of the Catalans. This lack of refinement is understandable if one takes into account the unceremonious life, with its constant movements from one place to another, which for diplomatic and military reasons (not to mention economic difficulties) the Catalan kings of the age were obliged to lead. The young *Infantes* were dragged around after the court on its constant journeys to Barcelona, Valencia or Zaragoza on horseback, on the croups of mules or in small litters. There would be stops of greater or lesser duration in the uncomfortable and not always friendly noblemen's castles. One of the first journeys Alfonso made, when he was not yet two, was to Constantí (Tarragona) where, to flatter the Catalans, his brother Jaime (later to become his faithful ally) was baptised.

Muntaner, in another burst of admiration and affection, assures us that the young *Infantes* were the wisest princes in the world, «the most proficient at arms and all kinds of deeds», and that on these journeys from province to province they would take part in the lively hunts for deer, wild boar and bears, which helped also to supplement the insipid travel rations. The tournaments and military sports which were organised in the castles would improve the children's handling of clubs, lances, cross-bows and other weapons — a training vitally necessary in that world of constant wars.

Pedro the Great distinguished himself brilliantly at all physical sports and would soon impose his inclinations on his son who, however little he may have inherited of the splendid physical vigour of his grandfather the Conqueror and the fine bearing of Don Pedro, must have been a strong and healthy child and doubtless very fair and handsome, as were his Catalan forbears and his mother's Teutonic family, the Hohenstaufens. However, in addition to games and hunts, Alfonso soon had to get down to lessons, tutored by the Aragon baron, Blasco Jiménez de Ayerbe, and strictly supervised by his father, who was a poet of some merit and who must also have inculcated Alfonso with his intellectual tastes. The frequent visits of Guillermo de Cervera and other troubadours and mummers helped to enliven the boring palace life with verses which usually transmitted the state of opinion of the people and probably aroused the imagination of this lively, conscientious and possibly rather pedantic boy. In his political and diplomatic education he had much to learn from the royal advisers and especially from the uncompromising Gilaberto de Cruilles, who collaborated so effectively with Pedro III and later with Menorca's conqueror himself.

Alfonso's life in world affairs began young, and although he took no active part in the matter, on 2nd October 1273, when he was not yet eight years old, he was promised in marriage by the Treaty of Sor to Princess Eleanor, daughter of Edward I of England. This marriage pact, which implied Anglo-Catalan *rapprochement* on the diplomatic level and a balance of force against the French, was to accompany him with its ups and downs throughout his brief life, although the marriage itself never took place. But his real incorporation into the life of the country began with the death of his grandfather, the Conqueror, and the coronation in Zaragoza of his father, the *Infante* Don Pedro, as King of Catalonia, Aragon and Valencia. When the sumptuous coronation festivities were over on 16th November 1276, the vassals of the new King swore homage and fidelity to his heir, Prince Alfonso, an important political innovation designed to bring to an end the eternal arguments and disagreements between the nobles of the kingdom.

Don Alfonso did not delay putting into practice the lessons learnt as a child. Following family tradition, at the age of fourteen he found himself responsible for handling an insurrection of Catalan barons led by the Count of Foix. His father the King, occuped in repressing the Moorish rebellion in Valencia, gave him wide powers, and although he had to rush hurriedly to his son's aid at the beginning, he later appointed him commander of the Valencian and Aragonese troops at the siege of Balaguer, where the rebel barons were strongly fortified. The city was reduced in July 1280 and Don Alfonso led the conquered nobles to Lérida. To quote the words of Desclot, a contemporary historian: «... and here he took them to a palace, had them clapped in irons and well guarded». As well as being his first major feat of arms and his first contact with the reality of the dangerous spirit of rebellion of the nobility, this experience was also his initiation into political life, for his father conferred on him the power of being arbiter and absolute judge in deciding the fate of the Viscount of Cardona, the Count of Pallars and Bernat Roger de Erill, leaders of the rebellion. Alfonso resolved to fine and pardon them, rehabilitating them to their former estates. His reconciliation with these men, who in the future would become faithful allies of the Crown, gives early evidence of the flexible attitude of the Prince and the healthy respect he thus merited from his vassals.

The *Infante* Alfonso hardly had time to complete his apprenticeship before his father, Pedro the Great, appointed him Regent and universal heir to his kingdoms. At this moment, 6th June 1282, Pedro was about to embark from Portfangós on the remarkable undertaking which was to be the conquest of Sicily. The King put to sea in the ships of Ramón Marquet and had them painted in gay colours — white, red, yellow, green and blue — specifying that «on all the paintwork there shall be the royal arms in every galley and ship». Several months later he landed in Trápani to avenge the death of King Manfred and liberate the kingdom from occupation by the House of Anjou, invested as sovereigns there by the Holy See.

At seventeen Alfonso found himself up against the difficult problem of governing his country and trying to find a solution to the labyrinthine diplomatic problems which his father had created with the Sicilian war. His immediate worries were to obtain the economic resources which the King demanded and to provide him with the horses, arms and troops necessary for his Sicilian campaign; to watch over and keep at bay the ever uneasy barons, and to guard against a possible Moorish uprising in the south. But his main concern was to seek some way of placating the wrath of the Vatican and of stopping the threats of the French monarch: rather oppressive tasks for the young man, however obedient, devoted and ardent a collaborator with his father he might be.

The conquest of Sicily unleashed a Franco-Papal fury which gave rise to a whole series of disasters in the kingdoms of Catalonia and Aragon, which from that moment on were under the constant threat of internal strife and foreign invasions. During the dramatic years of 1284 and 1285, Alfonso covered hundreds of kilometers on horseback and was at the head of innumerable battles from Albarracín to the Valle de Arán, amply demonstrating his mettle, his dynamism and that flair for meticulous organisation which so distinguished him. He arrived in the Ampurdán region during the early months of 1285, to prepare the defence of Catalonia against the fateful crusade mounted by the French Pope, Martin IV, as a result of the excommunication which had been imposed on Pedro the Great because of his conquest of Sicily. More than 100,000 crusaders were concentrated in Tolosa, and the fully armed French fleet was cruising off the coast of Catalonia.

The month of January found Don Alfonso in Gerona,

Figueras and Torroella de Montgrí. In March he was in Besalú and again in Gerona. After that he went to Peratallada, staying in the castle of his faithful Gilaberto and Bernat de Cruilles, engaged in the systematic work of preparing castles, troops and victuals.

The King, back from a hazardous visit to Perpignan — an event which confirmed his suspicion of the disloyalty of his brother, Jaime II of Mallorca, and of his alliance with the French — arrived in the Ampurdán and took charge personally of the army. Don Alfonso retired to the rear and took energetic measures to enforce general mobilisation, a task made difficult by the lethargy of the people, provoked by ecclesiastical opposition and widespread want in Catalonia due to the insecurity of the region.

The *Infante* soon returned to the front, but in June the crusaders — aided by a traitor — crossed the pass of Massana, invaded the Ampurdán, took possession of Perelada and besieged Gerona. Alfonso distinguished himself by his bravery in the fight against the invaders and remained in command of the troops along the line of retreat established between the rivers Ter and Fluviá from Gerona to Besalú.

Military affairs on Catalan soil were anything but favourable to Pedro the Great, while, by contrast, the royal fleet under Roger de Lauria won great victories in Naples, Malta and on the Calabrian coast: indeed these actions became legendary in Mediterranean waters. During these moments of danger, the King once again put his trust in the experience, discipline and dash of his seamen and gave urgent instructions to seek out his Admiral, cruising with the fleet in Sicily. While awaiting his arrival he ordered his old and trusted officers, Ramón Marquet and Berenguer Mallol, to harass the French fleet which, occupied in revictualling the invading forces, had anchored in Cadaqués, Rosas and San Feliu. The Catalan flotilla succeeded in carrying out a brilliant action of great prowess against the naval power of the French King and entered victorious into the port of Barcelona with a great many enemy ships in tow.

Roger de Lauria at last arrived in Barcelona at the end

of August, and with no loss of time set sail to find the French fleet. The naval battle took place between Calella de Palafrugell and the bay of Rosas, and during the night of 3rd to 4th September Pedro the Great's fleet won a final victory, destroying the French fleet and the sea-borne communications of the invading army. Desclot immortalised the action in the famous and arrogant phrase of Roger de Lauria when refusing to grant a truce to the French King: «Not even the fish would dare to rise from the sea if they did not have the Catalan colours painted on their tails». With the French demoralised and stricken by disease and their King, Philip the Bold, dead, the crusaders undertook a disastrous retreat and were annihilated in the pass of Panissars.

With the liberation of the Ampurdán, Don Pedro and his son felt able to enjoy a few days' rest and took part in the festivities organised in Barcelona to celebrate the victory. On 27th September the King set off in the direction of Salou where he had ordered a fleet to be fitted out with the object of organising a military expedition to invade Mallorca, in retaliation against the treachery of his brother, Jaime II, and in order to reunite under a single crown the dominions of his father, the Conqueror.

But the King was suddenly taken ill on the way and, nearing death, he ordered a halt at Villafranca del Panadés. He called for Alfonso and solemnly charged him with the Balearic expedition, ordering him to go ahead with the 500 horsemen, 2,000 *almogávares* and the 60 armed galleys captained by Roger de Lauria, Ramón Marquet and Berenguer Mallol which were waiting, fully rigged, in Salou.

The *Infante,* weeping, bade farewell to his father, kissing his hands and his feet. The King embraced him and blessed him repeatedly as they parted. Some days later (during the night of 10th November 1285) «this Lord, Don Pedro of Aragon, the finest gentleman in the world and the wisest, the most generous of all people, raised his eyes to heaven and his soul gently left his body, as though he were an innocent child».

Don Alfonso had already landed in Mallorca and had

advanced to Torres Llavaneras without meeting resistance when he received the news of his father's death. He was in the midst of negotiating the unconditional surrender of the island, and the new King, with the good sense and strict discipline that characterised him, did not make public the death of Pedro the Great until he had received the capitulation of Mallorca and the oath of allegiance of the syndics in the capital. Ibiza also surrendered and Alfonso achieved the first conquest of his reign without loss of men, demanding of his troops the same generous behaviour towards the populace that he himself had shown to their rulers.

II

Alfonso II of Catalonia, III of Aragon and I of Valencia and Mallorca was just twenty years of age when he ascended the throne in January 1286.

In the gothic painting in the Catalan Museum of Art in Barcelona he appears as a tall young man, slim, fair haired, with a pale complexion, penetrating eyes and sad expression, and with extremely refined and sensitive features. The fair moustache and beard scarcely hide the full, finely chiselled lips and the well-rounded firm chin. This portrait of the young King reflects not so much the man of action as the intelligent and compassionate dreamer. The high forehead, the straight large-boned nose, and the big ears give some indication of the man of controlled strength, courage and energy, which indeed he was.

Despite his extreme youth, which naturally deprived him of some authority and wisdom, Alfonso III ascended the throne well-equipped to rule. His great physical courage had been amply demonstrated on the battlefield; his work in government was carried out with a tenacious, teutonic meticulousness and an inexhaustible, altruistic vitality, qualities which had characterised him since adolescence.

Perhaps this very youthfulness was the cause of a marked tendency to express the contradictions evident in his character. He would turn easily from a position of intransigence to one of excessive capitulation, and from an exaggerated generosity to incomprehensible hardness. This apparent insecurity — which he disguised with a systematic ordering of his affairs — showed itself at times as prudence and generous good faith, while at others it turned into the cruelty typical of his time.

Brave and headstrong, orderly and benevolent, moderately intelligent: from these brush-strokes emerges the picture we have of him across the centuries. At all events, his undoubted natural propensity towards a greatness of spirit would lead him to grant franchises and liberties to the vassals of his kingdoms and would earn him the titles of «the Liberal» and «the Generous».

However, these attributes of clemency and liberality did not diminsh the force of his warrior spirit, nor did they make him forget the diplomatic and military principles inherited from Don Pedro; and the faithfulness and obedience which had governed his relationship with his father were to continue throughout his short reign, giving him a code and an ideal to pursue. Alfonso the Liberal began his reign with optimism and energy; his first action was to confront the Franco-Angevin-Papal alliance, sending his brother Jaime, who had inherited the crown of Sicily, a promise of unconditional aid, by which he bound himself to defend against any enemy the kingdom of Sicily. This action highlights his sense of family solidarity and his very personal spirit of faith in the international political development of Catalonia. It was, however, an action which would expose him to an infinity of problems, not only in connection with his powerful foreign enemies but also as regards his national policy.

The Aragonese Union showed itself to be both strong and discontented, constantly aiming at the submission of the throne to its own capricious will. Sancho de Castilla, subtle manipulator of his alliance with the French, proved as hostile and disloyal as he had been with Pedro the Great. Jaime de Mallorca, taking refuge in his states of Roussillon, Cerdagne and Montpellier, was constantly threatening the Pyrennean frontier and, supported by the French King, Philip the Handsome, organised frequent — albeit unsuccessful — incursions against the Ampurdán. But it was the Angevins and their Papal allies who were the enemies most to be feared, as much for the military power of the House of Anjou in the Italian peninsula as for the diplomatic and moral power exercised by the Holy See throughout the Christian world.

Despite this, the King of Catalonia and Aragon had good reason to view the future with confidence and to feel strong enough to confront the danger of the foreign alliance.

Against his uncle, Jaime II, he was able to count on the undeniable prestige and territorial advantage conferred upon him by his conquest of Mallorca; and against Sancho de Castilla, on the fact of holding the Castilian *Infantes* prisoner in Játiva. Another hostage of inestimable diplomatic value was the young Prince of Salerno, son of King Charles of Anjou, taken prisoner by Roger de Lauria in a naval battle which took place off Naples shortly before the death of Pedro III and jealously guarded in the castle of Siurana. A second legacy from Pedro the Great to his son, of considerable importance in facing his foreign enemies, was the victorious Ampurdán campaign and the humiliating retreat of the French. But, as so often seems to be the case in mediaeval Catalan history, the greatest strength of Alfonso the Liberal lay in his navy. It was his naval superiority which would make possible the conquest of Menorca and would be essential for retaining the island.

It was the right moment — and politically necessary — to annex Menorca, that island which occupied a geographical position of the greatest importance in Mediterranean naval strategy. Although Menorca at present paid tribute to the Crown of Aragon, her feeble vassalage left her exposed to the risk of falling easily into the hands of the harassed enemies of the King, which would be a grave danger to the fleet charged with protecting Catalan trade with the Levant and ensuring the safety of the vital maritime route between Catalonia and Sicily.

Alfonso the Liberal thus set sail from Salou on 22nd November 1286 with the expeditionary fleet which was to invade Menorca. Like his grandfather when he conquered Mallorca, the young King was exactly 21 years old.

II. Menorca - the object of conquest

I

«In the direction of Sardinia, towards the wind which sailors call the «*Gregal*» (the «Greek» or North-East), there is another island, governed by Mallorca, which they call Menorca and which is about thirty miles away. This island possesses a pleasant, level city close to the port which faces the main island. There are also other groups or clusters of houses, villas and very beautiful mansions built in an ostentatious style. The land, however, is not abundant in wheat, though it is most suitable and nourishing for livestock, both large and small. There are mountains in the interior, not so high as those of Mallorca, and on one of them there is a very fine strong castle which the Saracens call Santa Águeda; it is not situated on one side of the island, but almost in its centre. The island has four ports, Ciudadela, Sereyna, Fornells and Mahón, the last-named of which is famous among and above all the ports in the world because, according to what some maintain, it is almost five miles deep and on either side there are many safe coves which anywhere else would themselves be called ports. In the middle are two islands, not far apart, which are very suited to rabbits. Its waters are not sterile but are very good for oysters and for the wide variety of other fishes of that sort. They are also favourable for the formation of mother-of-pearl and beautiful pearls themselves. The inhabitants of the island have abundant meat, milk and cheese; of bread and wine they have sufficient, but somewhat little compared with other countries.»

This is the enthusiastic picture of Menorca given by the old sailor Pedro Martel, a citizen of Barcelona, on describing the Balearic Islands at a banquet offered for Jaime I which inspired the conquest of Mallorca.

The attractive island of Menorca belonged to the Saracens for almost four centuries, after the Caliphate of

Cordoba annexed it to its empire in 903; later it became part of the kingdom of Denia, and subsequently was under the dominion of the Almoravide and Almohade dominions. Moslem *Menurka* was always under the direct jurisdiction of the ruler of the *wadi* of Mallorca who, although he appointed the governor who ruled the island, left its people to enjoy a certain liberty and autonomy. This lieutenant-governor grouped his domains together in an orderly manner, charging his officials with responsibility for the administration of the four principal districts: Hasmuljuda, Beni Saida, Beni Fabin and Alscayor; whilst the powerful *jeques* controlled the numerous villages scattered mainly in the southern, warmer and more sheltered part of the island. The governors and other gentlemen of distinction inhabited luxurious palaces in *Medina-Menurka* (Ciudadela), the capital and largest town, living in the style and good taste of the Arabs of that time. The authorities must have had no fear of foreign invasion because the castles of Mahón, Ciudadela and the chief one at Sent Agayz (Santa Águeda) were the only ones of any consideration in the island and, moreover, if the truth be told, were not very effective, for even Sent Agayz was really no more than a luxury walled palace where the Moorish authorities spent their summers.

In this small island, looking on the map rather like a dried-up haricot bean, and girded by a coastline of cliffs and sheltered beaches, the Menorcan people lived a quiet life, devoted mainly to agriculture and cattle-raising. Their wealth was based on the legendary wisdom of the Moors in matters of husbandry and cultivation and on their incredibly efficient system of irrigation, by means of which they converted barren land into amazingly fertile gardens. Ditches and wheel-wells, some more than a hundred meters deep, irrigated the plants and trees in gardens and orchards, hidden in narrow valleys or *barrancos*. Olive, almond and fig trees grew among the well-tended vineyards on the slopes of the pine-clad hills. On the stony high ground and in the wind-swept plains, wheat, oats, maize and some esparto grass were cultivated, protected by carefully erected stone walls. Winter pastures covered the slopes and plains of the centre of the island, where the numerous cattle, the principal wealth of the island, grazed. The islanders concentrated above all on the task of augmenting and improving this natural fecundity by importing animals for wool and milk, thus increasing their economic and nutritional resources.

The greater part of the population lived in the countryside, both the nomadic bedouins who worked at cattle-raising wherever the land was suitable, and the land-owning *jeques* who cultivated the fields around the scattered farmhouses to which they gave their names, leaving their particular stamp in the architecture of the white-washed walls.

Eminent historians agree on the fact that the Moorish population before the conquest must have been considerable. Pedro Riudavets says in his history of the island that «within a few years of taking possession of it, the Africans were able to aid the Bey of Bone with 15,000 men»; and later Hernández Sanz writes: «Menorca at that time was so densely populated ... that her lands could not be sown with sufficient for a tenth of her population;» and although Muntaner exaggerates the figure considerably in his description of the conquest, «when women, children and men had been taken prisoner, the total amounted to some 40,000 people», there was unquestionably a large number of inhabitants.

At the present time, after 700 years, very many places retain their sonorous Arabic names, with the prefix «Bini» (which may be translated as «house of the sons or successors of») and, particularly in the southern part of the island, there is a profusion of place-names with the prefix «Rafal» (from the Arabic «*rahal*» meaning large property) and «Al» (equivalent to the definitive article «el» in Spansh): Ben Taufa, Bini Beque, Benialy, Benissaid, Rafalet, Es Rafal, Alcaufar, Alfavaret, Algendaró and Addaya, among others. Riudavet states that at the beginning of the eighteenth century there were still 85 place-names with the prefix Bini (indeed they still exist today). On the basis of this information we have tried to estimate the population of *Menurka*. Taking into account Moslem polygamy, some fifteen or twenty people (including servants and labourers) may have lived in each farmhouse. This would give a total of approximately fifteen thousand rural inhabitants, including the Berber nomads. To this figure must be added the population of the four most important towns which, small though they were, would each have some two or three thousand inhabitants, giving a further eight or ten thousand. The result of this, with no exaggeration, comes to twenty-five or thirty thousand people. Muntaner, after all, was not so far from the truth.

In this serene, pre-Christian Menorca, with constant comings and goings in its magnificent ports, not all the islanders were Moors: there was a considerable colony of Jews and Christians, natives of the island, who worked in industry or commerce. For the main part, these were the people who dealt in exports to the Barbary coast and to the markets of Provence, Pisa and Genoa, and in imports of products needed by the island.

Commerce in general benefited from the freedom which was granted to Jews and Christians. Travellers who happened to be passing through were allowed to reside in the consultates and to meet in the *alhóndigas* (public corn exchanges) where the buying and selling of grain was carried out.

A. de Besers was the owner of one of these public granaries and his Christian faith was not allowed to stand in the way of his obtaining, in 1285, authorisation to manufacture and sell wine from the grapes of the island. Another of the Christians living in Menorca at that time was Ramón de Montsó, a native of the island; according to contemporary documents, he received a large estate near Mahón under the distribution of conquered lands made by Alfonso in 1297. In Mahón there was a church dedicated to San Blas in which, it would appear, the Aragonese were able to hear Mass shortly after the conquest. Further proof that the Menorcan Moslems were always tolerant of foreign faiths appears as far back as 1135, when an ecclesiastic named Gabino signed a notarial act in Amalfi under the title of Bishop of Menorca. And at the time of the *Taifas,* a governor named Ali-ben-Muyahid ordered that all Christian churches in his realm should come under the episcopal jurisdiction of Barcelona.

II

The peace and tranquility which Menorca had enjoyed for years under Moslem rule was suddenly interrupted in 1229 with the news of the invasion of Mallorca by Jaime I. After a hard struggle the Moorish king of Mallorca was defeated and his kingdom subdued. The Conqueror left again for Catalonia, leaving the island of Menorca if not forgotten, at least relegated to some future occasion in which his presence on the Peninsula might be less essential. Menorca remained, therefore, converted for the time being into an independent kingdom, governed for two short years by the *Almojarife Caid*, Abu-Abdullah-Mohamed, until in June 1231 the Catalan-Aragonese King again visited Mallorca. Jaime I took advantage of this journey to annex the lesser Balearic Island, Menorca, a necessary step in his expansionist policy and one which would wipe out, at this juncture, his recent failure in Navarre.

Jaime I reached Mallorca in the spring of 1231 and landed in Portopí with the aim of subduing a group of Moors who had taken refuge in the mountains and were proving an obstacle to his plans for the organisation of the country. On the urging of his lieutenant-governor, the Templar Raimundo Serra, who assured him that the mere threat of an invasion of Menorca would be sufficient to obtain its surrender, the King conceived an ingenious and cunning plan which would prove its worth by achieving the peaceful submission of the island.

The three nobles, Berenguer de Santa Eugenia, Asalid de Gudar and Serra himself, embarked in the three galleys which had brought the monarch to Mallorca. Accompanied by a handful of soldiers, they set sail for Ciudadela. The inhabitants of that city together with their nobles and the mayor, on seeing armed galleys approaching their shores, rushed to the defence of their beaches, fearful of a sur-

27

prise assault; but on finding that the ships were flying the standard of the Catalan King, they went out to give them a friendly welcome.

The emissaries of the Conqueror continued their course straight into the narrow harbour; then they turned and prudently anchored astern, despite the show of cordiality on the part of the Menorcans. They sprang ashore and presented their credentials to the Moorish authorities which were ceremoniously read out in Arabic by the interpreter, Solomon, an Aragonese Jew who accompanied them. The Moorish chiefs invited the royal representatives to remain on shore and offered them the hospitality of the city, whilst they deliberated with their own people the proposals — or threats — of the Christian King. But the Catalan nobles, distrusting such friendliness, preferred to spend the night aboard the galleys, where they received a gift of two hundred chickens, a hundred sheep, ten cows, and bread and wine in abundance.

Meanwhile Jaime I had set up camp with a small retinue in Cap de Pera, the nearest point to Menorca on the island of Mallorca. As darkness fell he ordered a number of fires to be lit among the bushes on the promontory, so as to lead the Saracens in Menorca to believe that a considerable army was about to invade them should they not accept the conditions offered. «And we lit fires in more than three hundred places in the bushes, scattered about as though a large army were encamped there.» Thus the King himself describes the episode in his famous chronicle. The Menorcans fell into the trap and the following morning the *Almojarife* or *Caid,* his brother and the top municipal authorities hastened to present themselves to the envoys of the Christian King, to acknowledge his sovereignty and offer him a share in the poor produce of the island which, they assured the envoys, was hardly enough to feed one-tenth of the population. In exchange for royal protection Abu-Abdullah-Mohamed promised to make an annual tributary payment of 3,000 quarters of wheat, one hundred head of cattle and five hundred lesser farm animals; two hundred ships were to be provided to transport the cattle to Mallorca with the two quintals of butter demanded by Asalid de Gudar; and he also ceded command of the forts and castles of the kingdom. The treaty itself was quickly drawn up, but the procession of the three hundred most important *jeques* who presented their oaths of obedience took three days. Once this ceremony was over the representatives of the *Caid* moved to the Christian camp at Cap de Pera in Mallorca, where the Conqueror received them amid clusters of fennel with which he had decorated his tent — a courteous attention on his part towards the legendary luxury of the Arabs. Jaime ratified the treaty and sealed it with his ring, accepting the Moors as his vassals.

One of the representatives of the *Caid* Abu-Abdullah-Mohamed who visited the camp of the conquerors was Aboac ben Aben Haken, a strange personality who was soon to usurp the leadership of the Menorcan hierarchy and carry out faithfully the terms of the treaty of vassalage during the fifty years of his reign.

Abu Othman Caid ben Haken Al Karashi, to give his official titles, was born in Talavera on 29th January 1209 and, as well as being a good and just governor, was a man of great culture, a writer and poet with a keep knowledge of law and medicine. He had collected for his court library a considerable number of beautifully bound scientific books, and this attracted the visits of wise men — both Moors and Christians — to the intellectual gatherings he organised. On the other hand he had an untoward reputation of being bloodthirsty: he went so far as to inflict the penalty of torture and death on anyone who drank wine, and he punished with similar severity those guilty of equally minor offences.

However that may be, his qualities of intelligence and generosity were great indeed. His loyalty to the Catalan King was without question: he even presented Jaime I with one thousand cows for the crusade to the East which the latter had organised in 1269 but which, because of his advancing years and bad weather, did not take place.

Abu Othman died in January 1281 at the age of seventy-seven. He was succeeded by his son, Abu Omar Haken ben Caid, who, like his father, was a well educated and cultured prince; he was, however, of weak character and altogether a lesser man than his father, although less violent in his habits. He soon displayed his shortcomings and his lack of loyalty to the King of Catalonia and Aragon when, only a few months after taking over the government of the island, he committed the unpardonable crime of betraying his lord and master. This was a fault which Pedro the Great was never to forgive and which, years later, would provide the pretext for taking away the lands of the Moorish *Caid*.

Pedro III, resolved to undertake the hazardous Sicilian campaign against the House of Anjou (who had occupied the kingdom which by right of succession and inheritance belonged to Queen Constanza by virtue of the death of her father, Manfred, in the battle of Benevento), fitted out a powerful squadron of 150 vessels with the object of gaining some bases on the north coast of Africa, from whence he could operate with greater facility in his future theatre of war. He set sail from Portfangós with his fleet commanded by Ramón Marquet on 6th June 1282 and made for the port of Mahón, keeping the secret of his ultimate destination well guarded. After a bad crossing the fleet cast anchor in the centre of the spacious Mahón roads and the King disembarked on Rabbit Island (later known as Isla del Rey, or the King's Island), the very island on which, four years later, his son Alfonso would land with less peaceful intent. Abu Omar Haken ben Caid presented himself to pay homage: he was accompanied by the principal *jeques* of the island, Abdilla, Ali, Mahomet and Binichae. The customary offerings of cattle, eggs, cheese, butter and fresh bread were duly accepted, as well as other gifts such as gold and silver jewels which the governor of Menorca presented personally to the King. The monarch, cautious, did not allow his troops to go ashore without special authorisation, and after a few days' rest in the island the squadron raised anchors and put to sea again for an unknown destination.

The secrecy surrounding the mission of such a large naval formation aroused the suspicions of the Menorcan *Almojarife*. Noticing that the Christian ships were making for the south, he hastily manned a light settee with expert crew and despatched them to Alcoll with orders to warn his allies, the Moslems of Bone and Bougie on the Barbary coast, that a large and well-armed fleet was about to descend upon them.

When, after a week at sea, Pedro the Great reached Alcoll, it was to find the town completely abandoned. His friend the Lord of Constantine, on whom he had counted to establish a bridgehead between Africa and Sicily, had been assassinated. The King learnt from some Pisans anchored in the port that Abu Omar had been behind the disaster. Furious at the treachery, he swore to avenge it by conquering the island. (A clever strategem this, on the part of Pedro, because at that time it was not to him but to his brother, Jaime II of Mallorca, that the *Almojarife* of Menorca owed vassalage.)

Pedro the Great died before he was able to achieve this, but he made his son Alfonso promise solemnly that he would bring about the conquest of Menorca and inflict hard punishment on the island.

III. Reasons and preparations
for the conquest

I

Alfonso the Liberal undertook the conquest of Menorca at a time of serious internal difficulties and no less grave external problems, but apprenticeship at the side of those great statesmen, Jaime the Conqueror and Pedro the Great, had not been fruitless and, following their example, he faced impending danger by attacking.

With his expedition to Menorca, Alfonso endeavoured to find a solution which would resolve worthily his internal problems. The Catalan nobles, while united in their support of the royal cause, were also involved in rivalries and discords amongst themselves; and the Catalan people, impoverished by the constant threat of warlife incursions from Roussillon, needed a distraction and the promise of new riches. In addition, a military undertaking of this sort would quell the amibitons of the powerful Aragonese Union, avid for excessive privilege and always ready to rebel.

The conquest of Menorca was regarded as a necessity, not only to maintain the military prestige of the King in the eyes of his people and those of his foreign enemies, but also as a means of skillfully winning Papal blessing — essential for his external policy — by a religious war against the Moslem heretics. And a new territorial victory would favour him greatly in his future diplomatic negotiations with the Christian world.

Nor did the King forget the importance of Menorca as a strategic point — both offensive and defensive — in the Mediterranean struggle. The proximity of the island constituted a continual threat to his possession of the kingdom of Mallorca, so recently annexed to the Crown of Aragon. A virtually independent Menorca in the hands of a disloyal and suspicious governor would form an ideal springboard from which Jaime II, Alfonso's uncle, backed by the French army and soldiers from Roussillon, might attempt to recover the lands seized from him. And there was always the danger that his uncle might conceive ambitions to occupy the magnificent ports of the island, making them even more necessary to Alfonso as a safe refuge and revictualling centre for his ships which were constantly patrolling the Mediterranean.

Alfonso the Liberal duly justified the invasion of Menorca by maintaining that it represented a well deserved punishment for the treachery of the Menorcan *Almojarife* towards his father at the beginning of the latter's plan to invade Sicily, a treachery which had cost the life of the Lord of Constantine, an ally of Pedro III, and had thwarted his military plans.

Muntaner relates that Alfonso sent clear and precise warning of his intentions to the Menorcan leader, saying that «he would consider evacuating the island» and that «with the help of God he would avenge the lord King his father for the treachery (of the Caid) when he warned the Barbary coast that he (Pedro III) was on his way there.»

The arguments which persuaded Alfonso to invade Menorca were sufficient justification in themselves, but it was also essential to carry out his plan with the greatest possible speed. Apart from the difficulties of organising in so short a time a campaign which presented the dual problem of military and naval coordination, he was impelled to find an urgent solution to his eternal economic difficulties.

The King devoted himself first of all to naval matters, and in May 1286 wrote to Ramón Marquet and Berenguer Mallol (who were both in Barcelona) seeking their advice.

These famous maritime figures, owners of the largest Catalan merchant fleet of their time (probably the first shipping company with capitalist partners), were always at the service of their King, their ships ready to be fitted out and hired by the Crown. During the reigns of Jaime the Conqueror and Pedro the Great, Ramón Marquet had cooperated closely with the royal house (even contributing discreet financial suport), receiving in return for his services the honorary rank of Admiral whenever he led a maritime expedition. Alfonso again showed his great confidence in this citizen of Barcelona by reappointing him Admiral of the fleet which was to conquer Menorca. Marquet was then over fifty, an expert navigator, a man of great integrity and proven fidelity.

The expedition having been agreed, the monarch spent the spring and summer issuing orders and gathering together his nobles and vassals, whilst at the same time raising the subsidies required to finance the war. The many royal letters written from Valencia, Tarragona, Cervera, Cardona and Lérida tirelessly exhort private citizens, as well as cities and municipalities, to supply men, horses, arms, ships and money.

He let his plans be known to his brother, Jaime II, King of Sicily, asking him to send the Admiral, with 40 armed galleys, and he told him that he wanted them for the aforementioned expedition to Menorca. He also wrote to Roger de Lauria, telling him to proceed to Barcelona with the galleys.

Roger de Lauria, an admiral in the service of the Catalan-Aragonese Crown, is without doubt the most outstanding figure in the maritime struggle for Catalan hegemony in the Mediterranean during the early Middle Ages, and one of the most important seamen of all time. His exceptional gifts of command, his naval genius, his astuteness and bravery, merited his being appointed commander of the Admiralty by four Catalan Kings. This Calabrian, who came to the court of Jaime I as a child with his mother, Bella de Amichi, lady-in-waiting to Constanza, and who lost his father in the same battle in which Manfred, King of Sicily, also died, was, according to Muntaner, the «most perfect Catalan», and his life was one glorious tale of naval prowess, hazardous incursions — the very daring of his actions had at times a distinct savour of piracy, not entirely divorced from cruelty — and of uncompromising loyalty to his kings. Naturally, therefore, Alfonso the Liberal could not dispense with the services of this exceptional seaman, and he determined to send for him at once to support his Menorcan campaign.

The young King took an active part in the preparation

of his fleet, but the Catalan navy — and also the merchant navy — were governed by a series of laws and rules established over the years by the Board of Officials of the Port of Barcelona and recorded in the *Ordinationes Ripariae* and in the numerous chapters of the *Llibre del Consolat de Mar*. These wise and strict laws, which the Barcelonese of former times had drawn up for the good order and discipline of their fleet, were the very foundation of the advanced training and the valour of their seamen, on whom the Catalan kings depended so much for their wars overseas.

Love of the sea was always a characterjstic of the Catalan people and, unlike the practice in other nations, enlistment of seamen was voluntary; they swore loyalty to the Crown at a colourful ceremony presided over by the King and the higher command of the Admiralty. All duties performed on board were regarded as honourable, «even the task of rowing, not yet made infamous by laws nor dishonoured by faithless slaves», and each man received for his services his stipulated pay plus whatever booty he could capture — less the one-fifth which the King reserved for himself.

The elegant galleys, *dromos* and *leños*, with their terrible bronze rams in the prow, carried a crew of around 250 men, and many were the posts to be chosen in King Alfonso's warships — from captain, pilot, boatswain, purser, surgeon, carpenter, constable, bugler, etc., to the marines (who fought in boardings and all man-to-man affrays) and the highly-trained archers («the most superb archers in the world», as Muntaner called them) who, with the two bows and 300 arrows assigned to each, bombarded enemy ships. All Catalan seamen were a credit to their King. There were also a large number of oarsmen although the ancient lateen sail, typical of the Mediterranean, was in constant use so as to take advantage of the variety of winds in the difficult coastal navigation of these waters. As the galleys had no more than a sterncastle with a sort of rudimentary cabin, the crews were at the mercy of the inclemencies of the weather, so life on board must have been harsh.

In maritime expeditions, merchant sailing-ships (which the King hired from shipping companies and private owners and fitted out for such occasions) were just as important as galleys. The big-bellied *brisas* and *taridas* carried soldiers, horses, machines of war and other military material; their rounded bows and sterns and their high sides enabled them to carry up to six hundred people (no doubt closely packed); they could also take up to fifty horses, tied together with straps so as to take up the minimum possible space. To simplify embarking and disembarking, some of these vessels were provided with large doors in the bows, rather like those of modern landing craft.

Ramón Marquet and Berenguer Mallol, who had moved to Salou, got down to the task of fitting out and arming all these warships and merchantmen. Pedro Garcés was in charge of the Sicilian flotilla which put into Barcelona on All Saints' Day under the command of Roger de Lauria.

III

The King ordered the Aragonese nobles to organise their campaigns and get their knights and arms into a state of readiness, and also called on the Catalan barons to accompany him on his expedition to the Balearics. The nobility responded well and collaborated generously with men and supplies.

From all corners of the kingdom the barons arrived, wearing plain round helmets, mail and flowing greatcoats emblazoned with their devices and colours. Following them were their knights, armed with lances, clubs and swords, and behind them came the sergeants of the troops and the archers. Fifty horsemen, 100 archers and 200 soldiers attended the Count of Ampurias; the Viscount of Cardona had 50 horsemen, 100 foot-soldiers and a load of 200 bushels of barley plus 100 bushels of wheat. The Count of Prades commanded 300 men with shields, 100 archers and a considerable contribution of wheat; the powerful Count of Urgel brought an army of 500 foot-soldiers, with rations consisting of 200 bushels of wheat and barley; and Viscount Rocabertí from the Ampurdán had 200 knights under his command.

The Church and the towns also responded to the royal call-up: the Archbishop and the corporation of Tarragona organised 10 galleys with their crews; the men of the 15 galleys fitted out by Barcelona received three months' advance pay. The Bishop of Urgel mustered 150 archers and sent 300 bushels of wheat. The Bishop and city of Lérida armed 1,000 men between them, and Zaragoza prepared 25 knights and 300 foot-soldiers. Mallorca promised to man 10 galleys and five other ships and to train 200 soldiers for landing operations, as well as the 300 soldiers which would form part of the army itself. Finally, a contingent of 6,000 Sicilians was expected with the Admiral's squadron.

The young King, an expert warrior, trained his army in the discipline and coordination of arms, the basis of his military structure, as indeed it was of other kings of Aragon and Catalonia. Alfonso perfected his soldiers in the arts of combat, which in the thirteenth century, as at all times, began with a bombardment, followed by a massive charge of armour, finishing up with an advance and the taking up of new positions by the infantry. Arms were different and far less lethal than they were later, but the basis of assault was the same and, then as always, without close cooperation between archers, knights and foot-soldiers, the battle could be lost.

In October the King began to send to Tarragona and Salou the ammunition and men involved in the campaign. The battalion of lancers and archers composed of people from Camarassa, Cubella, Montgay and other Catalan towns were ordered to assemble in Tarragona during the last week of October, there to await the arrival of 4,000 further recruits raised from the Aragonese villages of Ribagorza, Pallars and Tamarit. (These village lads were called up and obliged to fight unless able to free themselves by paying a stipulated price.) At the same time various army officers were told to meet in Salou, and from Cervera the King issued orders to Julián de Bosch to move to the port of Tarragona all the *taridas* to be found in Barcelona. Bernat de Centellas was ordered to report there with his men with the greatest possible speed. Orders were sent from the King to Pedro de Ulbiá and Ramón Escorná, officers in the army, to embark the men and material under their command in the ships of Jaime de Cánovas anchored in Barcelona: 2,500 infantry, 450 horses, flour, biscuits, stone and other war supplies which were waiting in the port. The King advised his officers that he planned to have 6,500 more men to accompany him on the voyage, in addition to the sailors comprising the navy and the soldiers embarked.

These 6,500 men would probably be a detachment of *almogávares*,* a formidable *tercio* of *guerrillas* who responded to the call of the King in time of war. These much feared *almogávares*, brave and hardened in the many frontier struggles against the Moors, were the fulcrum of the intrepid Catalan infantry from the time of Jaime I to Pedro III.

Desclot has left a superb description of these brave fighters: «These people, known as *almogávares*, live solely by their arms and reside not in towns or cities but in the mountains and woods. They fight the Saracens constantly and penetrate into Moorish territory for a day or two, commit rape and pillage, take the Saracens prisoner, and much more. And they live on these earnings. They suffer many privations which other people could not bear, going for two days without eating if necessary, or eating plants from the fields. Their guides are called «*adalids*», people who know the land and roads well. They dress only in a large buttonless coat or short tunic, both in summer and winter; they cover their legs with tight hose, made of hide, and their feet are clad in stout leather brogues. They carry knives and a good strap and a firelock in the belt; and each of them has a lance and two javelins and a leather shoulder-bag, in which they keep a supply of

---

* A class of professional foot-soldiers who formed the most effective element of the army of Pedro the Great in his war against the house of Anjou and were later employed in Catalonia to make frequent incursions against the Moors.

bread to last two or three days. They are very strong people, swift in running and in scaling obstacles. They are Catalans, Aragonese and Serranos.» They had, it may be added, a very strange manner of announcing their dreaded presence. At daybreak, the time at which their combats usually began, the hirsute *almogávares* would knock their arms against stones, producing vivid sparks, and they would throw themselves at the enemy shouting «Via sus! Aür, aür!» (Wake up! Get armed!).

IV

Alfonso was occupied not only in the meticulous organisation of the army but also in seeing to every detail of its provisioning. He wrote repeatedly to his suppliers, placing orders for cereals, wine and wood. These purchases, destined to feed his troops, were scrupulously paid for by the King, and as the donations of wheat and barley from the nobles and town councils, although large, were insufficient for the needs of the expedition, entries for bread and barley figured several times in the lists of orders. It is recorded that the King paid Alberto Medonia 8,500 *reales* for a thousand quarters of wheat, and 50 *libras reales* for the wheat delivered to his officer, Pedro Sitges, whilst other sums were paid for the supply of various cereals to Berenguer Brun, Berenguer Coromina and Ponç Marqués. Among the merchants who undertook to supply the army with 8,000 quarters of wine, Arnau de Escrivá and Ramón Riusech were paid in promissory notes, and the King favoured Tomás Zaludo with the order for bows, irons and other arms for his soldiers, paying him 47 *sueldos* and 25 *dinars* for these items.

Alfonso was already in Mallorca by Christmas 1286, with only a few days to go before the proposed landing in Mahón. He was still concerned with the details of supplies for his warriors, and resorted to the extreme of demanding wheat for the voyage from the villagers of Pollensa, under threat of death and confiscation of their properties if they did not declare the amount of wheat in their possession. The record of supplies is made up almost exclusively of bread and wine, from which it is to be presumed that these were the only rations issued to the army and that supplies of all other foodstuffs must have been left to the rapacity of the soldiers themselves.

The dense forests of Catalonia and Aragon also rendered their tributes to the Menorcan campaign and in this, as in so many other matters, the King proceeded in a legal and orderly manner. In the case of the hills of the district of Bages, the monarch asked the council of Moyá to permit and aid Bartolomé Llop to fell the trees required for the fleet; he issued a acknowledgement of debt for 10,000 *sueldos* to Berenguer de Conques for timber sold.

In order to overcome his financial deficit, Alfonso had recourse to an endless number of measures to raise the money necessary to fund the war. He requested loans, signed promissory notes, imposed subsidies and demanded payment of taxes.

On 28th July 1286 the King thanked the municipality of Mallorca for their offer of 10,000 *sueldos* (and later claimed the money); and the Mallorcan Jews helped him with 20,000 *sueldos* from rents in Inca and other towns. He asked the Jews of Barcelona for a loan of 10,000 *reales* and the municipality for one of 30,000, in addition to the 60,000 which the citizens of that port had already promised to donate to their Admirals, Marquet and Mallol. The Church was obliged to pay the subsidies offered, and Ramón Cavaller was charged with obtaining 500 *sueldos* from the Abbot of Besalú; the priests and rectors of Mallorca came forward with 10,000 *sueldos,* and those of Zaragoza with 500 gold florins. The King signed an acknowledgement of debt in favour of Juan Lope de la Isola for 200 doubloons of Castilian gold, and another in favour of Pedro Garcés for the 50 doubloons he had advanced to Marquet for naval expenses. He demanded the agreed amounts from villages and towns which had redeemed their menfolk from military service: from Tárrega 3,000 *sueldos,* from Cervera 5,000, from Camarassa, Cubellas and Montgay 4,000 *escudos*; from Santa Linya and

Villafranca he demanded the stipulated number of soldiers or the price of their redemption.

Alfonso the Liberal did not hesitate to mortgage the rents and tithes of his lands. So sure was he of the successful outcome of his future campaign that he offered as guarantee the selling price of the slaves and the Moslem property he would obtain in Menorca. He sold two years' worth of the tithes on wine supplied to Guillermo Valentí in Mallorca, and pledged the quit-rents and revenues of the Albufera, quoted at 100 gold doubloons. He ceded the tithes on wheat from the parish of Montuïri to Guillermo de Corbins and his son for 140 doubloons. He obtained a further 60 on the security of the royal dues of Sineu and 150 on that of the tithes charged on the cattle of Mallorca. Alfonso signed a promissory note in favour of Bernardo Botín for 60 doubloons, which he guaranteed with the produce he would obtain from the conquest, and stipulated that he would pay for the barley purchased from Ramón Fraga and Juan de Mora with the Saracens and other booty of war he would obtain in Menorca.

When we bear in mind that in 1294 an ounce of gold was worth 60 *sueldos,* we can calculate the enormous cost which the conquest of Menorca represented for the Crown of Aragon and its subjects.

V

The King imposed meticulous order on everything concerning his army and navy, and before embarking at Salou he showed once again his subtle skill in diplomacy and the strength of his discipline when he dictated new orders and naval regulations, with the object of coordinating his commands and administering justice among his soldiers and sailors. The King appointed Pedro Cornell (one of the nobles who, in the parliament of Huesca the previous October, had opposed most of his war plans) as his lieutenant and Captain-General of his army. His appointed Admirals Ramón Marquet and Berenguer Mallol to be responsible for the fleet and its Catalan crews, while

Pedro Garcés was appointed Vice-Admiral in charge of the 6,000 Sicilians and the squadron due to arrive from Sicily. He designated Acart de Mur as delegate of the Catalan army, and García Garcés de Aranzuri as deputy for the Aragonese soldiers; a very human decision this, and sensible too, for the former was a Catalan and the latter Aragonese. And following this enlightened policy, the King showed himself to be in advance of his time by laying down that any accused man had the right to be judged in accordance with the laws and customs of his native region, and imposed a sliding scale of punishments in accordance with the crime committed.

Alfonso's organisation, however, went further than the mere appointment of his general staff: he drew up specific plans for the naval operations prior to the landing.

The monarch entrusted this activity, one of great responsibility and urgency, to Roger de Lauria, ordering him to put to sea with a small light squadron to explore the island waters and ensure that no enemy ships lay hidden in its bays. Roger de Lauria cruised along the coast of Murcia and the south of the Peninsula (occupied by the Moors), getting as far as Tunis to stop the Mahomedans from sending military reinforcements to the *Almojarife* of Menorca. The intention of the King in sending his Admiral to patrol Mediterranean waters was both a clever naval strategy against the Saracen ships and a tactical necessity for the protection of his landing army against the Provençal fleet which, encouraged by Jaime de Mallorca — anxious to recover his lost lands — could put the whole Menorcan campaign in grave danger.

VI

From this, some idea can be formed of the landing forces which the King had available in 1286. Although Muntaner gives the exact numbers of the maritime forces and the combat troops destined for the conquest of Menorca («so the admiral fitted out the aforesaid 40 galleys ... 700 armed horses and more than 30,000 *almogávares* were assembled», etc.), historians have considered these figures to be somewhat exaggerated, given the exuberant and enthusiastic style of the chronicler of Perelada; but if we follow step by step the preparatory stage of the campaign, we realise that Muntaner's story is fairly close to reality.

Muntaner had the unfortunate habit of calling all infantry troops «*almogávares*», whether they actually were or not, but in this particular case we do know from other sources that 6,000 Sicilians, 3,000 Mallorcans, 2,500 Catalan foot-soldier, 4,000 Aragonese, 1,000 Leridans, and 6,500 «men» (possibly *almogávares*) — a total of 23,000 combat troops — were ready to embark, without counting the sailors, the nobles and their servants.

The 40 galleys which arrived from Sicily with Roger de Lauria were naturally quite insufficient to embark this large body of men, as well as the 700 horses, the weapons of war and the provisions required for the campaign, and the consensus among many historians is that the total number of ships of all classes — transports as well as galleys — which took part in the action probably amounted to 125.

It would seem that the population of Menorca at that time was about 25-30,000, so that the estimate of the number of invading troops would appear to be highly exaggerated: almost one soldier per inhabitant. It is difficult to establish whether this really is an exaggeration or whether it was a military necessity of that age. However, one thing is certain: Alfonso the Liberal prepared the invasion of Menorca with a numerical margin sufficiently wide as to leave no room for doubts about the outcome of the campaign.

The King could not risk a defeat. The success of this war was vital to the Crown of Aragon and Catalonia, both for its territorial importance and for the political prestige it represented in the eyes of the world. Alfonso II of Catalonia and III of Aragon, audacious soldier and meticulous organiser that he was, handled this enterprise with skill and aplomb, even though he may have lacked that imaginative flair that can turn ordinary men into heroes.

IV. The conquest

I

Alfonso the Liberal chose Salou as the port of embarkation for his army and the anchoring ground for the navy that was to take him to conquer Menorca.

Salou is situated just south of Tarragona, in the lee of the Cape of Salou which protects it from the capricious Mediterranean winds and which dominates the beautiful sandy gulf of San Jorge. Supplied with water from the Riudoms river, surrounded by the fertile lands of Baix Camp, within a few leagues of thick forests and a hundred miles from Mallorca, Salou offered many advantages as the point of departure for a military expedition against the Arabs then in possession of Menorca.

It is a sheltered natural harbour and the bay was large enough for Alfonso's ships to manoeuvre easily. Men and supplies could be readily embarked from the wide beach; cereals, soldiers, knights and suppliers were able to reach it from Barcelona and Aragon along roads which in another age had been well planned and paved by the Romans. Not far from the coast were the thick woods which supplied the shipyards, and the countryside was rich in the raw materials needed for naval accoutrements: timber of all kinds, iron, pitch, tar, hemp and esparto grass. Its people were fishermen, good navigators, strong and hard-working men, with centuries of marine tradition behind them.

Thus, it was because of its open roads, the facilities for victualling, its deep harbour, its gentle breezes and its expert workforce experienced in organising naval expeditions that Alfonso gave orders for the considerable contingent of military forces from all capital cities in the kingdom to gather in the port of Salou, at the end of October 1286, and prepare to take part in the Menorcan expedition and landing.

A small detachment of Valencian troops congregated in Denia, whence it could cross more easily to Mallorca to meet up there with the bulk of the army and the royal fleet.

The King's first intention on initiating this campaign was to set sail from Catalonia in early autumn, but the very magnitude of the undertaking and the difficulties which arose forced him to postpone the date of departure until well into November — rather late in the year for an overseas war, with the consequent dangers of storms and bad weather, the principal enemies of all maritime expeditions at that time.

Marquet and Mallol had fitted out and armed the many galleys anchored in the bay; victuals, arms and machines of war filled the holds of the transports; Aragonese, Catalan and Sicilian troops were on the beach ready to embark; the nobles with their servants and horses were in the port awaiting orders from the King...

Alfonso signed his last letter and, at the head of his army, set sail from Salou for Mallorca on 22nd November 1286.

II

The combined manoeuvres of oar and sail must have been spectacular, as the fleet of a hundred ships weighed anchor in that chill November dawn and left the calm waters of the bay on the first stage of its voyage of conquest.

The royal fleet had to make the crossing of 128 nautical miles from Salou to Palma de Mallorca which, with favourable winds and a calm sea, should take about seventy hours. The first phase of the journey, while the fleet cruised in the lee of the waters of the Gulf of Lyon, was fast and easy, but on emerging from the protection of Cape Creus, which sheltered the whole coast of Catalonia, it found itself suddenly lashed by that freezing Provençal wind, the *Tramontana*. Galleys, transports and other ships were assaulted on the open sea by the full force of this mighty north wind, so much more dangerous when it is unleashed in winter. Throughout the ages sailing has been difficult and hazardous when the *Tramontana* blows; but to find themselves in a severe storm from the north with strong cross-waves, in the small open vessels of the thirteenth century, fitted with lateen sails and shipping tons of water, must have made that voyage a most distressing experience for raw troops and experienced seamen alike. And, in addition to the violent storm, the expedition had to endure rain and hail and extremely low temperatures during the crossing. The cold was so intense that the sailors suffered from frostbite. Muntaner, a young man of twenty-two at the time, who no doubt closely accompanied the King, suffered the same hardships as the rest. He has left us a graphic description of the joruney: «The winter that year was so hard that never had there been one with such snow, rain and hailstorms. What shall I tell you about it? It was so hard that we might have been in the Tana sea; so much so that there were galley oarsmen who lost the tips of their fingers.»

The King and part of the fleet were able at last to approach land in the port of Palma, and the remaining ships dispersed by the storm followed one after another until all were reunited in Palma on 18th December.

The bad weather had caused considerable delays, but Alfonso did not rest while awaiting his ships and on the very day of his arrival signed a number of documents which had been drawn up on the island. He went all over Mallorca, completing the preparations for the attack, organising the delivery of grain, getting together the vessels offered by the Mallorcans and demanding that promises of money and troops be made good.

The Moors in Menorca had received news of the preparations for war going on in Mallorca and of the great fleet anchored in the bay of Palma. Doubtless fearing the pulnishment of which they had been warned, the *Almojarife* sent obsequious ambassadors to the King, who endeavoured, by offering him their unconditional vassalage, to dissuade him from his belligerent plans against the island.

Less astute than his grandfather, Alfonso responded with a brusque ultimatum, couched in very hard terms, on 13th December. He sent as emissaries to the court of Abu Omar ben Caid the Aragonese knight Pedro Garcés, and an *alfaqui* (or Doctor of Law) called Bondany, with instructions to negotiate an unconditional surrender, making it perfectly clear that should the island not surrender the King would declare war; in his own magnificent words: «You have gravely erred against our rule by giving succour to our enemies and in other ways; we detach ourselves from you and cast you out from our love.»

Having declared war and made final arrangements for the army and navy, Alfonso ordered his Admirals, Marquet and Mallol, to embark on 21st December. It would seem, however, that perhaps due to the weather or perhaps so that Christmas coud be celebrated on land, the expedition did not leave until later. «After Christmas, which the King celebrated in the City of Mallorca, he gave orders for everyone to embark and set sail for Menorca,» writes Muntaner.

The powerful fleet left the bay of Palma in formation, hoping to cross the 181 kilometers separating Mahón from Palma in a few hours. Colourfully decked out, the royal ships had sailed in line past the island of Conejera and round the cape of Salinas when, in the middle of the narrow channel separating the two islands, near Cape Artruitx, the squadron met with another calamity. A tremendous storm suddenly arose, breaking up the fleet and scattering the ships in all directions. Dismasted and disorientated, they sought refuge in the bays and coves of the Mallorcan coast. Some found shelter in Cabrera, others in Cap de Pera, while the King's ship moored in the calm waters of Porto Petro, from where Alfonso issued royal orders on 29th December.

This new storm was doubtless another violent north wind typical of these waters, call it *Tramontana* or *Mistral,* which in winter, when it snows heavily in the Alps, rages fiercely down the Rhône valley, churns up the waters of the Gulf of Lyon, sweeps across the island of Menorca and turns the sea between the Balearic Islands into an infernal cauldron, with waves and surf surging so strongly from coast to coast that even today, when the *Tramontana* blows hard in winter, passenger ships do not pass along this channel. It should be remembered, moreover, that this occurred in the December of an exceptionally hard winter and that the ships, the size of a recreational yacht of today, were laden with soldiers, horses and the impedimenta of war.

This storm caused a considerable setback in the plans for the Mahón landing and, had it not been for some amazing strokes of luck, could have led to a tragic outcome of the conquest of Menorca.

Alfonso waited impatiently for the weather to change. A few days later, before allowing time for his fleet to reassemble, and with all the confidence and recklessness of his twenty-one years, he put to sea with twenty galleys and entered the port of Mahón. After a feeble show of resistance on the part of his enemies, he disembarked on what was then known as Rabbit Island, situated in the centre of the spacious roads. «He landed in the port of Mahón, with only twenty galleys, on Rabbit Island,» as Muntaner wrote. On 5th January 1287 the King signed certain documents on the island and it was henceforth known as Isla del Rey, or King's Island.

The weather continued harsh. Muntaner puts into the mouth of the King the concern he felt for his troops: «They were in the depths of winter and his people suffered greatly with the bad weather.» And the minute size of the island on which they had landed no doubt aggravated the lack of comfort of those hundreds of men precariously camped there. To keep the soldiers occupied, or simply because they lacked water, Alfonso gave orders for wells to be sunk on the island, with the miraculous result that at only a few meters' depth fresh water flowed abundantly, giving to the spring the name of «Sa Font del Rei n'Anfós» (the Well of King Alfonso). These and other matters occupied the King while he waited day after day, with growing anxiety, for the arrival of his fleet, under the eyes of the enemy forces who, like a nest of ants, watched him from the banks of the port.

It seems incredible that the Moors did not take advantage of this really unique opportunity to annihilate the invaders in one short battle. The Christian King was encamped for twelve days, without receiving reinforcements, on this rat-trap of an island, at the mercy of the Almojarife, and the Moors did not even try to approach it. Knowing as we do, moreover, that the Menorcan chief was provided with a well-organised army («the men of the island were very good soldiers and included excellent Turkish horsemen which the Almojarife had in his pay»), and also that a considerable contingent of troops, flouting the vigilance of Roger de Lauria, had arrived from North Africa in response to his appeal for Moslem help against the invasion by the King of Aragon, it appears doubly incomprehensible that the army of Abu Omar Haken did not decide to assault Rabbit Island instead of awaiting the inevitable enemy invasion which would of course be more difficult to contain. «The Almojarife of Menorca, who had prepared to defend himself with the large reinforcements he had received from the Barbary coast,» according to Muntaner, could depend on an army of some 20,000 men and 700 horses, of which 5,000 foot-soldiers and 500 horsemen had arrived from abroad.

III

«Later on, as the weather became kindlier, now a galley would arrive in the port, now two, now three, all of them mooring as best they could.» Thus Muntaner describes the arrival of the stragglers of the fleet of Alfonso the Liberal.

The King, unable to contain his impatience any longer, was eager to rush on to land with 200 horsemen, but fortunately this impetuous attack was not put into practice, although the news of movement in the enemy camp served to intimidate the Menorcan Almojarife into redeploying his forces into the fortress of Mahón. The Moors' indecision again favoured Alfonso and gave him time to organize his army which, although numerically inferior to that of the enemy, at least amounted now to a respectable number of combatants. Four hundred horsemen and a large detachment of almogávares where drawn up in battle formation on Rabbit Island.

The King called together his general-staff and ordered them to give battle without more delay. The Admiral and the nobles were strongly opposed to an attack under these conditions and begged him to await the arrival of his navy and horsemen, but Alfonso waved aside their objections and commanded that his orders be obeyed. On 17th January 1287, the feast of St. Anthony Abbot, the troops, horses and arms were embarked before dawn in the small launches carried by the galleys and in other boats of shallow draught, and slowly crossed the narrow waters which separated them from the shore.

The Moorish forces were deployed on the high land on the north side of the port, where they lay in ambush for the Christian squadron to prevent its landing. Expecting that the invading force would attack by way of Cala Llonga or Cala Rata — the beaches nearest to Rabbit Island — they armed an improvised stronghold in a small farmhouse overlooking the island and the *calas* where they could fortify themselves if necessary.

Alfonso carried out his offensive cleverly, directing it towards a small cove on the north shore of the port where the land was less steep and easier of access than elsewhere, and here he landed, to the rear of the Arab forces, at the landing stage known as «es Berebí». Observing this strategy, a small detachment of Moors assembled at the foot of the hill to impede the operation, but Alfonso, at the head of his *almogávares,* succeeded in repelling them and skilfully covered the landing of the bulk of his army.

The King deployed his troops and advanced over enemy territory to confront the Arab legion. The unexpectedness of the attack on the enemy's flank gave the King's forces a momentary advantage, but the combat soon moved to a hill (later known as San Jorge) which was in the hands of a strong Moorish contingent, who put up a tough resistance, fighting with courage and bravery. At one moment the Saracens dominated the field of battle, obliging the invading force to give ground. But the young monarch inspired and encouraged his men and, at the head of his troops, assailed the Moorish soldiers with renewed force,

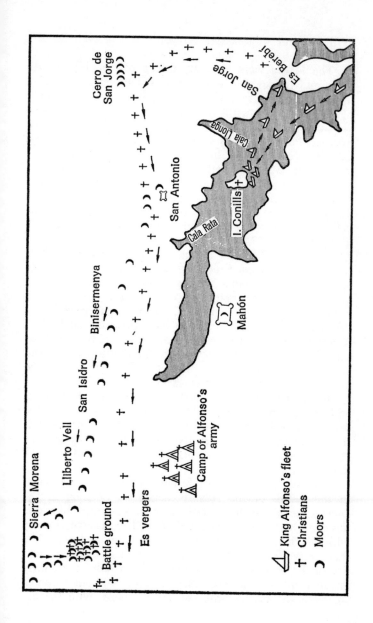

Sierra Morena

Lliberto Vell

San Isidro

Binisermenya

Battle ground

Es vergers

Camp of Alfonso's army

Cerro de San Jorge

San Jorge

Es Berebi

Cala Llonga

San Antonio

Cala Rata

I. Conills

Mahón

△ King Alfonso's fleet

† Christians

ᕼ Moors

to the cry of «Catalonia! Aragon! St. George! St. Anthony!».

The Moors were violently driven off the hill of San Jorge and retreated to other high land nearby, regrouping their forces and fortifying themselves in a strong point which became known as San Antonio. There the Christian divisions attacked again, dislodging them and pursuing them to the high lands of Benisermenya, San Isidro and Lliberto Vell, wooded hills which enclosed the port. By midday the Moslems had climbed to the highest part of Biniaixe (or Sierra Morena), where they regrouped their men and fortified themselves. Alfonso gave orders to remuster his own forces, which were deployed among the fields of San Pons, and set up camp at the foot of the hill occupied by the Moors.

While the Christian troops rested, the Moors received reinforcements from Ciudadela, and an imposing mass of armed Moorish troops were gathered on the heights of Sierra Morena. But before they could attack their enemy encamped below, a reckless Catalan knight provoked a skirmish and found himself so hard pressed that he had to appeal to the King for help. Alfonso rapidly mobilised the whole of his army, drew it up in battle formation, and led his men in a charge against the Moorish forces who marched in serried ranks to meet him.

Flags and standards waving to the sound of trumpets and nakers, and in an unbridled clamour of war cries, the invaders attacked with full fury the Moslem horde. Writes the chronicler: «And when the hosts were one against the other he attacked with all his people and the *Almojarife* did likewise.»

The battle reached an infernal paroxism, and the King, in the centre of the fray, breached an opening in the enemy ranks, attacking with lance and sword like one possessed until, his weapons destroyed, he fought furiosly with his club. «The battle was so cruel and merciless that everyone was hard pressed; but the King, who was one of the best horsemen in the world, assailed the enemy on all sides and none of them escaped without wounds, so much so that he broke all his weapons, with the exception of his club with which he wrought such havoc that no one dared face him.» Indeed, so terrible was the slaughter that the high ground where the battle took place became known by the people as «Cerro del Degollador» (Cut-throat Hill).

The Saracens were utterly defeated, and without even attempting a last defence in the fortress of Mahón they fled in disarray towards the interior, the *jeques* taking refuge in the castle of Sent Agayz on the summit of a hill in the centre of the island.

A large Christian camp was set up in the fields at the head of the port — the Pla dels Vergers — near to where the battle had been fought, and there the army of Alfonso rested for some days. The victorious troops attended the first Mass of the campaign to be held in Mahón, before setting out on the march through thick woods towards the final retreat of the islanders.

The battle was without doubt hard and bloody, and the troops on both sides fought cruelly, with the age-old hatred between those of different race and religion. There were countless dead and wounded, and although Muntaner exaggerates when maintaining that few Arabs were left alive («all were killed»), one must assume that they would defend their country to the death and that the wounded would be treated without pity. Many years after the battle, historians put Christian losses at 334 dead and those of the Arabs at 4,300; but one must consider these figures to be as biased as they are hypothetical.

The absence of strategic skill and of coordination among the leaders were surely the main reasons for the spectacular defeat suffered by the Arabs at the hands of the well-trained Christian army. There was the further factor that they found themselves invaded after having led a peaceful life on the island for hundreds of years and were quite unaccustomed to warfare.

The arrival in the port of Mahón of the bulk of Alfonso's fleet, with large reinforcements, completely demoralised Abu Omar Haken ben Caid, and after deliberating with his advisers he ordered the white flag to be raised and sent as ambassadors the lords of Binimodén,

Binicodrell, Binimahoma and Binidofá to agree on a peace.

The conditions imposed by the victors were harsh in the extreme, but the *Almojarife* could not but accept the demands of his enemies, and the document of peace was signed on 21st January 1287. The Aragonese noble and former tutor to the King, Blasco Jiménez de Ayerbe, swore in the name of His Majesty that its terms would be justly complied with.

IV

Alfonso the Liberal, now master of the island of Menorca, moved on to Ciudadela, its luxurious capital. There, on 2nd February 1287, in the Moslem mosque now converted into the principal parish church and consecrated to the Glorious Virgin Mary, a solemn Te Deum was sung, followed by a procession. Immediately afterwards the monarch travelled through his conquered lands, raising the Catalan flag and imposing the obligations arising from his victory.

Knowing Alfonso's kindly nature, his inhuman attitude towards the vanquished enemy seems incomprehensible and can only be excused on the grounds that he was simply behaving in accordance with the customs of the age, whereby in every country conquered by force of arms all its material wealth and its inhabitants — in disregard of all moral laws — became the exclusive property of the King and served to augment the royal treasury as a reward for victory. If, moreover, it was a case of lands wrested from infidels, the punishments and demands were even harsher.

The terms of the treaty of surrender were: total possession of the island, its cities and forts, and of all its wealth in whatever form that might be found there. Men, women and children were to become slaves of the King, unless they were able to pay within six months a ransom of seven and a half doubloons per person for their freedom, to be paid in gold, silver or pearls. This tribute would guarantee their departure from the island, but all their goods, jewels and property, with the exception of personal clothing, would be confiscated. They would be subject to the humiliation of personal search, though women were granted the privilege of being searched by other women.

The *Almojarife* deserted his subjects in exchange for his own liberty, stipulating in his pact with the conquerors that he and 200 members of his family should be exempt from payment of the ransom and should be accompanied to Ceuta, or some other place in the Barbary coast, by Admirals Marquet and Mallol in a ship to be provided by the King. His relations, however, had to leave their treasures behind and were only allowed to take as luggage their books, fifty swords and their bedclothes. It was agreed that the wives, daughters and other Saracen females who accompanied Abu Omar Haken would not be raped or otherwise dishonourably treated and that their faces would not be uncovered. Those who accompanied them would also be guaranteed immunity from attack. It is sad to think of the bitter fate that awaited those islanders who did not have the protection of this concession.

The fate of the *Almojarife* was, however, tragic, beginning with his transfer from the castle of Santa Águeda to Mahón where, whilst awaiting embarkation, his living conditions were so hard that the King himself gave orders that two mattresses be sent to him and sufficient grain to feed both him and his suite. After two weeks they at last embarked in ships captained by Nadal de Roses and the Genovese Raffo de Serion (not accompanied by the Catalan admirals, as had been stipulated), probably bound, according to Muntaner, for Ibiza for a cargo of salt. The King, however, continued to protect him to the end and, in a letter dated 8th February, ordered his officers and subjects not to molest the defeated *Caid* in any way. At the request of Abu Omar, they were taken to Almería, whence they crossed to Ceuta to visit the tomb of the *Almojarife's* father, after which they spent a long period in the palace of the *Emir* of Granada. But in 1288, off the Algerian coast, on their way to Tunis, «the storm overtook them and their ship was destroyed so that no one escaped». Thus perished the last and ill-fated Arab governor of Menorca.

The fate of the inhabitants of the island was in general

no less unfortunate. Two thousand Moors remained in Menorca working on defence projects in the ports of Mahón and Ciudadela, but the major part of the population was taken into captivity and many were sold as slaves by the King and exiled to distant parts of his kingdom.

These people, dispossessed of their land and separated from their families, were sold ignominiously as slaves at auctions held within a few days of the signing of the peace treaty: their fates varied from concubinage to forced labour. Nobles and soldiers in the King's army would attend these auctions held in the public market, and buy thousands of Saracens which the Leridan Ramón de Calvet was authorised to put up for sale.

The scale of prices for men and women was rather informally set: men were worth more than women, and white Moors were more sought after than black. But the great difference in price between one slave and another is difficult to explain, even taking into account their varying physical characteristics. We note that Jaime de Caminou paid as much as 50,000 *sueldos* for one man, and Pedro de Burgues only 7,500, while Bernardo Fuster's slave cost him 100 doubloons. We may also observe, among the many bills of sale for these slaves, that a single buyer would in general acquire a number of slaves. Pedro Delayet, for example, purchased one black slave and one white one; Eiximen de Nadal, two black and one white; Juan de Cabanyes, three white ones; Rodrigo de Luna, three men and five women; R. Turricell, one white male, two black males and four white women; R. Molina and Juan Castellany, nine males and two females respectively. No doubt re-sale was not unknown in those days.

The debts contracted by the King were more than covered by the sale of a contingent of slaves which he ordered to be auctioned in Mallorca, Valencia and Barcelona. Alfonso took advantage of the occasion to send slaves as gifts to several of his friends and relations. He sent two male Moors and one female to his aunt Constanza, ex-empress of Greece, and another Moorish woman to her family maid. He made a present of ten men to Lope Ferrench de Luna, and three more to the *Infantes* of

Castile. The Marquesa de Saluces received two slaves, as also did Friar Juan Splugues, the superior of the priests' college in Mallorca. Among the many prisoners who entered the royal service, thirty worked in the naval dockyards in Barcelona. One of the more fortunate of these slaves, by the name of Hassen, completed his sentence as a precious-metal worker so well that His Majesty, well pleased with him, ordered Calvet to send a ship to pick up his mother, wife and children, adding that should they have been sold he was to repurchase them immediately and send them to Barcelona.

At all events, not all the inhabitants of the island were condemned to the sad fate of slavery, and there are records of the sums paid by those able to redeem themselves (no doubt through generous contributions from friends on the Barbary coast, since all possessions of the Menorcans had been confiscated by the Crown). In many instances the King accepted less than the seven and a half doubloons stipulated, with the object of squeezing every possible monetary advantage from his victory. The result was that the sums paid were very unequal and varied between twenty-six and six or seven doubloons, sometimes being as low as one doubloon and a quarter per family; one group was so fortunate as to have to pay no more than half a doubloon for their liberty. Thus, whereas a group of 143 men and 150 women paid, on 27th February 1287, the full price of 2,197.5 doubloons, another consisting of 101 men and 125 women paid only 333 doubloons. There are even cases on record where the King granted liberty to certain Saracens without any payment at all, enabling entire families and their servants to leave the island.

But unfortunately this generosity had, on more than one occasion, a sequel as tragic as it was pathetic: some of those placed at liberty never reached their promised homeland because there were then, as now, vile abuses on the part of carriers. The boatmen paid to transport the redeemed Moors simply dumped their human cargo into the sea within a few miles of the coast. The punishments for such crimes could not have been applied very strictly, for Bernat Siquer, for example, was pardoned by the King himself and let off the punishment to which he had been sentenced for so criminal an act. And this was not the only case. From a royal letter, written in Valencia on 23rd April, forbidding the landing of one Domingo Vedell for having illegally exported a number of Menorcan slaves, we see that there must also have been other kinds of abuse. The King, in order to protect his booty and prevent its falling into the hands of soldiers and sailors, gave orders that no boat could put to sea without a note-of-hand showing an inventory of everything carried on board. The sordid lists of these spoils of war include every class of goods, even simple household objects like straw mattresses, blankets, cauldrons, rush mats and table utensils. Those in charge of inspecting and searching all galleys and other boats and checking permits were Guillermo Olomar and Pedro de Olivella.

The King also took good care to safeguard the goods confiscated from the islanders, and charged various officers with the job of cataloguing in detail the castles and houses, with their clothes, jewels, arms and other articles (including the water in the cisterns), and planned the future use of his lands with such precision that he ordered Bernat Espanyol and Guillermo Cerdá to draw up a census of cattle and to take charge of harvesting the wheat at the appropiate time.

It is possible that the harsh attitude of Alfonso the Liberal towards those he had conquered, in apparent contradiction to his usual indulgence, was no more than the consequence of his teutonic methods of organisation, or of a rather natural insecurity in the face of an unfamiliar problem. However this may be, the King remained in Ciudadela until the beginning of March, watching personally over the affairs of the island, administering the division of lands and appointing the future governing officials of Menorca.

The monarch structured the political organisation of the country in accordance with the customs of the kingdom of Aragon. The Aragonese noble Pedro Garcés de Nuz was appointed Lieutenant and Governor, a post which combined military, civil and judiciary powers. The functions of procurator and treasurer-royal, with the power to distribute the lands and possessions of the royal estate, were given to the distinguished Valencian citizen Pedro de Lebiá, «a very wise and outstanding man».

Universidades, or municipal corporations, were set up, and on 27th February the King signed a decree appointing as Bailiff-General Bernardo Sangenís, who thus became the authority responsible for civil administration and public order. Later, in 1288, an island police force was organised, composed of twenty armed knights, the owners of the *cavalleries* or fiefdoms, who in the course of time became the forbears of the island's nobility. (It would seem that at that time lands were awarded to the following knights: Gomila, Lozano, Olivar, Jiménez and Martorell, all names of distinction in Menorcan history.)

The office of public notary or scribe was held by Pedro de Bosch, whose duty it was to witness all the *escrituras* or deeds of the new properties and record notarial proceedings in the island.

Jaime de Garrius was put in charge of the ports of Mahón and Fornells and of the arsenal and port of Ciudadela; his duties included the collection of harbour fees from boats trading with the ports of the island. To judge from the many vessels which moored in the port of Mahón, this must have represented a considerable source of income for the royal coffers.

The first urgent task of the monarch and his oficials was to repopulate the island, cleared so violently of its former inhabitants. It was the Catalans who were designated as the future inhabitants, probably due to the proximity of Catalonia and the good customs of its people, a decision of which Muntaner approved: «So the island of Menorca was settled by good Catalan stock, as no place could be better peopled.»

The royal administration was so efficient that hardly more than a month after the conquest the King signed the

* The term «Universidad» was used in ancient Spain to mean the governing body of a group of citizens, especially in the sense of «Municipal Corporation».

document for the land concessions granted to his Catalan vassals, stipulating only that they should take possession of their properties and reside in Menorca. The positive, and mainly practical, significance of this repopulation may be seen in the lists of concessions of houses and businesses, more numerous at the beginning than those of rural properties and land. Among the new owners of estates appear the names: Arnau Ticert de Almudévar, some houses, lands and a pair of oxen; Bernat de San Genís, the bread oven formerly the property of Abenfixon in Ciudadela; Berenguer de Lupesti, the houses which had belonged to Ahomar Jahioch of Ciudadela; Pedro Socau, the houses and enclosures of Ali Ben Suyetar; Ramón Mercadal (whose family later became deeply rooted in the island), some large houses in Ciudadela which gave on to the main road and adjoined the property of the *Almojarife* situated opposite the palace; Silvestre Mercader de Luna, the farm known as Alfurí and its appurtenances, with the obligation as usual of residing in it. (Presumably these new residents bought a good number of Menorcan slaves to work the land; this would explain the conservation of Arabic place-names which indeed go on to the present time.)

Alfonso the Liberal gave special attention to the proper establishment of the Church, to which a third of the royal tithes of the island was granted for its upkeep. He made a generous contribution of 138 *sueldos* from his privy purse to Friar Galcerán de Tous to pay for bells and an altar in the parish church of Ciudadela. The King also set up chaplaincies under royal patronage in Mahón, Ciudadela, and the castle of Santa Águeda where the Governor was to take the oath of allegiance.

On 1st March the King dealt with the major part of the cultivated lands adjudicated to the religious orders of Mallorca, Catalonia and Valencia under the condition that they set up houses on the island. The Poor Clares founded a convent in Ciudadela, and Sisters Agustina and María of the Santa Clara convent in Mallorca received the deeds. These nuns were exempted from payment of tithes and «first-fruit» offerings. The Franciscans of Barcelona and the priests of the Merced in Valencia accepted the concession of various houses and lands, free of all taxes; and the Trinitarian friars Juan de Bas, Nicolás de Fort and Bernardo Dominico were granted a mosque, a house and a yard for the specific purpose of building a monastery and hospital. The communities of Our Lady of Mercy, who had accompanied the King, were granted lands in the rural districts of Ciudadela and Mercadal, and came to acquire Monte Toro. (Alfonso III has been criticised for the liberal way in which he distributed Crown lands; it seems to us however that it was a healthy and necessary measure for the future development of Menorca.)

Once these problems were resolved, and after leaving all important administrative matters in the hands of his representatives, Alfonso embarked for Barcelona on 5th March 1287, arriving there on the 9th.

The conquest of Menorca was, without doubt, a bloody and pitiless affair, but this territorial acquisition pointed the way to the solution of many future problems and brought considerable gains in security and prestige to the Crown. The fleet once again showed its predominance, safeguarding maritime routes and keeping away from the Catalan coasts any danger of incursion by Saracen pirates. The Balearic Islands were now united to the kingdom of Catalonia and Aragon, and Alfonso III could face the complex political embroglios of the Mediterranean, having proved beyond doubt his military strength and his personal worth.

Four years after the conquest of Menorca, when he was twenty-five years of age, and supremely happy about his imminent marriage to Eleanor of England, Alfonso the Liberal died in Barcelona on 17th April 1291 of septicaemia caused by anthrax of the groin.

Writes the chronicler: «And he crossed himself, and blessed first himself and then all his people and all his kingdoms, and clasping the crucifix and reciting holy prayers, he passed from this life to the next... And without any doubt whatever we may believe that he is with God in paradise, as befits someone who leaves this world a virgin, for he never had intercourse with any woman.»

That he is with God in paradise we do not doubt, but not exactly for the reason which Muntaner puts forward with such faith, for in a codicil made a few hours before his death he requests his successor to protect Dolça, daughter of Bernardo de Caldés, and to educate honourably the child which is to be born to her.

Alfonso was succeeded by his brother Jaime II («the Just») who, as a result of the treaty of Agnani of 1295 and pressed by Pope Boniface VIII, was forced to return to his uncle Jaime de Mallorca the lands which Alfonso the Liberal had so competently conquered for the Crown of of Aragon, including Menorca.

Menorca was again incorporated into the House of Barcelona in 1349 as a result of the conquest of the kingdom of Mallorca by Pedro III («the Ceremonious»), and finally became a part of what in the future was to become Spain as a consequence of the marriage between Ferdinand of Aragon and Isabella of Castile on 19th October 1469.

16th CENTURY

THE PIRATES

What had been the important mediaeval kingdoms of Catalonia and Aragon went into decline in the fifteenth century. Their territorial acquisitions in the eastern Mediterranean basin were left to the mercy of the power of the Osmanlis, centred in Turkey, and their commercial empire became paralysed for want of markets.

The French historian A. P. Prieur believes that the main cause of the decay of the eastern coast of Spain was that «Barbarossa closed the sea to the resplendent navy of the Catalan-Aragonese confederation which had brought the illumination of the civilised world to the most sealed-off regions of the Mediterranean. From then on Barcelona, rival of Genoa, would languish, and the exodus of businessmen and thousands of families would bring her to the deepest and longest crisis of her singular history. After this epoque the eastern coast of Spain would have a stormy existence, provoked by Mohamedan depredations.»

The causes of this political and military collapse were complex. The declining importance of Catalonia as a result of the union of the Spanish peninsula, her relegation to a marginal position in the discovery of America, and her economic collapse, accelerated in part by the implantation of the Inquisition in the territories of the Catholic Monarchs, and in part by the lack of maritime security in the Mediterranean, were the prime reasons for her deterioration.

The fascination of Ferdinand the Catholic for that new and vigorous Castile, his absenteeism and the lack of interest he showed in his Catalan-Aragonese lands, his wish to exclude them officially from the conquest of Granada, added to his obsession for Castilian hegemony, all gave rise to an extraordinarily lethargic attitude in his own states which kept them on the fringe of the Renaissance. Catalonia and Aragon, from being a kingdom of vital and adventurous people became a second-rate province, turned in on itself and prevented from following the historical path which Spain was beginning to take.

Without incentives or directives, the ancient fighting spirit of the Catalans gradually decayed. The rigour of her military discipline disappeared, her naval power declined and her commerce stagnated. In these conditions of anaemia and isolation, the country was readily invaded by the new functionaries and the new institutions.

The Inquisition was imposed: that masterly political discovery of the Catholic Kings and their successors which, like no other legislative measure, forced the unity of their provinces under the sole authority of the Tribunal of the Holy Office, controlled by the monarchy.

Barcelona attempted in vain to oppose the setting up of the Castilian Inquisition when it discovered that its establishment involved, among other things, a considerable loss of trade and the escape of people and capital abroad. The mere news of the arrival of the Inquisition in 1484 led the city councillors to write: «This has caused much sadness to all, from the greatest to the least, as if they saw this city totally lost and destroyed. For even before receiving this news some had left and many had transferred their goods elsewhere.» The Maritime Consuls also protested, referring to «the great disturbance and distraction so deeply felt in the market, due to this cause».

Later, the expulsion of the Jews from all the kingdoms of their Catholic Majesties, decreed in March 1492, aggravated this commercial crisis: foreign ships, intimidated by the new laws (which controlled the goods of «converts to, fugitives from and those under suspicion of the Holy Catholic Faith»), abstained from dealing with the eastern ports of the Peninsula. Converts and Jews fled from Spain, taking with them not only their privileged financial contacts with the rest of Europe but also their own human potential, their high degree of industry and their administrative competence, very necessary in a country devoted by nature to the quixotic development of its gentlemanly characteristics at the expense of its commercial qualities.

And if the Crown of Castile found some compensation

for these setbacks in the adventure and gold of America, Catalonia — a land of seamen with a long commercial and maritime tradition — was left on the sidelines of the most important colonising operation of all times. With one stroke of the pen Isabella the Catholic excluded the entire Levantine coast of Spain from participation in the discovery and colonisation of the New World. In her famous Testament of October 1504 the Queen declared: «Whereas the Mainland and Islands beyond the Ocean and the Canary Islands were discovered and conquered at the expense of my kingdoms and of their inhabitants, it is reasonable that business and commerce with them be carried out by my kingdoms of Castile and Leon and that to them should go everything brought from those lands... For this reason I order and command that this be complied with, both in the lands already discovered and in those which may in the future be discovered, wheresoever they may be.»

Thus by order of their sovereigns, the Catalans were denied an opportunity of renewed maritime activity and new markets, which would compensate for the loss of commercial routes to the Levant. In future Catalonia's sole concern would be to uphold as far as possible her constitutions and political privileges against the authority of the monarchy, and her war effort would be united to that of the Crown only when it was a matter of defending her frontiers against the French and her coasts against Turkish pirates.

Catalonia recovered somewhat from her passivity when Spanish policy-makers contemplated a possible, and necessary, expansion into North Africa at the beginning of the sixteenth century. The promise of exclusivity in commercial dealings with the Barbary ports and the hope of keeping the Moslems at a distance from her coasts encouraged Catalonia to fit out several warships and call up soldiers to take part in the capture of Meir-el-Kebir in 1505. The Catalan parliament, moreover, ever clinging to commercial interests, voted the large contribution of 208,000 *libras* together with the supply of 12,000 bushels of grain to the expeditionary army for the conquest of Tunis, Algiers and

Bougie in 1510. But until Charles V — fearful of the supremacy which the Turkish empire had achieved over sea-going activities in the whole of the Mediterranean — gave orders for the fitting out of a powerful fleet for action against Barbarossa in 1535, Catalonia could not renew any of her old naval production.

Ferdinand shrewdly manipulated the Inquisition to support his efforts to bring about the unity of Spain and the hegemony of the monarchy. Castile, having no parliament of its own, was politically the most indefensible and thus most manageable part of the country, and it was there that Ferdinand directed his main support. Catalonia was therefore the region which suffered most from these changes — particularly because of her maturity and lack of flexibility — and with her declined the neighbouring areas which depended entirely on her vitality. Naturally the more isolated the area the quicker it became impoverished, and the decline of Menorca was particularly rapid.

With the Catalan merchant navy paralysed by the Turkish and Berber blockades, the flourishing Menorcan ports came almost to a standstill, and during the reign of the House of Austria the island suffered one of the most catastrophic periods in her history. The monarchs, engaged in the political, commercial and territorial aggrandisement of Spain, forgot her in her geographical isolation, and such was the extreme state of inaction reached in Menorca that she did not even have the energy to support the revolt of the *Germanías* in Mallorca in 1520, remaining virtually cut off from all historical and material evolution. Agriculture was abandoned, cattle debilitated through lack of renovation of stock, and trade disappeared. Many of the inhabitants emigrated, leaving the population reduced to a few isolated families scattered throughout the island. Mahón and Ciudadela together hardly numbered three thousand souls. In the face of such disaster, Menorca fell easy prey to pirate raids, which increased the misery of the island to a dramatic degree. These destructive assaults, principally that of Barbarossa in 1535 and, twenty-three years later, that of Mustafa and Piali, removed the last vestiges of her security.

The devastation of Mahón in 1535 by the fleet of Khair ed-Din Barbarossa was the bloody epilogue to — and final revenge for — the defeat he had suffered at the hands of the Emperor Charles V in Tunis. And the invasion of Ciudadela in 1558 by the Turkish admirals was the consequence of the new Mahomedan supremacy in the Mediterranean after the failure of the Spanish off Algiers in 1541.

These historic events which so fortuitously affected Menorca laid the foundation of the tradition of her people.

I. The brothers Barbarossa

I

Barbarroja, Barbarroja,
Tú eres el rey del mal;
No hay dolor ni cumplimiento
De carácter infernal
Que no fuese acontecido
*Por pirata sin igual.**

Thus ran the popular ballad hummed by sailors and fishermen in the Spanish ports of the Mediterranean during the first half of the sixteenth century. Of all the pirates, the name of Barbarossa was the most dreaded in those towns terrorised by the brutal incursions of the Mahomedan corsairs.

It is curious to note the modest origins of this man and the reasons which drove him to attack the Christian world with such hatred and to defend the Islamic creed with equal intensity.

His father, a humble Christian fisherman on the Albanian coast, was captured by soldiers of the great Mohamed II on one of his periodic forays in search of oarsmen for the ships of the imperial fleet. This poor Jacob, a God-fearing and almost mentally retarded man, forsook his religion to save his life and came to form part of the long chain of rowers, stevedores and slaves on board the luxurious merchantmen of the Turkish prince which cruised the Aegean Sea and the African coasts.

On one of his voyages he fled his ship and took refuge among the poor fishing community of Mytylene, on the ancient island of Lesbos. There he married Catalina, the young widow of a Greek priest and the mother of several young children. They had four sons and two daughters. The sons were called Elias, Aruj, Khair ed-Din and Isaac

---

* Literally: «Barbarossa, Barbarossa, / You are the king of evil; / There is no pain, no deed / Of infernal character / That was not brought about / By this pirate without equal.»

— the famous Barbarossa brothers.

The renegade Jacob (or Mohamed, to give him his new name) led a sad life, persecuted by the incessant mockery and contempt of the inhabitants of the Bonava promontory where he worked as a potter. He succeeded in building a boat in the little port of Mola and used this vessel to ply a coastal trade between the ports of the island. He educated his sons in the strictest observance of the Koranic faith, inculcating them with a strong religious discipline, no doubt in order to demonstrate his devotion to his new religion and to alleviate the insults and humiliations with which his own life was filled. Mohamed perished in a storm, but his sons inherited his complex of suffering and the brutality so often inherent in mental weakness.

The brothers grew up surrounded by the constant movement of ships and sailors, learning quickly and easily the secrets of navigation and the various languages of those who did business with the island. Strong and silent, energetic and resolute, their youth concealed the hatred and the arrogance, the obsessive passions and the homicidal instincts which were to turn them into the most dangerous and abhorred men in the western Mediterranean.

Aruj was the first to leave the island to seek his fortune, and it was not long before he distinguished himself for his bravery and naval expertise. He soon received his baptism of fire in the Turkish fleet cruising towards the west to capture Christian vessels and rowers to fill the holds of its ships. In a skirmish with the fleet of the Knights of Rhodes, a Christian force which intercepted Moslem commercial traffic in Mediterranean waters, Aruj was taken prisoner and spent two years chained to a rowing bench.

He at last succeeded in escaping by cutting off part of the heel of his foot to free himself from the iron ring with which he was held prisoner. Lame and filled with the fiercest resentment against his captors, and with rancour against Cristianity, Aruj deceived, betrayed and assassinated in order to pillage three ships which he then captained under pirates' colours. His brothers joined him and he made them captains of his galleys, which became stronger and more numerous every day, whilst the wealth

71

of his booty of war accumulated, reaching fabled proportions.

His victorious forays, devastating the Mediterranean coastline, made him famous. Perhaps because of his full name, Baba Aruj, or because he did indeed sport a handsome red beard, he soon won the nickname of «Barbarossa» («Red-beard») in the Christian world. Aruj was the first of his dynasty, and this name was also applied to his brother Khair ed-Din, actually the most notorious of the Barbarossas.

The future corsair-kings of Algiers were far from being mere common pirates: their ambitions, religious intolerance and bravado put them on a level with the finest war leaders of the Renaissance. Although Aruj, deceitful, cynical, cruel and given to immeasurable anger, went to war to make his fortune, his principal motive was always a spirit of revenge and fanaticism. Khair ed-Din (whose name means «the good of the Religion») was to follow his elder brother faithfully, but he surpassed him in political skill and self-control; his prowess, maritime strategy and subtle diplomacy were to make him a worthy rival of the most distinguished European admirals and princes.

The Barbarossas soon understood the necessity of having at their disposal a safe port where they could revictual their fleet and deposit their prisoners-of-war, as well as a trading centre for the sale of slaves and other riches robbed from enemy ships. In 1504 they approached the king of Tunis and drew up an agreement under which, in consideration of payment of one-fifth of their booty, they could anchor freely in the ports of his domains. The corsairs established themselves in La Goulette — the port of Tunis — and on the island of Djerba off the Tunisian coast, admirably situated in the wide Gulf of Gabès, a secure shelter where they organised a naval base which would soon become the centre of the pirate world.

There villains, deserters, adventurers and criminals came to enrol under the flag of the Barbarossas, and a good number of independent pirates, through intimidation or blackmail, brought their ships to enlarge the already powerful fleet. At the Sea Gate in the principal port of the island an exotic and colourful market was set up. Merchants, dealers and swindlers of all races and creeds trafficked in the spoils of the pirates. Slaves, girls, horses, jewels, carpets, brocades, arms and armour were weighed and quoted amidst the shouts and rivalry of the buyers. The pride and the power of the Barbarossas grew to vast proportions with the humiliating dependence of men and the rapid accumulation of easy riches.

Baba Aruj and Khair ed-Din fortified the island and built large arsenals and dockyards, importing timber, cordage, rigging, pitch and tar, so lacking in that beautiful island of palm trees and olive groves, for the construction of their galleys. With sails lowered, the long light warships and the heavy transports would moor in the port. There would be mail boats with lateen sails, Spanish *faluches* and Italian *tartanas*; small Turkish *cektinas* and *moanas* engaged in the traffic of the port; heavy coracles on coastal trade, with huge square sails and many cannon; graceful galleys and combat *galeazas,* heavily armed and propelled by sails and innumerable pairs of oars; all of them seized from the nations of the Mediterranean and destined for the pillage, boardings, forays and commando raids of the pirates.

The voyages of the corsairs were not usually unfruitful, and their well-organised sorties were based on their extensive knowledge of the traditional routes followed by the Spanish and Italians, and on the strict discipline maintained on board, comparable to that of any national army. Their maritime campaigns took place between April and October. They would cruise on the high seas, just within sight of the coast, in a compact formations of light squadrons, quick and easy to manoeuvre. Their pilots and captains, who also served as guides and spies, were renegades and Spanish Moors, often natives of the very shores they were to assault. The tactics they used were characterised by their sailing under false colours, by the brutality of their surprise attacks and by the rapidity of their evasive actions. Christian convoys of merchantmen, barely protected by an inadequate navy, fell easily into the hands of the pirates, who availed themselves of their special genius for strategy and of their mastery of camouflage and imposture.

In the sixteenth century the Spanish import and export trade was centred on the ports of the eastern seaboard and formed the main basis of the country's commercial structure. Aragon's commercial interests in Africa — in Bougie, Tripoli and Alexandria — and the Catalan textile monopoly in Sardinia, Sicily and Naples, were born in the port of Barcelona, and it was there that the wool products of Aragon were embarked. Valencia exported her silk manufactures and cloths, and the Castilian wool of Villacasín was shipped from Alicante. Salt from Cádiz and Almería, leather from the Barbary coast made up in Seville and Cádiz, Andalucian and Mallorcan oil, sugar from the Canaries, the products of the American treasure route destined for Mediterranean markets, as well as grain imports from Sicily and (via Leghorn) from northern Europe, and spices and oriental fabrics arriving from Genoa; all this vital trade was at the mercy of the pirates. In the triangle formed by the ports of Valencia, Barcelona and the Balearic Islands, and in the Sicilian channel, gateway to the eastern Mediterranean, the ships of the Moslem captains gathered and lay in wait.

The disastrous news of the Barbarossas' deeds reached the Cristian courts and added to the already existing fear of the growing pressure of the Turkish empire. Spain at last reacted. Ferdinand, a fervent Catholic always ready to wage a holy war against the infidels, and a great politician eager to counter Ottoman power and to defend his country's commercial interests, prepared for war in Africa. Supported by Cardinal Cisneros and by a strong army of 10,000 foot-soldiers and 4,000 cavalry — the veteran regiment of the Italian war, captained by the great warrior, Pedro Navarro — the King gave embarkation orders to the galleys under the command of the Catalans, Ramón de Cardona and Bernat Vilamarí. Spanish troops conquered Oran, Bougie and Tripoli in 1509 and 1510. Reinforcements, consisting of the natives of those islands so particularly exposed to the pirate menace — Mallorca, Menorca and Sardinia — took part in the assault on Bougie.

II

Around this time Aruj and Khair ed-Din were drawing up ambitious plans. The idea of combining their naval operations with offensive territorial wars would strengthen their religious fanaticism, avenging the enemies of Allah, and would crown their personal achievements by conquering an independent kingdom on *terra firma*.

To achieve their own ends, the *emirs* of the African countries recently annexed by Spain had involuntarily to support the pirates. The fame of the Barbarossas was so great that first the *Bey* of Tunis, Moulay Mohamed, and later the *Bey* of Algiers, Selem Eutemi, had to enlist their aid in order to expel the invaders from their territories.

But the prelude to these new plans of the corsairs was to end in disaster. In 1512 Baba Aruj went to Bougie with fifty armed Turks and a well disciplined fleet. The place had been fortified by Navarro, and in the face of the bloody resistence put up by the Spanish cannons, the attackers withdrew. Aruj lost an arm in the affray and, badly injured, took refuge on his ship in La Goulette.

The indomitable pirate recovered, but from then on he displayed a luxurious silver hand and arm, which earned him the new nickname of «One-armed Barbarossa».

The appearance of this fabled pirate must have seemed incredible. Relatively young, he was lame, not very tall, strong and robust, with thick eyebrows and penetrating black eyes. His well groomed beard looked splendid amidst the elegance of his Asiatic silks and majestic plumed turban. To all this magnificence was now added a brilliant mobile silver arm.

Meanwhil Khair ed-Din put out to sea, destroyed a Genoese fleet and made for Menorca. He attempted to assault the island, but was repelled and driven off by three hundred furious Menorcans. With bloodthirsty intentions, he let loose a horse to roam the island with a doleful message hanging from its neck. It was written in Spanish and read as follows: «I am the punishment of Heaven. My revenge will not cease until the last one among you has perished and until your wives, your daughters and your children have been reduced to slavery.» It bore the signature and seal of Barbarossa.

In the following years the activity of the Barbarossas was prodigious. Their life was nothing but a series of captures, sudden coups, subterfuges and quick bloody boardings. But it was becoming more and more imperative to put into practice their obsessive dreams of ruling lands and peoples and gaining possession of a country of their own which would serve them both as rearguard and warehouse.

The King of Spain having died in 1516, Selim Eutemi of Algiers sought the support of the pirate brothers to liberate him from his vassalage to the Spanish monarchy. Aruj was well aware of the enormous advantage which the conquest of Algiers could bring him: it would be a centre for his piratical operations and, moreover, the capital of an empire which could be his.

«Algiers the brilliant», as the Arabs called it, exercised an unquestioned hegemony over the other cities of North Africa and enjoyed a life of abundance, peopled by Moors who had fled from Spain and brought with them their agricultural and artisanal experience. «On the edge of the sea, on a high hill, it enjoys all the advantages of an exceptional position between the gulf and the plain,» wrote that indefatigable Valencian traveller of the tenth century, Mohamed-el-Abdery.

The brothers therefore accepted the proposals of the *Emir* of Algiers. They arrived there with sixteen ships and a small Turkish army, installed themselves comfortably in the city and were acclaimed by the populace as liberators. Aruj, clever and treacherous, soon raised a powerful army among the neighbouring Kabyles. Master of the situation, he presented himself at the king's palace on the pretext of a courtesy visit, and assassinated him in his bath. The King's supporters and members of his family were quickly eliminated in their homes, and his wife, the beautiful Zafira, poisoned herself rather than submit to the amorous advances of the tyrant.

Baba Aruj took possession of the ancient city and proclaimed himself sovereign of Algiers. He imposed a draconian yoke on his vassals and applied atrocious tortures to any who opposed him, even decreeing mass cremations for his victims. Made proud by such an easy and extraordinary ascent, the corsair believed himself to be the envoy of Allah and, invoking his protection, achieved his wildest ambitions, aided by the perennial anarchy of the African states. He used firearms in his invasion and conquest of Tenés, and a little later the incautious nobles of Tlemcen called on him to support their party in the dynastic strife of that country. He arrived with a well-equipped army of Arabs and Turks and, as a first measure, cut off the heads of the nobles who had called him in, assassinated the heir to the throne and all his sons and, with the cloth of their turbans, hanged sixty members of the royal family. Baba Aruj then proclaimed himself king of Tlemcen.

The citizens of Tlemcen, terrified by the treachery of Aruj Barbarossa, asked Abou Hamou — one of the pretenders, who had fled to Oran — to liberate them from the despot with the help of the Spanish.

Two strong columns left Oran under the command of its governor, the Marquis of Comares and Captain Martín de Argote. In the course of various skirmishes with the Turkish army on the way, many Spaniards and Turks lost their lives, among them Elias, another of the Barbarossa brothers, whose blooded head Argote sent to Oran as a trophy.

The Spanish army surrounded Tlemcen and camped under its walls. Aruj was aware that his position, caught between a community incensed against him because of his crimes and a powerful enemy ready to fight him, was desperate. He called together his faithful captains and, laden with considerable booty, fled by night in the direction of Algiers. The alarm was soon sounded in the Christian camp and Comares quickly went after them. He reached them before they got to the river Salado, but Aruj, astute as always, made a last desperate attempt to save the situation. He ordered all the gold, silver, jewels and coins which his army had with them to be flung on to the road, thinking that greed would detain the Spanish. But nothing could stop these men in their impatience to put an end to their prey. Like a cornered beast, Aruj took refuge in a stable and defended himself with the imperious courage he had always shown.

After a short fight, the sword of García de Tineo pierced the body of Baba Aruj and the knight cut off his head, holding it up triumphantly aloft. The beard, red with blood, and the imperious expression still stared defiantly at the soldiers as they roared out their victory.

III

When Aruj Barbarossa died, Charles I was already King of Spain, Sicily, Naples, Sardinia and the Low Countries, and a year later was elected Holy Roman Emperor as Charles V. His dominions extended over half of Europe. This Spanish and northern-European prince, who was not yet twenty-one, is lucidly described by the Marquis of Lozoya in his history of Spain: «Very young, and gifted with a strong and concentrated intelligence, he realised the greatness of his position, which made him the first figure in Europe. His great merit lay in accepting this responsibility honourably and worthily and in sacrificing himself for its sake. The efforts of the Emperor should not be to submit to the wishes of other monarchs, but rather to preside over them with authority in order to coordinate their efforts towards two ends, one defensive: to contain the tremendous offensive of the East against Europe; the other missionary: to extend and spread the teaching of the Gospels over the face of the earth and to bring the barbarous nations into the fold of Christian culture.»

But Charles V, in the attainment of both his defensive and missionary ends, was up against a powerful adversary: Suleiman the Magnificent. Let us again listen to Lozoya: «In Constantinople... a strong and intelligent power, who had behind him the whole of the inexhaustible resources of Asia, prevailed against a disunited Christendom, blind to its danger... With Suleiman the Magnificent, Islam, now directed and motivated by the Osmanlis... had recovered its enormous expansive power... The Ottoman army and fleet, with their great human reserves and ably directed, frequently by renegades, appeared invincible...»

These impressive monarchs, the one the master of the major part of the north coasts of the Mediterranean, the other of the south, both of them ardent defenders of their respective faiths and possessors of comparable qualities of lordliness, intelligence and indefatigable tenacity, disputed the hegemony of the Latin sea. The Holy Roman Emperor appointed Andrea Doria as his paladin in this struggle. Suleiman, «The Great Turk», appointed Khair ed-Din Barbarossa.

Khair ed-Din, on proclaiming himself successor to his brother on the throne of Algiers, had to face serious internal and external problems. The eternal conspiracies and intrigues, the infidelities and treachery of the African peoples — and indeed of his own followers — upset the power of Barbarossa, and the constant menace of the Spanish squadron placed his kingdom in danger. More subtle and far sighted than Aruj and, moreover, a consummate politician, he saw in the Turkish empire an ally and a prodigious reinforcement which would back up his own authority. The pirate went to the «Sublime Port» and put himself at the service of the Sultan, offering him his vassalage. He was well received and was appointed Pasha Captain, or Governor of the Sea, with a considerable navy and an army of janissaries under his command. Protected by Constantinople, Barbarossa enlarged the Moslem empire on adding Algiers to its already vast territories of Kurdistan, Persia, Syria, Mesopotamia and Egypt. And even more than this, he was able to offer Suleiman a foothold in the Christian world.

The victories of these two allied forces were innumerable, and from the Dardanelles to Gibraltar they held the Castilian navy (at no time very powerful) in check. On a number of occasions they placed in peril the armies of Charles V, never very concentrated due to the protracted conflicts of so extended a kingdom which inevitably kept them occupied.

From then on — we are in the twenties and thirties

of the sixteenth century — the organisation, the power and the naval mastery of Barbarossa were to considerably enhance his former prowess; he would indeed become «the terror of the Mediterranean». For the first time he brought war to the sea. He used a compact organisation, with well-ordered methods of training and discipline, revictualling, and naval construction, and an exact system for the formation of assault troops, schooled in the difficult manoeuvres of rapid and concentrated raids. Khair ed-Din's fleet was now no longer limited to a few ships in search of any prey they could find. It had become an important navy, in constant battle formation, with responsible and experienced officers.

The first towns to receive the attentions of this new force were, ominously, those of the Spanish eastern shores whose incessant pleas for protection by a coastal force had gone unheeded. Their position was aggravated by the fact that a high percentage of the inhabitants of these lands were Moors, forced to renounce their beliefs, customs and costume; these people constituted a dangerous, subversive element ever ready to inform the Mohamedan corsairs on the state of the fortifications, concentrations of the Spanish navy, and vulnerable points along the coast.

Barbarossa's lieutenants went up the Ebro and attacked Amposta; they landed on the beaches of Badalona and burnt the city; they destroyed the town of Xilxes, penetrated the ports of Denia and Alicante, and sacked Parcent; and to crown all these «victories» they captured off Formentera the flagship of the commander of the Granadine fleet, killing its general officer, Rodríguez de Portuondo, and his son Domingo. The royal standard and the figurehead were presented in triumph to Suleiman II.

But not all their attentions were reserved for Spain: Italy, Sicily and Sardinia were also stormed and sacked. The only safe coasts were those of the south of France, protected by the alliance between Francis I and Suleiman the Magnificent; a revolutionary alliance this, which the Gallic king aimed against his enemy Charles V in particular.

At that time the appearance of the captain-king must have been most impressive. His spectacular oriental ostentation and his taste for the most luxurious refinements enhanced his well-proportioned body and the imperious aquiline nose of his classical Latin features. In singular contrast to his thick beard — red, if we are to believe the historians — keen, jet black, menacing eyes disclosed his enslaving pride, his energy and his total lack of fear. Sandoval tells us that he stuttered, but that he knew a good number of languages. He spoke Spanish fluently, and was surrounded by Spanish servitors. He judged with nicety and maliciousness; his studied grace and tolerance overcame his visionary's pedantry and his extreme love of carnal pleasure. His courage, his prudence in war, his foresight and above all his steadfastness in the face of reverses of fortune made him a great historical personality. It was his hair-raising acts of brutality which converted him into a legendary figure, and Christendom made the most of them to justify its own defects.

Because of intrigues and discords among his people, Barbarossa lost Algiers but soon recovered his throne and, in a stronger position than ever, he reinforced Djerba and methodically extended his dominions along the shores of North Africa. He took possession of Bone, conquered the Moors of Alcoll and Constantine, accepted for a second time the vassalage of the king of Tlemcen, and annihilated the Spanish garrison of *Peñón de Argel* (Rock of Algiers), a small outpost of Spain in Moorish lands.

Shortly after these victories he appeared again in Balearic waters. Through letters written to the Empress, the councillors of Mallorca expressed their deep anguish at the power of Barbarossa, «enemy of our faith», and gave their view, quite aptly, that «the destruction of this tyrant will be more arduous and difficult later on than now». They conveyed the news also of a bloody assault on Menorca, where «about sixty people» had been kidnapped; of frequent naval battles, with heavy losses of men and ships; and of the danger involved in living in the coastal regions of the islands «for fear of being killed or captured».

But neither the tragic end of *Peñón de Argel* nor the

warnings of the Mallorcan authorities succeeded in alerting the Christian world. Her kings and armies were too busy over their own differences and wars to restrain the ambitions of the Turkish Sultan and the victories of his admiral which, in the first third of the sixteenth century, brought the Ottoman Empire to its apogee.

Following European politics closely, Khair ed-Din — backed up as ever by Suleiman's army — took advantage of the weakness of the naval power of his enemies to take possession of Tunis in the summer of 1534. This daring conquest of the lands of Muley Hassan (a vassal of Spain), strategically situated opposite Sicily, unleashed on the North African coast the most concentrated and most effective offensive of the Christian countries against the Sublime Port.

IV

The proximity of Barbarossa in Tunis, almost at the gates of Sicily, was becoming constantly more intolerable, and the presence of the Ottoman Empire, which pressed to the maximum its blockade of the Christian Mediterranean countries, ever more dangerous. Charles V, taking advantage of the moment of peace solidly established with his European adversaries, at last succeeded in finding the time to devote himself to his enduring ideal: to place himself at the head of a crusade against Islam. In the spirit of a Mediaeval crusade in defence of Christianity, he obtained the support of the Pope and of many Western princes and states. But the undertaking was mainly Italian, Portuguese and Spanish, the former two, like Spain, possessing wide interests in Africa and the Mediterranean. France, naturally, was excluded (by her treaty with Suleiman) from participating in the project, and sent arms to her Mohamedan allies.

In the spring of 1535 Barcelona was the centre of the concentration of crusaders' fleets and armies prepared for the struggle against one who was essentially a pirate. With unheard of pomp, the greatest princes and warriors of the day were congregated in the city, and the arsenals of the port once again witnessed the splendour and activity of the past when the Catalan navy had defended the coasts so effectively.

Charles V personally directed the naval construction works and also supervised the military organisation. The King of Spain recovered all the enthusiasm of his early youth, borne up by the self-sacrificing efforts of the Spanish people, always prepared to give their money and their lives for a heroic struggle in defence of their ideals.

On 14th May 1535 the brilliant army marched through the streets of Barcelona before an enthusiastic throng. At the head of 12,000 soldiers, the knights — richly bedecked in their armour, brocades and velvets — adorned the theatrical military parade. The nobility of the whole of Spain supported the adventure of the Holy War, and the most famous warriors of the day had enlisted.

Once the formidable offensive apparatus of the Tunisian war had been mobilised, Charles devoted the final days of the month to a spiritual retreat in the monastery of Montserrat.

The navy put to sea on 30th May 1535.

The King's galley, the luxurious *'Bastarda'*, sailed between ships of the Portuguese fleet which led this «floating forest», and the galleys of Don Álvaro de Bazán brought up the rear. The convoy called briefly at Mahón on 5th of June, where the King attended Mass, and on the 11th he made a short visit to the Sardinian port of Cagliari, which he left on the 12th having absorbed into his own army the forces of the Marquis of Vasto. In all, the expeditionary force now reached a total of 420 ships and 40,000 landing troops.

News of the preparations for war by the Christian nations reached the court of Tunis, but Kair ed-Din Barbarossa could not bring himself to believe until the last moment that he was about to be attacked, still less that his opponent would be the King of Spain in person. He appealed in vain to Constantinople for reinforcements; but Suleiman was in Asia with his army, and the pirate was forced to organise the defence of his kingdom without the help of the Sultan. He issued a general call to war

— a war which to him too was holy — but the Berber tribes on whom he depended resisted, remaining loyal to the dethroned *Bey.*

Barbarossa placed 5,000 well-trained soldiers on a war footing, as well as the Moorish navy and the janissaries, but the bulk of the army, some 30,000 men, were no more than an undisciplined horde, ill able to defend themselves against the professionalism of the Emperor's forces.

Khair ed-Din organised, as well as he could, the defence of his strategic point, mounting cannons on the fortified towers of La Goulette, a bastion built on an arm of land which protected the road that separated the bay from the inner harbour. This harbour, or inland lake, extended from La Goulette to Tunis, and in it he enclosed his reserve ships, putting Sinan at the head of 6,000 of his best sailors. The army was concentrated in Tunis at the opposite end of the lake. As a wise precaution the cunning pirate hid fifteen light galleys in the bay of Bizerta, running them aground on the beach and burying their masts, cannons and oars in the mud.

On 15th June the fleet of the Christian allies anchored in Port Farina, opposite the remains of Utica. The laborious task of disembarkation lasted two days, and the troops landed on the dunes to the west of Tunis, near the ruins of historic Carthage. Here they erected a vast camp. The blockade of La Goulette was soon begun, a key action in the Tunisian war. Under the burning desert sun the impressive mass of the imperial army began to march, followed by the heavy artillery drawn by innumerable pairs of mules and able-bodied soldiers, who advanced with some difficulty along the beaches and dunes, until they entrenched opposite some defence towers between Carthage and La Goulette. The incessant sorties of Khair ed-Din at the head of his squads of cavalry continually undermined the enemy positions, hindering any positive advance by the European force, already weakened by the terrible heat and by lack of water. Turkish assaults, skirmishes and ambushes against the enemy positions went on for almost a month, while at the same time La Goulette was subject to bombardment by Christian cannons. In the bay, the galleys of Andrea Doria and Álvaro de Bazán were at one time or another driven far from the coast by unexpected storms, delaying the demolition of the fortress walls from the sea.

On 15th July Charles V mustered his heterogeneous army, reinforced by the Moors of Muley Hassan, and taking advantage of a breach which had been opened in the main tower of the bastion by the artillery of the *'Santa Ana'* — a powerful galleon belonging to the Knights of Malta — the Emperor gave orders for an assault on the bastion by sea and land. That same afternoon, after a ferocious struggle, the Emperor, accompanied by the *Infante* of Portugal, made his triumphant entry into La Goulette. Barbarossa's fleet, consisting of 42 galleys and more than 80 smaller ships, was captured in the lake, and among the rich booty which fell into the hands of the Christians were many batteries from the defence works stamped with the crest of France.

A few days later, allied forces mustered again, and after a painful march of five miles over burning sand (especially hard with the heavy European impedimenta of war and the weighty armour of the combatants) reached a place opposite the city of Tunis.

An implacable and definitive battle was unleashed on the plains of Kassar-Mexevi; the hosts of Khair ed-Din Barbarossa were defeated. The captain endeavoured to redeploy his forces in the city and to continue the struggle, but 11,000 Christian captives, who had been locked up there for years, succeeded in breaking their chains; they overcame the local population and opened the doors to the Emperor. It was 21st July 1535.

Muley Hassan recovered his throne, signed a strict vassalage agreement with the King of Spain, and La Goulette became a Spanish possession. But before Charles V left the country for Sicily, Spanish and German troops (no doubt following the normal practice of pirates) cruelly sacked the city, and thousands of Africans were chained to the rowing benches of the Christian galleys: always the immediate sequel, it would seem, of any holy war, regardless of which side emerged victorious.

How Barbarossa, accompanied by Sinan, Ali Caraman and his janissaries, managed to escape remains inexplicable. A thousand legends of his capture and death circulated throughout the camps of the victorious European confederation, but nowhere was his head exhibited and no one found his treasure. The pirate had disappeared into thin air.

Barbarossa, bearing on his shoulders the most humiliating defeat of his life and having lost a large part of his treasure, set his expert ingenuity to work: he had embarked for Constantinople in the ships hidden in the sands. Pursued by Andrea Doria, he stopped first in Bone — a city which the admiral assaulted — and at last took refuge in his own kingdom of Algiers.

Once more in his long and hazardous life, Khair ed-Din — stimulated by the fanatical rage which so characterised him — concentrated all his passion on avenging his defeat by the Emperor Charles V. With amazing speed the king of Algiers mustered a small fleet, and only a few weeks after the disaster of Tunis he was again cruising the waters of the Mediterranean, in command of 22 galleys and 9 *fustas*.

His objective was the port of Mahón.

II. The assault on Mahon

I

The monotonous austerity of Balearic life was broken with the news of the surrender of Tunis. The inhabitants of the islands organised great festivities to celebrate this Christian victory, which meant new hope of revival and liberation from the constant terror in which they lived. The effigy of Barbarossa was burned repeatedly on the bonfires lit along the coast, and the entire population awaited impatiently the arrival of the King.

After his flight from Tunis, Barbarossa set sail from Algiers with his fleet, determined to inflict a brutal and resounding punishment on the enemy so as to show the world once more that neither his daring nor his power had been defeated. Cruising off Palma, the pirate interpreted the jubilant illumination in the city — which could be glimpsed dimly far out at sea — as a sign of military preparations against his arrival. He manoeuvred warily and set his prow at Menorca.

The cautionary experience he had suffered at the hands of the Menorcans some years ago stimulated Barbarossa's spirit of revenge, and the scant defence of the island confirmed his bravado, based as always on his cautious good sense.

On the morning of Wednesday, 1st September 1535, the look-out on Monte Toro announced the presence of numerous ships which showed signs of approaching the narrow mouth of the port of Mahón. The fleet which was drawing slowly near seemed to be flying the royal standard, but it stopped inexplicably to surround some Portuguese galleys which were just putting to sea, captained by Gonzalo de Pereira, and did not cast anchor in the roads until midday.

The good news of the arrival of the ships of Andrea Doria spread rapidly around the town. Peals of bells were sounded in the churches. The people of Mahón hastened

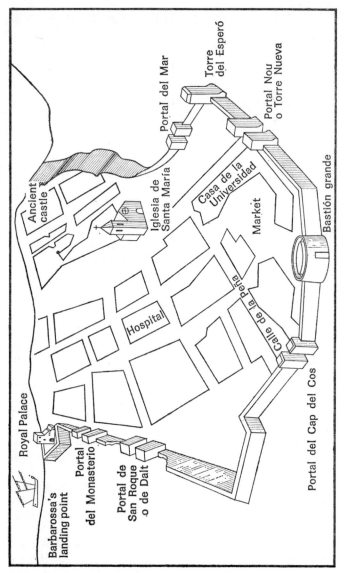

Royal Palace

Barbarossa's landing point

Portal del Monasterio

Portal de San Roque o de Dalt

Ancient castle

Portal del Mar

Torre del Esperó

Portal Nou o Torre Nueva

Iglesia de Santa María

Casa de la Universidad

Market

Bastión grande

Hospital

Calle de la Peña

Portal del Cap del Cos

(From a drawing of Andrés Murillo)

to prepare baskets of fruit and food with which to receive the conquerors of the infidel Barbarossa. Carried away by their enthusiasm over such an unexpected visit, two Franciscan friars, Bartolomé Genestar and Francisco Coll, went out in a small boat to welcome the galleys, now busy folding their sails.

On drawing near the anchored ships the friars realised with horror that their crews were Turkish pirates armed for attack. Rowing for all they were worth, the two friars returned to warn the people of the imminent Moorish assault.

The town of Mahón at that time had little more than 1,500 inhabitants, or some 300 homes, built in a small walled precinct which overlooked the deep bay. The streets and lanes of this small town had grown under the shelter of an old mediaeval fort, defended on the landward side by walls and towers and on the seaward side by high rocky cliffs. The town was surrounded by a wall of stout stone bastions, divided by three gates which opened on to the fields, known as the Mirador, the Dalt (or upper gate, which later became the arch or gateway of San Roque) and the Cap de Cos which gave access to the main street. Another gateway, the Portal del Mar, was the only one which communicated directly with the port. In the case of attack this tight encirclement assured the town of a stout defence, although the small number of its inhabitants and its enforced isolation detracted somewhat from its effective protection. Indeed Mahón had lived a miserable, poverty-stricken and apathetic existence for years, after her maritime lines of communication, the principal basis of her economy, had been practically cut.

The two friars having warned them of the dangerous Moorish presence, the people of Mahón prepared to fortify themselves with the few arms at their disposal. The gates were blocked and house doors were barred. A contingent of 350 able-bodied men, though scarcely trained in the use of arms, entrenched themselves on the walls, prepared to cover all points of access to the town.

On his side, Barbarossa did not delay, and soon after anchoring directed the landing of his people towards the most vulnerable part of the coast. The historian Rafael Bosch Ferrer, who followed the episode step by step, related: «Early in the afternoon the corsairs began to disembark near the Puente del Rey.»

The nobleman *Mosén* Jaime Scalá, Bailiff of Mahón and governor of the castle, organised the hasty protection of his town from the very beginning. He placed the authorities of the *Universidad* in strategic positions, appointed Councillors Gil Calderer and Jorge Uguet as captains of groups of defenders, and Francisco Mir to control the two pieces of artillery on the bastions.

By about three in the afternoon it was clear that Barbarossa intended to surround the town, supported by several combat cannons. Scalá, conscious of the grave danger, sent an urgent messenger to the capital, Ciudadela, with news of the assault, explaining the desperate situation and requesting urgent help from the general authorities in Mallorca.

Stopping only in Alayor, the horseman bearing the bad news crossed the entire island in six hours, reaching the capital before nine in the evening. On receiving the letter, the Governor and Captain-General of Menorca immediately summoned the General Council and as a first measure decided to ask for help from the Viceroy and General Councillors of Mallorca, since the neighbouring island, under a privilege granted by King Sancho, had the obligation to help Menorca and Ibiza with 300 men in the event of an invasion.

Without wasting time, within two hours of sunset, they wrote as follows:

The first of September,

at two in the night, with much haste.

Most magnificent and wise Sirs. At this time, which is two in the night, we have received by letter the certain news that the fleet of the perfidious Turk, Barbarossa, has entered the port of Mahón, and that a landing has been made at the Puente del Rey in that town. And likewise by this letter we understand that the people of the town of Yalor (sic) have thrown themselves into the task of helping those of Mahón, but there are few people and we, with much care, as the case demands, will not cease to provide whatever may be in our power, though the resources of this island are slight and the people and munitions very few: for this reason, with great urgency, we ask for your aid, for the service of our Lord and Sacred Majesty, and for the custody and defence of this island, which we take as lost if such aid is not provided in the name of Our Lord and of the trust we have in your aid; we ask and require you, for the service of God and His Majesty and every Spaniard and, above all, of the Island, to provide very promptly men and other aid for this poor island, which we take to be lost without it; a loss which you can realise how much it will mean to His Majesty, as well as touching Our Lord God and the Christian faith. Your aid can be sent to Ciudadela because the enemy's field or army is in Mahón, and will you please do this with great urgency because new letters reach us every hour and delay is perilous, because the Turks are landing and they have artillery. We, so that the Governor may inform the Viceroy by letter, we have not failed to have recourse to you, whose lives and health may God preserve. Given in Ciudadela at the said hour, with much haste, on 1st September MDXXXV. God, may you send aid promptly.

The Councillors of the Island of Menorca.

The inexplicable delay in replying to this deferential and anguished letter — which explains so clearly the lack of men and arms and the urgent necessity of receiving reinforcements — was, in part, the cause of the tragic denouement of the assault of Mahón and of the consequences it had for the island. Another letter, with precise details of the places where Mallorcan aid could disembark, also went unheeded.

The Governor of Ciudadela, a man of advanced years, organised in the capital a small contingent of 300 men, and this column was added to by people from Mercadal and peasants of the great farmhouses. But, in all, the support which was mustered did not exceed 500 volunteers, plus some 40 from Alayor, and men from the country around

Mahón who had come forward to help the besieged town. At the head of the expedition went the Governor in person, supported by *Mosén* Juan Oliver, captain of 300 men, and by Gabriel Leonardo Martorell, in command of the company of horsemen, accompanied by his sons Juan and Guillermo. These forces left Ciudadela in the morning of 2nd September, a few hours after the general call-up to all able-bodied persons on the island had been announced.

Meanwhile, early on that same day, Thursday, Barbarossa had completed the landing of 2,500 janissaries who, divided into three groups, had blockaded the town of Mahón on the landward side in an enveloping operation. He placed his sling artillery on a hill facing the Great Bastion and from there he bombarded the Cap del Cos gateway and the Torre del Esperó. The people of Mahón, besieged within their walls, defended themselves tenaciously with the bastion cannons, with which they succeeded in killing some three hundred of the enemy. These preliminary actions seemed to be going against the Moors — who did not succeed in breaking the walls — and various companies of pirates who had ventured into the countryside, disposed to sack whatever they could find, were also repelled, a good number of them being killed. However, a small detachment got as far as Alayor, where two captured Moors confirmed the news that the operation was directed by Barbarossa himself, accompanied by his lieutenant, the dreaded pirate Cochidiablo, well known in the islands and on the Catalan coast for his devastating forays.

For the first few hours the mood of the population was optimistic, and judging by the results of the preliminary skirmishes people thought that the Moors — although superior in numbers — must have arrived poorly armed and that they would soon be defeated by the ferocity of the islanders and the Mallorcan reinforcements. This hope of outside help was soon to be confirmed by the arrival of news that the Ciudadelan expedition was on its way, the information being brought by a pardoned bandit who had succeeded in crossing the enemy lines. Confident of the imminent arrival of the Governor and his men, the

Bailiff, Scalá, gave the keys of the western gateway — Cap del Cos, at the end of the Calle de la Peña — to his son Bernardo who, accompanied by Bartolomé Gañalons and Gabriel Pou, had orders to expedite the entry of the relief forces.

Barbarossa, realising the danger to which he would be exposed if he failed to achieve the assault in the shortest time, intensified his bombardment of the city walls. The batteries emplaced on the hill again went into action, and, after a heavy cannonade, succeeded in demolishing part of the Great Bastion. But the attempt to force an entry on that side failed and the Moorish attack was repelled. Losses among the defenders were considerable.

After a long day's journey by the broken roads which crossed the island from one end to the other, the Governor's forces at last reached a point opposite the walls of Mahón on Friday, 3rd September. They did not delay in engaging the besiegers, and the battle was concentrated on the slope between the Cap del Cos and Dalt gateways, at the beginning of the Ciudadela road.

Juan Oliver, commanding his company, had orders to be the first to enter the town, supported by Bernardo Scalá, the son of the Bailiff, who came out of the town with some troops with the intention of opening a way through the enemy for the newcomers and covering their entry by the Cap del Cos gateway. Scalá was repelled violently by the Moors before he could reach the island company and, without being able to accomplish his mission, was forced to retire behind the bastion. Trapped between the walls and Barbarossa's janissaries, Oliver's companions-at-arms were mercilessly attacked by the Turks with their scimitars. Their leader was felled by a dagger and many of his men were killed. The aged Governor was also killed in the fierce battle, as were a hundred of his best men, including the knight *Mosén* Gabriel Leonardo Martorell — a descendant of one of the original Catalan settlers in the island — and Vicente Andreu, a young man from Alayor who had voluntarily come forward to help the besieged port. The death of their leaders and the numerical superiority of the enemy decided the outcome of the battle, and the men of the expeditionary force were almost entirely wiped out. A few survivors succeeded in entering Mahón through the gates, left inexplicably without guards; others retraced their steps and took refuge in nearby farms, but many were taken prisoner by the Turks and carried off to the galleys anchored in the port.

The defeat of the relieving militia gave rise to one of the most shameful episodes in the history of Menorca. Such was the demoralisation which spread throughout the beleaguered town that subsequent events present an extraordinary record of treason and cowardice, difficult to explain; for although means of defence were practically non-existent and hopes of immediate relief eliminated with the annihilation of the island column, an organised and stoical defence of Mahón from the parapets of her walls would still have been possible, particularly taking into account the fact that the pirates could not plan a long siege, conscious as they were of the danger of the inevitable arrival of the forces requested from Mallorca and of the return from Tunis of the Spanish navy. But the terror which Barbarossa inspired in the peoples of the Mediterranean must have been so great that all sense of honour and duty dwindled before his threats; people even forgot the fact that the pirate's victories were based on quick and sudden raids, a tactic which he would inevitably have been obliged to use in this case.

After scarcely two and a half days' fighting (with only slight losses on the Mahonese side) Barbarossa, having been informed of the state of morale of his enemies, succeeded in initiating the terms of surrender of the town without even having to attempt a new assault.

On the morning of Saturday, 4th September, the third day of the siege of Mahón, a white flag appeared over the Torre Nueva, although nobody took responsibility for having raised it. Convinced that the town was lost and that the Moors would not delay their attack any longer, a small number of Mahonese began to cross to the enemy's ranks. Among the first to scale the walls were the barber, Antonio Rotger, with Lucas Saura and Bartolomé Mir, who presented themselves in Barbarossa's camp. The pirate took advantage of their surrender to send Rotger to parley with the besieged townfolk. Manacled and carrying a white flag, he was escorted by two renegades serving the pirate to the Torre Nueva, where they met the Syndic, Jorge Boscá and his people on the bastion. While listening to what the barber had to say, Councillor Antonio Olivar came forward and, climbing to the highest point of the town, informed the emissaries that the top officials were not present at that moment. The Syndic, Jorge Uguet, was sent urgently to find the Bailiff, but, informed of the latest happenings, Jaime Scalá had already emerged from his house and a little later the chief of the defence of Mahón appeared on the Bastion to listen to the propositions of the Moorish embassy.

The first reaction of the *Alcaide* was to reject any enemy proposal and, to the promise of sparing the lives of the inhabitants, including women and children, if they would surrender the land, Scalá replied that it would be defended by «cannon fire, even if fifty men be lost in the defence».

The representatives of the Town Council (Gil Calderer, Antonio Olivar, Bartolomé Saura and Jorge Boscá) were joined on the walls by many of the townspeople. Faced with the menacing words of one of the renegades who escorted Rotger, «that should they offer any resistance they would all have their throats cut», and that the town would be taken «and given over to fire and blood», they requested a two or three hours' truce to study the Moorish proposals. Scalá, against his will, transmitted the wishes of those around him and succeeded in getting Barbarossa to agree to a two-hour cease-fire.

The debate which ensued at the meeting between the people and the Syndics to discuss the enemy's proposals took place in the hospital building. It was characterised from the very beginning by a radical divergence of views, and although the majority of the Council voted to resist the blockade, there were already some who openly expressed the opinion that Barbarossa's proposition should be acceded to. The Bailiff was roundly opposed to this and threatened to resign if a surrender were accepted: «If they

want to accept agreement and enter into pacts with Barbarossa they had better not count on him to act as Bailiff
in future, nor as Captain nor as anything.» Even with
these words Scalá could not win support for his determination to resist. At a second meeting, held in the *Universidad*
building, he sought the support of the principal citizens
of the town and of the Council. With a crucifix in his
hand he exhorted those present to defend their land and
their lives, and succeeded in convincing the majority of the
dishonour of a surrender without resistance. Jorge Boscá
and Pedro Juaneda supported him and bravely offered
their lives, but some Councillors allowed themselves to be
influenced by Councillor Gañalons, owner of the Son
Mercer farm, who suggested that lack of powder dictated
the prudence of reaching an agreement with the enemy.

In the face of this division of opinion the Bailiff decided
to approach the clergy, convinced that among them he
would find some moral strength, and from the *Universidad*
building he sent his son Juan, a priest, to the church of
Santa María to put his views to them. But with the exception of another priest, Guillermo Olives, and Juan
Scalá himself, the clergy let it be known that their
unanimous decision was to recommend submission to the
demands of Barbarossa «as the lesser evil». This unaccustomed show of weakness influenced the assembly at
the *Universidad,* which passed the cowardly resolution to
negotiate with the enemy.

When it became known that the decision of the
authorities was to surrender the keys of the town to the
Moors, with the condition that the inhabitants should in
no way be molested, the people who had witnessed the
talks came crowding out of the *Universidad,* inciting
the populace to join in the surrender. The panic which the
pirate inspired in the Mahonese grew with the loss of
confidence they left at the lack of courage of their own
leaders and, terror-stricken, they rushed hither and thither
about the narrow streets of the town, spreading every sort
of rumour, not knowing which side to take.

The warm summer morning was now over and with
it the two hours' cease-fire. The Council ordered the

96

Bailiff, Jaime Scalá, to go to the enemy's camp and accept their conditions. For the third and last time the Bailiff refused to participate in this desertion, but after that he could no longer oppose his colleagues and thus, like most of them, he was responsible for having betrayed his high office.

Bartolomé Saura — accompanied by Jorge Uguet and Antonio Olivar, both particularly prominent throughout this episode — came forward as a volunteer to take the message to Barbarossa, «because there are many captains who know him», he said rather ambiguously and mysteriously. Also mysterious was the news that two priests, Grau Boscá and Martín Pou, were in the besieging camp, having already gone over to the enemy, without leave, before the town was attacked. (This is understandable only if one accepts the version of those historians who assure us that in earlier years, under a tacit pact, Menorcans agreed that pirates could revictual on their coasts; thus it is possible that these people would already have made contacts among the enemy.)

Emboldened by so easy a victory and aware of the defeatist attitude among the Christians, Barbarossa answered proudly to the envoys of the *Universidad* «that he had come there not for clothes but for slaves», and against the will of the people demanded the sacking of the town and the delivery to him of a hundred boys and a hundred girls over the age of seven.

When these new and imperious demands of the pirates became known, the people of Mahón gave themselves up once more to the most pitiful bewilderment and, terrified at the prospect of seeing their land destroyed and themselves taken prisoner, the majority agreed to give in to the enemy's demands. But the reaction of the syndics to Barbarossa's criminal proposition was quite lamentable. They went so far as to offer the lives of their children in exchange for their own immunity, although the poor children which Bartolomé Saura proposed to sacrifice «were consumptive and almost dead», according to the cold explanation of the Bailiff's wife.

The only person who, in the face of the general

demoralisation and cowardice, raised his voice in stout opposition to any parley with the besiegers, was one N. de Ávila, who tried in vain to convince the authorities that no more than a few days' resistance would be necessary until the hoped-for aid arrived. (Indeed, Mondéjar arrived in Palma with his navy on his return from Tunis the following Wednesday, 8th September, only four days after the surrender.) «But the authorities, who had already begun to bungle, were plotting partly and in particular the loss of the town, provided they could save themselves from the general ruin, which they considered inevitable,» as Rafael Bosch Ferrer, the historian, was to comment later.

When Antonio Olivar and Jorge Uguet returned again to the Moorish headquarters with orders from the Council to seal the new pact, the atmosphere in the besiegers' camp was one of joyous victory, accepted by the two collaborators, Bartolomé Saura and Francisco Mir, who were conversing openly with the Mohamedans. As was to be expected, Barbarossa was not satisfied with the hundred boys and hundred girls he had previously demanded and imposed additional and terrible clauses: the capitulation of the town of Mahón, the sacking of its houses and the surrender of its inhabitants. He caustically granted one perverse mercy: he would respect ten homes, to be designated by the ambassadors.

Participators in these base negotiations, Olivar and Uguet were quick to name five houses each, putting their own houses and safety first of all and then those of their relations and friends. In this way, the houses of the Bailiff Scalá, the Councillor Gil Calderer, and the syndic and mayor of the castle Pablo Serra, as well as those of Montserrat Gomila, Pedro Gomila, Blas Uguet (brother of Jorge), Jorge Boscá and Pedro Juaneda (the latter having distinguished himself by his bravery in the first moments of the siege) were saved.

Olivar finalised with Barbarossa the details of the surrender, agreeing that the flag on the bastion would be raised twice in succession as a sign of acceptance, that those chosen for immunity would carry an arrow, and that Barbarossa would enter the town accompanied by only a hundred of his men.

In the evening of that 4th September 1535, Bartolomé Saura, involved in negotiating the surrender of Mahón, showed himself on the Great Bastion, accompanied by a Portuguese. Here he raised the standard twice, thus announcing the surrender of the town. A little later, Antonio Olivar culminated his own treachery by opening the Portal del Cos to the clamorous horde of Turks and Moors.

More than a thousand armed ruffians penetrated the town that night. In an unbridled avalanche they invaded the deserted streets, and breaking down doors and windows they cruelly raided the homes of the people. Respecting neither age nor sex, they knifed and raped the unfortunate inhabitants, sacking their houses. No corner remained secret, no cupboard was safe against robbery; money, jewelry, cutlery, ornaments and clothing were sacked by the assaulters, and hundreds of captives, their clothes torn from them, were taken naked to the galleys. As a warning to the populace, the Town Hall was burned and the parish church desecrated, its treasures taken, its statues destroyed and its archives burned. By the light of the flames, fabrics and clothing were dragged through the streets, and pieces of gold and silver thrown to the ground in a Dantesque carnival of destruction. And, to add to the confusion and outrage, people who succeeded in evading the pirates turned to robbing the houses which had been forcibly abandoned; or bought their liberty by showing the sackers where treasures were hidden. There were also people who rushed to pick up coins and other objects thrown away by the invaders, leading to the most grotesque and pitiful sights.

Few were saved from the ruins and even those who had sacrificed the town in the hope of their own immunity received the punishment of the insatiable Barbarossa. Taken safely to the galleys, Olivar and Uguet were manhandled in order to make them divulge the hiding places of the money of those captured; Gil Calderer was tortured until he gave up «a little box which contained some gold and silver jewels and spoons». The Bailiff, Scalá, was luckier: he was able to save himself by showing the pirates «a large amount of money, clothes and jewels which were hidden».

All in all, the most innocent martyrs were the friars who had gone out in such haste to meet what they thought was the royal navy. Barbarossa sought them out in the Franciscan monastery situated some miles outside the town, where they and the caretaker-priest, Friar Miguel Capó, were beheaded by the Turks, who then burned down the monastery.

The atrocities went on all night, and in the morning the victorious pirates boarded their ships laden with the wealth of the town. They took with them as captives 800 Menorcans, and although some of the prisoners were members of the volunteer force which had come to help the besieged town, Mahón lost more than half its popula-tion. To add to the bitterness, the deportees were young men and women, fated now to work in the holds of the galleys and in the bed-chambers of the seraglios. A few succeeded in flinging themselves from the ships and swimming to the opposite shore of the port, but the majority ended their lives in the most terrible hardship and humiliation and were never heard of again.

Barbarossa left Mahón on the morning of Sunday, 5th September, having achieved a resounding triumph and leaving the survivors of the disaster sunk in the most desolating tragedy among the smoking ruins of their town.

II

The first news which ran through the island concerning the catastrophe which had befallen Mahón was confused and contradictory. Conjectures and rumours — repeated with horror and pity by some, with condemnatory severity by others — soon became clear and the truth was revealed to all: the authorities had been responsible for the treason implicit in the pact of surrender and the barbarous sacking of the town which followed.

The death of the Governor in the battle which took

place outside the walls, and the flight to the farm of Binimaymut of many members of the Town Council, left Menorca without command and Mahón without leaders. Nevertheless, within two or three days of the surrender the judicial machinery of the country began to function again. The Fiscal Procurator (placed temporarily in charge by the government) arrived in Mahón from Ciudadela on 8th September and opened an enquiry against those believed guilty.

As a result of information testified by witnesses it was not long before the following were accused: the Bailiff of Mahón, *Mosén* Jaime Scalá; Councillors Antonio Olivar, Francisco Mir, Jorge Uguet, Gil Calderer and Nicolás Calderer; Bernardo Scalá and Bartolomé Mir. These men were later detained and taken to the royal prison in Ciudadela. There began for them what was to be a long year of imprisonment and torture: though their crime was great, their punishment was to be appalling.

Meanwhile, the expeditionary force from Palma, consisting of 220 men, had arrived in Ciudadela — too late, of course, to be of any use. The General Councillors of Mallorca were so out of touch with the grave events which had taken place in the neighbouring island that it was not until 1st October that they reported the details to Charles V through Don Pedro de Figuerola, son and lieutenant of the Viceroy, after he arrived in Ciudadela at the end of September. The letter, somewhat exaggerated, no doubt in order to draw the monarch's attention to his neglect of the islanders, reads as follows:

«Barbarossa and his Turks had entered the town of Mahón, sacking and burning everything, killing or taking captive all its inhabitants, both men, women and children, save a few who have been found and are now in prison in Ciudadela, as it is believed that they were the schemers who in the end had plotted to give the town to Barbarossa.»

Figuerola was made Governor of Menorca, having as his adviser Rafael Ballester, fiscal lawyer of His Majesty in the law court of Mallorca. The case against the criminals was commenced immediately. There were thirteen witnesses, and the process of declaration, mutual accusations, confessions exacted under torture, imprisonments and brutalities against the wives of the accused, was long drawn out; sentence was finally passed on 20th October 1536, over a year after the event.

The notary and clerk of the court, Bernardino Dalmau, read the sentence in the Plaza del Borne in Ciudadela: confiscation of all the criminals' property; their children, male and female, to be debarred from all prerogatives, privileges and office; that the comdemned men be dragged «through all public places of the town of Ciudadela»; and that in the main square «the right hand of Antonio Olivar, with which he opened the gates of Mahón to the aforementioned Turk, be cut off, and the right foot of Jorge Uguet, with which he entered the town of Mahón in the company of the perfidious Turk, be cut off; that thereafter all the above-mentioned criminals shall have their throats cut and then be beheaded and their members mutilated; and that the head and hand of Antonio Olivar, together with the foot of Jorge Uguet, shall be placed over the gates which Antonio Olivar opened to Barbarossa; that the head of Jorge Uguet shall be exhibited over the Portal del Mar; that the head of Jaime Scalá shall be exhibited in the centre of the main square of Mahón; that the head of Francisco Mir shall be exhibited on the bastion from which he descended to go to the Turk, Barbarossa; and that the head of Councillor Gil Calderer shall be placed at the entrance to the *Universidad*. The remaining members of all the aforementioned criminals shall be distributed and scattered throughout the most public places of the island, with the full knowledge of His Lordship (the Governor).»

The sentence was carried out on 24th October 1536.

Morally and physically destroyed, Mahón remained practically depopulated, few survivors taking refuge in Ciudadela.

In the face of the danger to which the island was exposed, and the risk of a fresh attack on the now deserted port, the Menorcan authorities wrote to the *Universidad* of Mallorca (with scant results) «imploring their immediate cooperation». They needed men, arms, corn, credits and, above all, a plan for the restoration and defence of the town. The construction of a castle was organished, the tongue of land at the southern side of the mouth of the port being chosen as the site. The land was part of a farm known as Torre d'en Serra (Serra's tower). The owner, Pablo Serra, was entitled to receive 537 ½ gold florins for its expropiation. He finally received this amount, after long litigation, in 1571. Charles V sent the Italian engineer Giovanni Batista Calvi to direct the works and the first stone was laid on 1st May 1554, the feast of St. Philip. It was decreed that both labour and money for this great walled precinct should be provided by the populace, but in view of the scarcity of both, it was almost twenty years before this «urgent necessity» was completed.

As the solution consisted in planning for the defence of the port of Mahón only, it was comparatively useless because the island was equally vulnerable at the other end, where lay the unprotected port of Ciudadela.

Epilogue

Khair ed-Din went on harvesting his triumphs for several years after his assault on Mahón. When very old and almost blind, he retired from the sea to his sumptuous palace of «Bixara» in the Pera district of Constantinople where, ostentatious as ever, he lived surrounded by slaves, beautiful women and treasures of immense value.

Despite his years, the figure of this unique personality was still impressive. Tall, corpulent, erect, with his great beard now white and his rich garments, he looked more like a venerable patriarch than the extraordinary man of the sea who had reduced all Christendom to a state of insecurity. Voluptuous to the day of his death, he fell in love like a young man with Doña María, a beautiful Spanish lady kidnapped in Reggio; and, according to Sandoval, this love affair precipitated his end: «He was very lecherous in two ways, and they say that he exhausted himself with Diego de Gaëtan's daughter.»

He died in May 1547 and was buried among palaces and gardens in the luxurious mosque which he had built on the shores of the Bosphorus.

For hundreds of years, on rounding the Golden Horn, ships raised the colours of the admiral, and with a salvo of gunfire saluted the tomb of the Lord of the Sea, King of the Pirates.

III. Ciudadela invaded and razed

I

Neither the power of the Turks in the Mediterranean nor the incursions of the pirates into Spanish coastal lands declined with the disappearance of Barbarossa. Suleiman the Magnificent was living out the last years of his very long reign; Philip II occupied the throne of Spain; Charles had retired to Yuste; and a number of corsairs had inherited from Khair ed-Din the «kingdom of the sea».

The daring and much feared Ottoman captains cruised around the well known and traditional routes which in the past had been so fruitful, and in the spring of 1558 Admiral Piali, accompanied by General Mustafa, was following what was almost the established itinerary. They crossed the Straits of Messina, attacked yet again the western coasts of Italy — already sacked a thousand times before — and in the ports of the kingdom of Naples, in the island of Procida, and in Sorrento they made off with considerable wealth and 9,000 captives.

These favourites of Suleiman united, probably for the first time, their land and sea forces into a single operation, because, if Admiral Piali was a man of great naval experience and one who had given frequent demonstrations of his aptitude for war, General Bajá Mustafa was a young man of twenty-four, a clever intriguer, well thought of in the Sultan's court. In the raids along the coast in search of booty the General had the advantage of serving his apprenticeship beside the expert Piali, an alliance which was to last for many years and which would bring the two men together as companions-in-arms on various occasions, including the invasion of Malta in 1565 and of Cyprus in 1570.

Piali was a Hungarian Christian who, at the age of sixteen, fell prisoner to the Turkish troops in the battle of Mohacs in 1536. Brought up in the court of Suleiman, he quickly won the affection of the Sultan, and while still young was appointed *bajá* and *visir*; he fought against the squadrons of Philip II and against those of the Italian republics, and ravaged the Mediterranean coasts in the name of the Ottoman empire. His naval victories were numerous and he never ceased to be one of the highest dignitaries of Constantinople.

Mustafa became the first favourite of Selim II. He was a grand-marshal of the court, *lalá-bajá* (or noble) of the empire, governor of Egypt and conqueror of Georgia; but he died in disgrace without having achieved his supreme ambition to occupy the post of prime minister.

Piali approached the Balearic Islands after his successes in Italy, in June 1558, in command of a formidable fleet — reinforced by some units of the King of France — consisting of more than 150 galleys and several galleons, large ships with considerable sail, powerfully armed with 24 long-range bronze cannons. 15,000 fighting men had embarked under Mustafa's orders, with «munitions and provisions for the said army and its horses», as the Catalan deputies said in their urgent letter asking for aid from the kingdom of Aragon, «in this most extreme and urgent necessity», when the many sails of the «Turkish navy» were sighted from San Feliu de Guixols, Tossa and Blanes. Barcelona, crippled by the plague, managed to obtain a reinforcement of 500 Aragonese, but Piali's fleet did not stop on the Catalan coast on this occasion — it was not long since Cadaqués, Rosas and Palamós had been brutally sacked — having learnt from experience to choose more isolated places where no help of any sort could be expected.

Nevertheless, it would seem that news of the proximity of Piali's fleet had reached the Balearic islands, since «it was common knowledge that it was against them that the expedition was directed». The Viceroy of Mallorca, Guillermo Rocafull, doubled the guards and endeavoured to repair some of the fortifications. Whether Menorca received this news or not is doubtful, although an old Mallorcan historian is of the opinion that, «as the Moor is such a domestic enemy in these waters and is so often to be seen from these islands, the inhabitants did not think this fleet would halt there». In any case, Menorca could not have appeared as a very valuable prey, since at that time it was going through years of deep crisis. Impoverished by the stagnation of its commerce, due to the lack of maritime safety; its population reduced by the hazardous conditions of life (it scarcely amounted to 10,000 at that time); its agriculture slowed down for lack of labour; its coasts left defenceless by the emigration of the peasants into the less directly threatened hinterlands; its people weighed down by payment of taxes and debts forcibly contracted (for the construction of the fort of San Felipe alone the citizens of Ciudadela had to contribute more than 221 *libras* a year); and on top of all that the constant danger of invasion by pirates, condemned Menorca to indescribable sufferings and hardships.

It is curious that Mustafa and Piali, informed no doubt of all this, should still persist, after their victorious raids on richer lands, in assaulting the island of Menorca. Be this as it may, the Turks arrived off Mahón on the night of 29th June 1558 and bombarded the partly-built fort of San Felipe with cannon fire. The *Alcaide,* Pedro Esquerra, resisted the attack, answering the fire with the castle's artillery, getting the culbrins — despite their short range — to «sink three or four galleys». Piali prudently retreated, sailed round the north coast of the island and, at about 7 o'clock on the morning of 30th June, the enemy navy approached Ciudadela from the side of the *Gregal* and *Tramontana.* *

Since the Arab domination, Ciudadela had remained the capital of the island, no doubt because, being on the west coast, it was the nearest port to Mallorca. Fortified since the beginning of the fourteenth century, the walled city was built over a long narrow inlet of the sea, which advanced inland until it became a shallow channel and eventually lost itself in the fields which at that time were situated to the north of the city. This little port was a safe refuge for the shallow draught vessels which moored

* Menorcan names for winds: «Greek» (North-East) and North respectively.

beside the walls of the city. Winding, suffocating streets were enclosed between the city walls, surrounded by moats, and five stout doors allowed entry to the capital. The one which opened to the east was called the Mahón Gate, and here began the road which led to that port. The western gate, known as the «Puerta d'en Salas» (possibly where the present day Paseo de San Nicolás begins), was the most important because it gave access to the great parade ground square — the Borne — and because it was placed on the Trabuco bastion which contained the Real Alcázar (royal castle), the seat and residence of the Governor of the island since the Arab domination. The luxurious palace of the *almojarifes,* later the residence of Alfonso the Liberal, was set into the wall of the port and communicated with the bastion. It was reinforced in the time of Alfonso by the Moors who had stayed on as captives, «whom the King ordered to make the Alcázar wall», as Muntaner relates. To the north of the city the gateway known as the «Portal de ses Fonts» gave on to the lane leading to the fields; and «la Baixama», the path leading to the port, wound underneath «es Portalets». The fifth gate, the «Puerta d'Artruix», gave onto a rocky slope which lead to the open sea on the southern side.

The precinct must have been fairly extensive, according to what the Menorcan historian Antonio Ramis y Ramis writes: in 1363 «it was planned that the boundary of Ciudadela should be under the protection of the corresponding wall, so that people on horseback could go round it without being molested by the enemy in case of invasion.» Even so, having been under threat for centuries, life for the thousand or so inhabitants of Ciudadela in 1558 must have been anything but pleasant. The recurrent calamities they had to bear would have contributed to the deterioration of their morale and of their houses, most of which were poor in the extreme. (Even the mansions of the feudal families who had fled from the country at the beginning of the century to take refuge in the city were modest and unkempt.) And the rigorous evening curfew, added to the strict religious supervision imposed by the many convents, no doubt heightened the general atmosphere of danger and unease in which the population lived.

In June of that year (1558) the Governor of Menorca *ad interim, Mosén* Bartolomé Arguimbau, a Ciudadelan by birth, held the post of Lieutenant of the Government, while awaiting the arrival of the Governor-elect, Juan de Cardona y Rocabertí; this turned out to be a fortunate occurence, because the Ampurdán noble was «not quite the man for that government», to quote the opinion of Princess Juana, regent of Spain while the King, her brother, was on a visit to England. But the interim Governor, Argimbau, was supported by *Mosén* Rafael Pons, assistant solicitor-royal; Francisco Arnau, administrator; and Miguel Negrete, captain of a small group of soldiers of the garrison and head of the armed forces of the island. These and other officials and officers in the royal service carried out their responsibilities conscientiously, but there was little they could do in the face of such adverse conditions.

II

It is possible that Argimbau may already have witnessed Piali's action against San Felipe, as it happened on the feast of St. Peter when he was in the fort giving the soldiers their monthly pay. Without being able to foresee the terrible consequences of his decision, he gave orders that the women and children in Mahón should take refuge in Ciudadela. As the Ciudadelan historian Cosme Parpal y Marqués explains, «the natives and neighbours of Mahón stayed in this city, clear proof that it was there (Mahón) where it was feared the attack would be directed.»

A few hours after his return to Ciudadela (it was after midnight by the time he got there) the Governor learnt of the arrival of the awesome Ottoman fleet off the capital. Accompanied by *Mosén* Guillermo Martorell, he immediately set off again for Mercadal, Alayor and Mahón in search of the greatest possible number of reinforcements, leaving Miguel Negrete in Ciudadela «to oversee and maintain the fortifications».

Argimbau devoted the whole of 1st July to going from one town to another, but he did not succeed in recruiting more than 110 men in Alayor, 100 in Mercadal and, although 50 men from Mahón set out, only seven or eight of them reached Ciudadela (a mysterious defection this, considering that the Governor himself went after them several times). The Governor overtook the small force and was back in Ciudadela before dawn, giving orders that Mallorca was to be informed of what was happening. He twice sent letters to the Viceroy through a sailor called Pedro Campllonc who, despite the danger, managed to slip through the enemy blockade and make a headlong landing, as he was to explain later, «running the bows onto the land, and leaving the boat and fleeing into the hills, with the danger of being captured by the Turks». But the only positive result of the pleas for help was the wreck of poor Pedro's boat.

When the Turks began their attack on the city on 2nd July the defensive position of Ciudadeda amounted to this: barely 230 island villagers, 400 men from the capital, 40 of Negrete's soldiers and possibly 150 recruits who, under the command of Pedro Gomila, had arrived from the castle of San Felipe. Precious few at all events were these approximately 800 inexpert fighting men against an invading force of 15,000 well trained soldiers.

There exists a curious and moving document, written in Catalan, dated in Constantinople on 7th October 1558 and signed by Ciudadelans who were taken prisoner by the Turks and who were eye-witnesses of the events which took place that year in the attack on Ciudadela. The signatories were: Bartolomé Arguimbau, interim Governor; Miguel Negrete, captain of infantry; Juan Martorell, knight; Martín Traver; Juan Aloy, blacksmith; Gabriel Mercadal, a farmer from Biniatzem; Rafael Bru, a priest; and the notary Pedro Quintana, who authenticated the document. The account of the bloody struggle, drawn up with simplicity and humility by people who without any doubt were its heroes, is read every year in the Town Hall of Ciudadela on 9th July. We will follow the steps of this singular testament, quoting its own words wherever possible.

The twenty-four cannon on the galleys soon began

their relentless and uninterrupted bombardment of the town, and for «seven successive days, by day and by night, they employed their batteries and destroyed the wall and bastions». After the first round of cannon-fire, which covered the landing of Mustafa's janissaries — probably at the spot now known as Cala del Degollador (Cut-throat Creek) to the south of the port, and in the fields around Cala Blanes to the north, as it was unlikely that Piali would venture to expose his galleys right up to the end of the narrow port — the enemy militia surrounded Ciudadela and dug themselves in, facing the walls in massive formation. The Turkish infantry which fell on Ciudadela was composed for the most part of janissaries, light shock troops particularly feared for their discipline and efficiency. Some historians maintain that these trained soldiers were recruited from the Christian children kidnapped in the pirates' raids and educated for war since childhood. They were easily distinguished by their colourful garments, consisting of loose-fitting apparel, large pointed caps and strong brass-nailed boots. The rapidity of action of their bows and well-sharpened arrows, the effectiveness of their curved sabres, and the speed of their movements — as well as their tactic of advancing in tightly formed squadrons — gave them enormous advantage over their enemies, who were armed with heavy cross-bows, or blunderbusses, and slowed down by cumbersome armour. Moreover, however fiercely the peasants defended the capital of Menorca, they had no appreciable quantity of arms of any sort.

Argimbau and Captain Negrete took command of the fighting, organising the defence of Ciudadela as best they could with such scant means that it is pathetic to read that, slipping through the close blockade, a few of the defenders managed to bring into the precinct some crude weapons for its protection: «They cut branches and despite the enemy placed them inside the town.» It was indeed heroic to try to defend their city with a few branches. And even more moving is the following paragraph concerning this episode. The Governor, seeing that a few meters away from the wall the enemy were constructing strong trenches in which to emplace the ships' artillery, and thinking that several cannons were already installed, «they armed six men with nails and hammers to spike the said artillery, and despite the enemy they went into the trenches, but did not find the artillery». But even though on that day the siege batteries, which Negrete's brave soldiers had wanted to silence with nails and hammers, had not arrived, the enemy soon attacked furiously. Protected by pallisades and trenches, the Turks bombarded the weak walls, which began to disintegrate, the very stones dislodged from the wall by the blows of the artillery fire, causing a large number of casualties.

Wives and daughters of the city's defenders were at their side, boldly helping them to repair the breaches, covering the openings with branches, wood and earth, to the extreme of using woollens, mattresses and sacks of clothing from their own homes in a valiant effort to reinforce the bastions. Both men and women fought day and night until they dropped from sheer sleep and exhaustion, to rise again and continue the struggle.

Despite the great damage which the walls and bastions had suffered, the cannons of Ciudadela succeeded in weakening the enemies' positions. «Those within fired with artillery and arquebusses, killing many of the enemy, dislodging many pieces of their artillery and destroying their trenches and bastions.» But, as was to be expected, the losses suffered by the Menorcans were enormous: «almost all the gunners were killed, as well as many other people on the said bastions.» Moreover, the Turks lost no opportunity to impose their special brand of war nerves, and night after night, from the first to the last day of the siege, a voice cried out to them from the enemy line, in Spanish, urging them to surrender the city: «They shouted to the said Regent and Captain, addressing them by name and demanding on the part of the Bajá and Captain-General of the fleet that they should surrender the city.» But to promises of pardon the answer was always a furious salvo of Negrete's artillery, delivered «where they would feel it», not without courteously warning the crier beforehand to retreat.

Eventually the Trabuco walls and the San Juan bastion

collapsed and the breach thus opened was so large «that a beast could pass through it». Mustafa took advantage of this to order an assault on the weakened enemy position; with a great show of flags the Turkish army concentrated a powerful attack against the Christian fortifications. Four times they were driven back and, after the last battle, which lasted three hours, the janissaries were defeated and obliged to retreat. Enemy losses in dead and wounded were heavy, but the assault had decimated the small Ciudadelan army to such an extent that when Negrete mustered his fighting men no more than 200 remained.

The situation was already dire enough in itself, owing to the few combatants still on their feet and the scarcity of ammunition, when a new calamity occurred to worsen the fate of the city. The gunpowder store, situated in the warehouses of the *Universidad,* caught fire, burning itself out in a few minutes. Not only the gunpowder was lost but also cord and bow-wire. In the end not a thing was left with which to repel the enemy.

Even so, Ciudadela continued to stand firm.

On foot and on horseback, Argimbau and Captain Negrete went tirelessly back and forth over the positions, «eating and drinking where they stood», inspiring the spirits of the defenders and organising what remained of the militia. In the absence of gunners the Governor took charge of one battery and, although badly injured in the chest by the grapeshot of a cannon which had exploded as the match-cord was lit, went on commanding the defence of the capital.

A little later Pedro Gomila also fell, wounded, grasping the royal standard.

At the end of a week's impressive struggle, and notwithstanding the tenacity and bravery of the besieged Ciudadelans, the situation of the city had become desperate in the extreme and any resistance was almost impossible. Food was becoming scarce, many buildings were in ruins, and the problem of burying the dead had become acute. Moreover, the Turks were threatening the other side of the walls and were building ramparts opposite the Salas gateway. Without any hope whatever of receiving the aid requested from Mallorca, a delegation of Councillors, captains and representatives of the people appeared before Negrete and Arguimbau, asking their permission to retreat in good order from the city, «considering the few that remain to fight and without ammunition to put up a good resistance against such a force of the enemy». The Governor and the Captain were opposed to this abandonment of their land without defending it *usque ad mortem* but, in view of the insistence of the populace and realising that they could not resist a fresh attack, they acceded to the wish of the Councillors, though not without recording an official protest before the notary and clerk to the *Universidad*, Martín Antonio Bonet.

Men and women rushed to the Mahón gateway and the retreat ran the risk of degenerating into a rout, when the Governor and Captain Negrete — still occupied in commanding the batteries on the walls — came to give the official order for the evacuation of Ciudadela. At nightfall a police patrol was twice sent to search the roads because, quite rightly, «it was suspected that Turks would be there». Once assured that there was nothing which would impede the free passage of the convoy, the men of Mercadal and Alayor were grouped together and headed the column, followed by women, children, the wounded and other useless people. Arguimbau and Negrete defended the rearguard with the forces remaining. When a large part of the populace was already on its way, those last to leave the city were warned that the vanguard had been attacked by a Turkish detachment and, faced with the danger of being horribly wiped out, the leaders ordered a precipitate retreat behind the walls of the threatened city.

Mustafa was soon informed of the anguished situation of his enemies and on the following morning, 9th July, he ordered his army to force an entry into Ciudadela by the Puerta de Salas.

The heroism of those people was admirable, as they defended their land, inch by inch, up to the last moment. A handful of Menorcans climbed the walls and continued the attack, but few remained to stop the Turkish hordes which before long reached the Plaza del Borne. A fresh resistance was organised in the centre of the city and, with clubs and sticks, the Ciudadelans managed to beat back the invaders to their batteries. But the advantage was only momentary. The Turks attacked powerfully, succeeding in reducing the defenders and completely mastering the city.

The barbarous sacking of Ciudadela, with its slaugter, rape, destruction and arson, lasted three days. Churches and monasteries, altars and holy ornaments, houses, archives, jewels, clothes, everything, fell under the devastating vandalism of the invaders. The savage hordes of janissaries stormed the countryside for many leagues into the interior: they attacked the farms, killed the cattle and burned the crops.

Almost half the population of the whole island was embarked on Piali's ships which departed for Constantinople with no less than 3,452 prisoners.

The Court of Castile, paraphrasing the reports arriving from Menorca, described the tragic event as follows: «The town of Ciudadela and the island of Menorca were taken by the Turks, by fighting and force or arms. Not only did they kill and capture all its inhabitants, who, like good and faithful citizens, endeavoured to defend themselves to the death, but with much cruelty and rage destroyed and burnt all its houses, churches and monasteries and put people to flight and laid waste the countryside for two leagues around, without leaving anything standing, so that the said town was depopulated and ruined.»

III

Barcelona was the first to receive news of the devastation which Ciudadela had suffered, and soon not only all of Spain but the whole of Christendom learnt of the heroism and capture of its inhabitants.

Faced with the loss of all the town's authorities, Mallorca sent Federico de Cors to assume temporary responsibility for the government of the island. It is hairraising to read in the city's archives that the first task of this worthy gentleman was «to bury the many dead bodies, both of people and animals», and that his first residence was to be «a cave, because all the houses were demolished and burnt». The guard was scrupulously kept every night «by ten or a dozen armed men» — although so little now remained to be protected that their zeal appears to have been rather useless; «and he gave orders to clean up the whole of the battery and close the breaches in the walls with dry stones». Hardly three weeks had passed since the disaster before this admirable organiser had appointed people to administrative posts. He selected the Bailiff-General, the Councillors and other officials from among the farmers and artisans.

Among the few survivors who remained to be sworn in to their posts on 31st July 1558, the same names appear as are constantly found in the long lists of deportees to Constantinople; Menorcan names repeated like a litany throughout the history of the island: the Quart family (Joanot Quart was appointed Bailiff-General) lost sixteen of its members; the Amellers (an Ameller was made Consul-Bailiff) nineteen; Mascaró (Treasurer) fourteen; the Saura family also fourteen; the Gomilas twenty-one; the Arguimbaus twenty; the Olivars sixteen; the Squeller family fifteen. The impetuous and brave Martorells — later to become the Marquesses of Albranca — lost twenty of their family, one of the survivors, Joanot Martorell, being appointed Military Councillor. The Uguets recovered their good name, sullied in the Barbarossa assault, as a result of the sacrifice of twenty-six members of their family in the taking of Ciudadela. Several nuns and novices among the twenty-four who were taken prisoner in the Santa Clara convent came from these families, and the Abbess, Sister Águeda de Ametller was martyred, being hanged and killed by arquebus fire in the garden of the convent. Piali's ships also had on board twelve friars from the San Francisco monastery, as well as hundreds of inhabitants of the municipalities of Alayor, Mercadal and Ferrerías, and many women and children from Mahón who had taken refuge in the capital. It is curious to note that the Castilian names (Moreno, Carretero, Segovia, etc.) which figure in the list of prisoners are those of soldiers from the garrison and their families. In these mournful pages, what stands out is the tremendous greed of the Turks for prisoners: they did not hesitate to put in chains even the forty patients in the hospital.

As «the town was now completely depopulated», the most imperative task, after appointing the authorities, was to find new inhabitants. The new Governor, Federico de Cors, enjoyed at that time, as on the many occasions when he had to have recourse to the Court, the unconditional support of Princess Juana. By the end of November the bureaucratic machinery of the Viceroys of Catalonia, Valencia and Mallorca had begun to function and the future inhabitants of the island were found from among their people. In order to make voluntary emigration more attractive, the newcomers were offered lands and houses free of tax for ten years. This is evident in a Royal Ordinance dated 14th December 1558: «Any persons at present living or dwelling in the said town of Ciudadela and who propose to reside there in future... shall in either case be free and exempt from paying tithes... for a period of ten years as from the date hereof.»

But as this was insufficient to restore the economy of the island, Princess Juana had to intervene again, asking the Governor of Catalonia to reduce the poll-tax and exhorting the Catalan creditors to reduce their interest rates. She prevailed upon the Solicitor-General of Mallorca to suspend temporarily the tax levied for the construction of the San Felipe fort near Mahón, and the Bishop was asked to pardon non-payment of church tithes. Doña Juana went even further in her charitable interest in the fate of Ciudadela when she interceded with Pope Pius IV to get him to authorise plenary and *pro difunctis* indulgences for the purpose of obtaining alms for the ransom of the Menorcan prisoners. But although this did not succeed in arousing the ever reluctant charity of the Christian world, the sums raised being insufficient to redeem all the captives, the efforts and the dedication of Marcos Martí, a native of Alayor, not to mention the risks he ran in his journey to Constantinople, did culminate in the liberation of many of his fellow islanders.

This future priest did not confine himself, in his selfless work, to ransoming those who signed themselves (in a letter included in Martí's extensive documentation) «the slaves of Menorca» and who complained bitterly: «Our servitude is so great that we suffer more in this country than anywhere else. Christians are flayed alive here, they are subject to greater opprobrium than in any other place.» He also devoted himself to redeeming *objects d'art* and documents sacked by the Turks in Ciudadela. A polychrome wooden carving, representing the Adoration of the Shepherds, was restored to the convent of Santa María and, even more important, he bought for 400 ducats the famous «*Llibre Vermell*» (the Vermillion Book). This book, bound in red leather, was the first and only testimony in existence of the laws and privileges granted to Menorca by Alfonso after the conquest, and also contained records of innumerable legal matters relating to the island. Its disappearance and presumed destruction had forced the royal functionaries to search anxiously in the Crown archives in the hope of finding some information about the legal position of the Menorcan people, their appointments, lands and franchises.

The «*Llibre Vermell*», albeit somewhat deteriorated, was brought back to Ciudadela from Turkey in 1560 by Doña Esperanza Alsina who, for this singular service, requested exemption from taxes for herself and her heirs.

But neither the freeing of the captives nor the recovery of the documents would ever erase from the historical memory of Menorca the horror of the Turkish invasion. The year 1558 would forever be the «*any de sa desgràcia*» (the year of misfortune).

Three centuries later, in the centre of the Plaza del Borne in Ciudadela, an obelisk was erected on which appear the words: «PRO ARIS ET FOCIS HIC SUSTINUIMUS USQUE AD MORTEM» (For hearth and home we here endured unto death).

Until the beginning of the seventeenth century, Menorca suffered from the systematic threat of incursions from the Barbary coast. And added to this danger were innumerable misfortunes which aggravated the miserable state in which the inhabitants of the island lived. Cholera decimated the population; consecutive plagues of locusts destroyed the crops; the hair-raising plagues of rats in 1574, 1600 and 1601 increased the agony and the privation; tremendous droughts burnt the pastures and the cattle died; people suffered from hunger; banditry, violence and immorality reigned in the land. In 1573 the number of Menorcan homesteads amounted to 852, and in 1588 there were only 1,195 families living in the island. Mahón had neither doctor nor pharmacist, and Ciudadela recovered so slowly from the dramatic «year of misfortune» that, inhibited by terror and poverty, her inhabitants begged His Catholic Majesty «graciously to grant permission for us to leave this land for some other, where it is possible to live in safety». (Nevertheless, when Philip II ordered the evacuation of Menorca in 1570, the Menorcans, backed by the Councillors of Barcelona, were vigorously opposed to the measure.)

Despite so many calamities, the constant obsession was the Turkish attacks. Island life became subordinate to defence work, and the *Universidades* united — rising above their many quarrels and litigations — to build defence towers along the coast, equip a fort in Fornells and fortify Monte Toro so that it could be used as a refuge in the event of a fresh attack. These works went on for many years, and so it was that the fort of San Felipe was not completed until 1608, and the reconstruction of the walls of Ciudadela lasted until 1614.

The watch towers (still standing today) which were constructed along the coast gave warning of the approach of enemy ships by means of fire signals. But in spite of this the pirates succeeded in landing and in carrying off peasants and cattle. Binidonaire, Colom Island, Torreblanca de Favaritx, Ses Coves, Cala Turqueta and many other places were the scenes of corsair attacks, bravely repelled by the country people, who suffered no small losses.

As a result of all this, but principally due to the pirate invasions, the island of Menorca endured, for almost two centuries, the most disastrous period of its history.

Part III

18th CENTURY

THE WAR OF THE SPANISH SUCCESSION

The English 1708-1756

The French 1756-1763

The English again 1763-1782

The Spanish 1782-1798

The third and last English occupation
1798-1802

The first half of the tumultuous and bellicose eighteenth century was characterised in Europe by a whole complex chequer-board of pacts and alliances, necessary to maintain the balance of power between the sovereign states. Dynastic struggles and endless wars imposed hegemonies, colonial empires and new commercial routes. England and France fought furiously for dominion of the Western world. The international power of Spain having been broken when the House of Austria was replaced by that of the Bourbons, Spain was tossed about like chaff by the powerful nations of Europe who submerged her in their conflicts and ambitions.

The strategic position of Menorca and the great possibilities of the port of Mahón brought the island once more into the centre of foreign interests and, for almost a hundred years, England and France took her and left her, by war or by treaty — almost as fancy pleased them — like one more token to be exchanged in the *bourse* of their diplomatic negotiations. If truth be told, Menorca did not lose out in all these comings and goings of the great powers; pampered, the island was reborn under the care of her new occupants.

For Spain, the eighteenth century began with the death of Charles II «the Bewitched». When he died without issue in 1700, Prince Philip, grandson of Louis XIV of France, was nominated heir to the Crown of Spain in the royal will. This surprising decision on the part of the last Hapsburg monarch immediately provoked war between the European powers and unleashed a long drawn out civil war in Spain.

The War of the Spanish Succession was to be waged on the one side by the formidable coalition of England, Holland, Austria and Portugal, who, anxious to keep French supremacy within limits, supported the Austrian pretender, the Archduke Charles. France, whose clever political intrigues had been crowned with success, seeing herself already the mistress of Franco-Spanish destinies, sided naturally enough with the Bourbon. A large part of Spain was to remain loyal and to fight for her French King, but the ancient kingdom of Aragon — which included Catalonia, Valencia, Aragon and the Balearics — would find in this dynastic struggle a hope, according to the Catalan historian Ferran Soldevila, «of changing its situation within the Spanish monarchy».

The antagonisms between Castile and Catalonia, and the different political aspirations of these two peoples, would find an echo in those foreign countries who were fighting for dominance of the European world. France, a model of state unification, represented absolute monarchy and centralisation; Austria and England, decentralised imperialism and «Enlightenment». It was only natural, therefore, that Catalonia, stimulated by the unconditional promise of protection from these two countries, and with expectations of future autonomy, should want to recover from her decadence and take the side of the Archduke Charles. And if, yet again in Catalan history, the effort to defend her federative tendencies turned out to be as disastrous as it was useless, examples of great bravery and unbreakable tenacity of purpose in her attempt to impose on the rest of Spain «this little king who had been made for them» were not lacking.

The first years of the war were favourable to the Archduke Charles. Accompanied by an English army and an Anglo-Dutch squadron, he disembarked in Lisbon in 1704 and that year took Gibraltar, thus giving the fleet of Queen Anne of England the key to the Mediterranean. A little later the Allies began the blockade of Barcelona, which capitulated, and the Austrian pretender made his solemn entry into the capital of Catalonia on 9th October 1705 to the joyous reception of the Catalans, who proclaimed him King as Charles III of Spain. The Balearics followed the example of their ancient capital: Mallorca revolted against the Bourbons a year later, and Menorca — oppressed by the strong garrison which occupied the island — declared a civil war, the Archduke being proclaimed King in Ciudadela on 20th October. The struggle between *Carlistas* and *Felipistas* lasted three months, until, in January 1707, Philip V sent a reinforcement of a French batallion to the Governor of the island, Diego Leonardo Dávila, who was again able to gain control.

On the Peninsula, the war continued with attacks and counter-attacks by both sides. Charles occupied Madrid, but Philip regained it. Peterborough and Lord Galway commanded the invading forces; the Duke of Berwick was at the head of the Franco-Spanish army and occupied Aragon and Valencia in 1707, suppressing their liberties. With the battles of Almenara and Zaragoza the Allies won a large part of Spain, but the Duc de Vendôme succeeded in driving them out as a result of his victories at Brihuega and Villaviciosa. In the north, Gerona was besieged by the French. Meanwhile England, not losing sight of her ambition to install herself firmly in the Mediterranean, occupied Menorca in the name of Charles III on 29th September 1708.

The War of the Spanish Succession lasted for more than ten years. Catalonia and the Balearics were bearing the brunt of it when an event of international importance occurred, which decided the fate of the Bourbons. The Austrian Emperor, Joseph I, brother of the Archduke Charles, died without male issue and Charles inherited the crown of the Holy Roman Empire. England, faced with the possibility — should Charles become King of Spain — of seeing reunited the extensive territories which had once constituted the empire of Charles V, radically changed her attitude. The German Confederation had become too powerful and would annul the English effort to maintain the difficult balance of power on the continent. The Archduke Charles and Catalonia were abandoned in exchange for two important tricks which would leave England with the winning hand in the gamble for the Mediterranean: Gibraltar and Menorca. The European peace treaty was signed in Utrecht in April 1713. Philip V, the Bourbon, was assured of the throne of Spain, and

England of her predominance of the western Mediterranean. Catalonia lost what liberties remained to her.

After a glorious and stubborn defence on the part of both bourgeoisie and peasants, Barcelona capitulated on 11th September 1714; Mallorca and Ibiza a year later. Only Menorca, under an English occupation which made no attempt at assimilation — and which was to last forty-four years — would retain her privileges and her own peculiar way of life.

Among the many and important consequences of the Treaty of Utrecht, one of the most immediate was the increase in England's overseas possessions, to the cost of French interests, in North America. Maritime and commercial competition between the two countries gave the French new energy to install themselves more comfortably on the American continent, by penetrating, from Canada to the Ohio valley, the very heart of the English colony. In 1755, with the frivolous Louis XV on the throne of France, hostilities broke out between England and France in America, and shortly afterwards a French squadron appeared off Ciudadela. Troops of the ineffable Marshal Richelieu took two months to dislodge the English from Menorca. In addition to purely strategic purposes, this occupation formed part of the diplomatic games of the French King, who was trying to place the Spanish monarch, by offering him the island, under the obligation of agreeing to a military alliance against England in the Seven Years' War. But Ferdinand VI, devoted to the task of slowly restructuring his country and defending the peace and neutrality of Spain at all costs, did not accept such a tempting offer, and Menorca continued under French rule for another seven years.

Later on, Pitt's government vigorously undertook, from England, the defence of its colonial empire. The decline of the French army and navy led to the fall of Quebec and Montreal, and Louis XV at last had to give up his American possessions. Under the Treaty of Paris in 1763, France ceded Canada, Nova Scotia and the whole of the region to the east of the Mississippi to England. George III, desirous of wiping away the affront received in the Mediterranean — and ever mindful of his strategic and commercial interests — demanded the restitution of the island of Menorca.

So, for reasons which, as far as the history of Spain is concerned, are purely marginal, but which are closely bound up with English colonial history, the flag of His Britannic Majesty was raised for a second time over Menorca. This new domination was to last for eighteen years.

In the second part of the eighteenth century a new order of human society emerged from the rivalry of political ideals and forms of government. In England, parliamentary democracy was already supreme; the Revolution would put an end to the absolutism of the French monarch. But the bellicose tendencies did not cease, nor did Great Britain neglect defending her already vast empire. By the end of the century the Directorate, the figure of Napoleon Bonaparte, and the French victories would complicate even further the fluctuating loyalties between states.

Charles III of Spain, on inheriting an organised and stable kingdom, would put into practice his own interpretation of «Enlightened Despotism» and would participate in European disputes by binding himself through the Third Family Pact — and in order to ensure support against England — to a mutual aid agreement between the Bourbons, not only in Europe but also in the colonised continents. Following this policy, and in defence of his own interests, when the English colonists declared their independence in 1776, France and Spain sent effective help to the rebellious colonists, with the consequent reprisals of the all-powerful English navy. The many humiliations imposed on Spanish ships by English corsairs, although perhaps trifling compared with other events in America, constituted outrages which were to serve as the basis for the outbreak of hostilities between the two countries in the summer of 1779. But the aim of these would, in part, be to recover Gibraltar and Menorca.

After a long and fruitless blockage of Gibraltar and various naval defeats, a Franco-Spanish squadron prepared to attack Menorca. The expedition set out from Cádiz under the command of the Duke of Crillon — a French military veteran in the service of Spain — on 23rd July 1781. A landing was effected without difficulty and, after six months' resistance, the English garrison on the island capitulated.

Menorca having been reconquered, a peace was signed in Versailles, with advantageous terms for Spain: she recovered, in addition to Menorca, the whole of Florida, Nicaragua, Honduras and Campeche, which had been occupied by Britain. Thus began a brief period of Anglo-Spanish peace, and Menorca remained reintegrated into the Crown of His Catholic Majesty until 1798.

The French Revolution, unleashed in 1789, turned Spain — for obvious reasons of monarchic principles — into an enemy of the French government. But on defending his ideological inclinations by allying himself with England, Charles IV created the problem of acting against his own strategic interests, shared as always with France. The resolution of this dilema was fatal. The counter-revolutionary struggle between 1793 and 1795 gave rise to the invasion of the Basque country and Catalonia by French troops. A new revision of alliances, the break with England, the pact with the Directorate and then with Napoleon, dragged a debilitated Spain into war. England, who continued to be the principal maritime power in the Mediterranean, struck once more at Menorca. The ships of George III besieged Ciudadela for three days, and on 16th November 1798 the third and last English domination of Menorca began.

A little later Napoleon paraded victorious throughout half of Europe, and a change of ministry in England — eager to seek relief for her closely pursued forces — counselled peace between the two countries. Godoy — who was in charge in Spain and who had strong links with France — took advantage of British weakness and managed, by the Treaty of Amiens in 1802, to recover Menorca.

Thus terminated the vicissitudes of the conquests and reconquests of this small island, so sought after by the powers who fought for hegemony in the Mediterranean.

I. The War of the Spanish Succession

I

When Charles II of Spain died withouth issue on 1st November 1700, and the royal will, whereby the Crown of Spain should pass to the Duke of Anjou, second son of the Dauphin of France and grandson of Louis XIV, became known, alarm spread rapidly throughout the provinces of the ancient principality of Catalonia and Aragon. A Bourbon on the throne would lead to a unified state on French lines, France being the model of absolutism and centralisation. Castile would take advantage of the protection of the most powerful monarch in Europe to conserve the centralising and unifying tendencies of the Spanish monarch, while the autonomist and federative tendencies of the kingdom of Aragon with its own system of privileges would be in danger of being attacked by those who saw in its regime and constitution «a static defence sign». For some, «collective and individual liberty seemed an anachronism in the face of the omnipotence of the Prince», as Soldevila, the Catalan historian, put it, in Machiavellian terms; to others, no form of political life could exist which did not incorporate these virtues.

The interests of Castile and Catalonia differed; their conceptions of government and of the structure of the state were opposed.

Austria, England and Holland took advantage of this antagonism between Castile and Catalonia to improve their positions in Europe, and when they signed the Grand Alliance in The Hague in September 1701 and later proclaimed Charles, second son of the Emperor Leopold I of Austria, as King of Spain, with the name of Charles III, the entire principality placed itself unconditionally on the side of the Archduke.

Meanwhile the Duke of Anjou had been crowned as Philip V of Spain.

With realistic vision the Catalans understood that the

Hapsburgs would be more respectful of local autonomies than the Bourbons, and urged on by the resounding Austrian campaign, which condemned the «oppressive despot» and praised Catalan laws and liberties, became the most fervent and loyal partisans of the House of Austria. But this did not lead them to lose their practical sense, and until they received in the summer of 1705 a guarantee of support of 8,000 foot-soldiers, 12,000 guns and 2,000 allied horses, and had assured themselves that, even if things should go badly, the integrity of their institutions would be protected, they did not proclaim the rebellion which was to become a bloody civil war.

In this struggle, apart from the political advantages which would result from possession of the Spanish provinces, Louis XIV was to seek enlargement of the House of Bourbon, «while dominion of the Mediterranean was the primary aim of English expansionism».

For more than a year Philip V of Spain had been fighting against Allied arms on the Portuguese front, while Anglo-Dutch naval forces were savagely harassing Spanish ports, and Gibraltar, garrisoned by barely a hundred soldiers, had to surrender to the powerful squadron of Admiral Rooke. Meanwhile, Allied propaganda had in-flamed the whole of the east coast of Spain in favour of the Archduke. Denia was the first Spanish fortress to acclaim the invaders, in August 1705, proclaiming the young Austrian pretender sovereign of Spain. And when, at the end of that month, «the first Charles III» trod Catalan soil, the people of Barcelona, to the cry of «Visca la pàtria! Visquen els furs! Visca Carles III!» («Long live the motherland! Long live its laws and privileges! Long live Charles III!»), they supported *en masse* the landings of Allied troops. The Viceroy, Francisco Velasco, resisted the blockade for a month but, faced with the hostility of the populace, was forced to capitulate on 8th October 1705. Charles made his entry into Barcelona with royal honours, and was proclaimed King a short time later by the corporation, the nobility and the people.

The welcome which the population of Barcelona offered

this young man of twenty was delirious, their devotion idolatrous. In the words of a contemporary ditty:

> *Viva lo Rey d'Espanya,*
> *Carlos Tercer es lo nom.*
> *És blanch com un Colom*
> *Vingut d'Alemanya.**

It went on to praise his beauty with these gallant phrases: «beautiful as a pearl», «his eyes are two stars».

In his person were placed the patriotic hopes of Catalonia. Nor did the Catalans defraud him of his confidence in them, defending the Carlist capital for almost ten years.

From the taking of Barcelona the uprising had extended throughout the whole of Aragon and part of Castile, until in June 1706 the Archduke was declared King of Spain in Madrid. On 24th September an Anglo-Duch fleet appeared off Palma, demanding its surrender. The authorities, supported by a politically violent populace, capitulated. The Count of Zavellá landed with 200 English soldiers — who were to remain as a garrison in the castle of San Carlos — and on 4th October 1706 the pretender from the House of Austria was proclaimed King.

Menorca demonstrated clearly her preference for the German, but open revolt was difficult due to the strong garrison defending the island. Nevertheless, on 19th October an insurrection against Philip V took place in Mercadal.

II

With the dawn of the eighteenth century, Menorca's tragic isolation appeared to have reached its end as she became once more one of the nerve centres of the western Mediterranean. Having recognised her strategic importance and the undeniable advantages of the port of Mahón, the last Hapsburgs (Philip IV and Charles II of Spain) were induced to augment the defences of the island. The fort of San Felipe was considered to be one of the first order,

---

* «Long live the King of Spain, / Charles the Third is his name. / He is white as a dove / Come from Germany.»

and more than a hundred large-bore cannon guarded the entrance to the harbour; in Ciudadela the small octagonal castle of San Nicolás was built to guard the mouth of the port. A considerable garrison of Castilian infantry defended the castles of Ciudadela, Mahón and Fornells, and the frequent visits of the royal fleet conferred a clear preponderance on Mahón over the capital, which was soon to lose the privilege of being the city of the Governor's residence when the post of Commander-in-Chief of San Felipe was combined with that of Governor of the island, a matter which naturally aroused the complaints of the *Universidad* of Ciudadela, always afraid that the military command would endanger the liberties of her people.

This constant coming and going of soldiers and war ships, bringing new currents of thought from the Peninsula, was looked at askance by the islanders. Menorca, still eminently rural, enjoyed a simple and austere existence and her people remained attached to their ancient customs. Neither the royal troops nor the Castellan of the fort of San Felipe were accepted with good grace, being particularly resented because of the abuses which the governors from the Peninsula — ignorant of the language, customs and character of the people — committed to achieve their ends.

Menorca was in fact still spiritually linked to Barcelona, although depending judicially on Mallorca and militarily on Madrid.

The island followed its own slow and organised rhythm of life. The political and economic administration was directed by the *Universidad* from Ciudadela. Controlled by meticulous councillors elected annually from among the nobles, bourgeoisie, country people and artisans, the regime was almost democratic, despite the obedience which all owed to the Governor, appointed by the King every six years. Nevertheless, the aristocracy exercised a great political and social influence over the people. Of the fifteen thousand inhabitants, some four or five hundred families — descendants of the original feudal Catalan knights — owned the land, which was worked by their labourers under archaic systems of husbandry. Residing in Ciudadela in what were beginning to be great, austere palaces, tastefully designed, they concerned themselves to some extent with their lands — «where they sow but a tenth part of the land they have» — but to a greater degree with politics and even more with gossip about their neighours, who were involved in endless trials and litigation. For this reason, or because of the natural tendency of the people to seek a higher education, jurists, lawyers, notaries and scribes abounded in Menorca, resolving such disparate matters as inheritances and gambling debts. Doctors, with their complex theories and disastrous practice, were also numerous. They and the surgeons — who at that time were barbers — belonged to the same guild as the pharmacists, druggists, grocers and candle-makers. In the same way, manual workers, peasants, sailors, blacksmiths, wool carders, weavers, tailors, carpenters and cobblers were also grouped into guilds and their rights protected.

But over and above the social establishment, the life of the island was ordered by the Church. The great religious sense of the Menorcans — and the lack of distractions — found its expression in colourful liturgical functions, solemn servcies and pastoral visits. The enthusiastic processions of the confraternities and the pilgrimages to the sanctuaries united these people of deep and simple faith, and the chimes of the bells in the parish churches and many convents governed their daily timetable. In spite of the puritanism and devotion, there was a flourishing brothel in the Calle San Juan in Ciudadela, many houses had Moorish girl slaves whose natural children were kept at home, while a certain trend towards witchcraft was also in fashion at that time. Even so, pleasures were few, meals were frugal and Menorcan *libras* (pounds) — divided into *sous* and *diners* — were amassed slowly and converted into lands. But bit by bit the well-to-do ceased investing all their savings in the country: the physionomy of the towns — enclosed within high walls — began to change, and churches, convents and lordly mansions were built in baroque and neoclassical styles.

In the countryside the peasant and his wife lived poorly, but the extraordinary cleanliness of the farmhouses, years later, was to surprise John Armstrong who, in his «History of the Island of Menorca», published in England in 1752, describes the beauty of the rural homes, regretting only the strong smell which emanated from the pork fat used in the candles. Lacking money and communications, the peasants solved the problem of their basic necessities by the exchange of produce, and cautiously stored provisions for the whole year in larders and lofts; in view of their long experience of constant shortages, first and foremost among these were pickles, salted meats and preserves. And excellent they were, many of them. A little after the conquest, pots of honey and capers (the latter still grow wild today among the dry-stone walls which divide the countryside into fields or «tanques») were sent to the King of Catalonia.

Another important task of the housewife was making clothes for her family. Flax spinning and weaving were practised in country places until quite recently, and the wives would make their own sheets, towels, shirts and aprons with this stout golden thread.

Due to the scant help which reached them from the Peninsula, the island had little to offer and few foreigners settled there, although even the exiled and persecuted were well received and readily assimilated into the life of the country. The result was that Menorcans at that time were insular and conservative to a degree, and their guiding principles were self-sufficiency and a fiercely protective attitude to their laws and privileges. Catalonia, which defended the same political liberties with equal tenacity, was not only admired but imitated, and the Catalan tongue — which for more than four centuries had been the only spoken and written language among the people of Menorca — was a close link between the two peoples.

It is not to be wondered at, then, that in the coming struggle Menorca should remain faithful to Catalan interests.

III

Menorca had accepted the accession of Philip V with ill grace. The festivities and cavalcades which should have celebrated his coronation were replaced by prayers for peace, by order of the General Council, «because we live in such calamitous times», they affirmed.

But the Menorcans did not long delay in expressing their true political opinions, and the island soon became a hot-bed of conspiracy. Encouraged by the enthusiastic proclamation of Charles III in Barcelona, the numerous partisans of the Archduke waited impatiently for the right moment to rebel.

The chief conspirator was Miguel Saura y Morell, a distinguished knight of the second branch of the Saura family of Ciudadela, and an ardent defender, like many of the nobility, of the ancient laws of the island. This man, already quite elderly, displayed a prodigious activity, so much the more effective because of the high esteem in which he was held by the Menorcans. But his work was made difficult by the increase in the normal garrison of the castles, reinforced by 300 men in 1702 and by more than 300 in 1704, all of them Bourbon loyalists. These reinforcements had arrived not through any warning of what was to occur but to oppose a possible English attack, which had been feared ever since the Allies had declared war on Louis XIV and his grandson on 15th May 1702 because they considered them usurpers of the Spanish crown.

News of the insurrection in Mallorca gave the final impulse to Saura and his men, who, to the cry of «Long live Charles III and death to the *Botiflers* *! », initiated the Menorcan uprising a few days later in Mercadal. The following morning the entire capital rose in arms against the established monarchy. Saura and his small volunteer army took possession of the keys of the city guards and of the access to the walls. Followed by the populace, they ran through the streets of Ciudadela, proclaiming Charles III as King and lord of Menorca.

The Governor of the island, Diego Leonardo Dávila, had arrived only a few months before with precise instructions to smother mercilessly any attempt at revolt, and

---

* *Botifler* (or botifleur), according to some authors, is a compound of the French *botte,* and *fleur,* flower, two details of the customary dress of Philipists (high boots and *fleur-de-lis*).

subsequent events clearly demonstrate the hard and intransigent character of this Castilian brigadier. He had under his command 2,000 well-armed veteran soldiers, as well as the security of the support of Spanish and French reinforcements, should the struggle take on an ugly complexion.

Meanwhile a plenary meeting was called in the *Universidad* of Ciudadela, composed of Councillors, knights and other members of the political establishment. *Mosén* Saura appeared before them, accompanied by a large number of the townsfolk, and ordered the scrivener to read the admonition of Charles exhorting the Spanish people «to return to the gentle yoke of his rule, because it is he who, in justice, should wear the crown». With but slight opposition, Charles III was recognised as King. Saura received the appointment of Commander-General of Menorca, a title which was later ratified by the Count of Zavellá, Viceroy of Mallorca.

The remaining *Universidades* in Menorca at once supported the movement and, in a new General Council, the constitution of an army was approved, with the hope of being able to reinforce it with 400 Mallorcans, as demanded personally by the recently elected Councillor-in-Chief, Bernardo de Olives.

Each of the *Universidades* of the island contributed to the formation of such an army according to its means. Ciudadela brought 150 men, Mahón 100, Alayor 100, Mercadal and Ferrerías together 50, making a total of 400 soldiers, divided into eight companies, plus 1,000 volunteers who responded to the call-up with rudimentary arms and a total lack of any military training.

The reinforcement which should have arrived from Mallorca was so much delayed that it was agreed in November to send an Augustinian monk, Fr. José Vergés, from the Monte Toro monastery to Barcelona, while Saura's brother went to Palma to seek military aid. These attempts did not succeed in raising more than 150 Mallorcans, under the command of Francisco Net, accompanied by Sergeant-Major Juan Fuster, three captains and other junior officers.

Quite clearly, the war of the «*Carlistes*» and «*Felipets*» — which began with a superiority on the side of Dávila's 2,000 professional soldiers over the 1,500 Carlist combatants who were to fight with more faith than experience — would be a patriotic contest, and the only attempt at an autonomous decision to be found in the history of Menorca.

United in arms under the flag of the House of Austria, the first offensive of the Menorcans was to dislodge the *Botiflers* from the fortresses of Fornells and Mahón, where the fleur-de-lis still flew.

The Mercadal battalion, commanded by Captain Juan Massanet and José Hernández, went to Fornells, and after two days of siege and intensive gunfire the captain of the San Antonio castle, Andrés Sans, was forced to capitulate, and the fort at the mouth of the port was occupied by Carlist soldiers.

This first victory strengthened the army of «Señor General Saura», as he was called; their numbers were also increased by some of the deserters from San Felipe and conquered troops from Fornells, but the fortress of Mahón, headquarters of Governor Dávila, «which is well fortified and equipped, with a considerable number of troops», repelled every attempt at attack. The situation alarmed the Councillors of the *Universidad* so much that they wrote to Mallorca demanding «ships to prevent any aid that our enemies might be able to bring to the fort of San Felipe, as well as men, victuals and ammunition to prevent whatever sorties from the fort the enemy might make»; the letter ended with the candid comment that «the fort might cause some unpleasantness to the island».

The position of the fort or castle of San Felipe, built on the rocky coast of the western side of the entry to the harbour of Mahón and dominating the Cala San Esteban, had enabled it to receive some outside aid, as the keeper of the keys had observed in his report to the General Council. But neither was the blockade of the castle from land complete: «The people of Mahón complained to the *Universidad* that they had always to go about armed, without being able to work, as they had to defend themselves against the daily sorties of troops from the castle looking for provisions, such as cattle, firewood, etc., and although they were helped by infantry from Ciudadela and Alayor it was but a small force in comparison with that of the castle, which remained obedient to the Duke of Anjou,» relates Rafael Oleo in his history of the island.

The Mahonese, moreover, were constantly harassed by the people from the Arrabal, the village which had grown up in the shadow of the walls of the fort. This cluster of hovels and cottages which had developed from the needs of the castle, sheltered every kind of ruffians, adventurers and loose women, a rabble which, no doubt from self-interest, remained attached to the troops of San Felipe and were to some extent their bodyguards. To defend themselves against their rapacious forays, the peasants of Mahón had to arm a company, which soon found itself counter-attacked by another, of armed women, under the command of Casilda Corbarán. This feminine militia had been formed with the object of mounting guard when the men were out campaigning. It was especially feared by the peaceful inhabitants of the farmhouses which had the misfortune to be on the very field of operations between San Felipe and Mahón.

Around 16th December, Saura's staff, comprising Francisco Net, Fuster, the Mallorcan officers, those of the Mahón battalion, and Captains Andrés Sans and Gonzalo Bustamante (who had come over from the enemy), went to where the front line had been established in the blockade of the fort, «to observe and reconnoitre». To the south of Mahón the Carlist positions extended over a stony plain from Cala Figuera to Binisaida, passing through Biniatap and Toraixer. It is possible that the front reached the coast, below the spot know as «Torre d'en Penjat» (the name possibly deriving from the gallows subsequently erected there), an extensive line, several kilometers long, almost impossible to cover with the small number of troops they had available. After having reconnoitred the terrain, the immediate objective was established: to set fire to the Torre del Rey, adjacent to the castle itself, since it dominated «the whole terrain and the field of our people».

(Later, as Saura would ingenuously excuse himself, «it was necessary to desist from such a major operation, because the few people who presented themselves at that time did not bring with them the instruments necessary for the task».) And, to add to the confusion which doubtless reigned in this general-staff of amateur philanthropists, a rivalry of commands broke out between the Mallorcan Sergeant-Major Francisco Net, and the Commander-in-Chief of the island, Juan Miguel Saura. Giving as his excuse an attack of gout in his hand, Net withdrew, offended, to Alayor, virtually refusing to continue the fight.

This dispute did not daunt Saura, who continued to direct his campaign despite the great difficulties and scant means.

At the beginning of winter — especially hard in that area fully exposed to the ravages of the *Tramontana* — the blockade of San Felipe continued without any positive result whatsoever; but Saura, in view of the possible arrival of enemy reinforcements, ordered «four iron cannon, eighteen-pounders, and two bronze swivel guns» to be sent from Ciudadela by sea to Cala Tamarells for the defence of Mahón. The cannon were to have been brought in a *guangüil*, but the small fishing boat (the only one available, as it appears) was engaged at that moment in the transport of wheat and ammunition for the Mallorcan troops, which caused an irreparable delay in the preventative arrangements Saura was trying to organise.

On 31st December 1706, three sails, making for the castle of San Felipe, were sighted from Monte Toro.

IV

Armand, Comte de Villars, was one of the eight sons of the Marquis de Villars, French Ambassador to the Court of Charles II in Madrid. Together with his elder brother, the famous Marshal the Duc de Villars, he had taken part in the Bavarian campaigns, being appointed Field-Marshal in 1704 and Rear-Admiral a year later. Saint Simon speaks of him as being an honourable man, modest and considerate. His first visit to Menorca took place in

139

1705 when he landed a battalion of the French navy, intended to reinforce the garrison which remained in San Felipe under the command of the naval Captain La Jonquière.

At the end of 1706, Villars set sail from Toulon in command of a flotilla, with orders to help the fort of Mahón and occupy the island of Menorca in the name of his monarch's ally, Philip V of Spain.

On the calm morning of 1st January 1707, the flagship of the Comte de Villars, accompanied by two good ships of sail, entered the mouth of the port of Mahón and dropped anchor in the eastern part of the roads. A little later three more vessels and various transports closed the harbour mouth. The fire from a handful of men shooting from the nearby shore did not prevent the landing of the first soldiers of the expeditionary force in a little cove just opposite the ships. From the bridge of his vessel the Count observed how the Foudroyant battalion, under the orders of the Chevalier La Rochalard, together with a company of grenadiers led by an officier called Goyon, occupied the beach and deployed themselves towards the adjacent hills, taking up strong defensive positions in a tower which dominated the coast. By evening, after overcoming some weak opposition, their positions were consolidated. The Rear-Admiral landed with a battalion of marines in Cala Figuera on the 5th and put himself at the head of the San Felipe garrison. La Jonquière had crossed to the other side of the port to join the landing forces.

Villars had been informed that the enemy was composed of a motley band of peasants, short of arms and with no military experience; he saw no difficulty whatever in carrying out the operation with which he had been entrusted in a very short time. Indeed, within a week of his landing, all opposition had been overcome, and shortly afterwards the French officer demanded the surrender of the island.

V

The news that enemy ships were entering the roads of Mahón spread rapidly on 1st January 1707, causing much anguish. Saura immediately summoned a meeting of his people in the Casa del Rey, «to resolve the most appropriate means of defence». As a first urgent measure, the north shore of the port had to be reinforced for fear the enemy should land there and take possession of the San Antonio farmhouse which dominated the shore from above. With this end in view, the Sergeant-Major of Mahón, Rafael Montañés, was ordered to cross the harbour by water (presumably because this was thought to be the shortest way) with 20 men, and to occupy the place known as the «Font» and the farm building. But Montañés's soldiers arrived late and were unable to prevent the French from landing in Cala San Jorge. On the contrary, it was the French who opposed the «landing of our men in that part». Meanwhile, Captain Fuster, Dr. Beltrán, Dr. Carbonell and a few others, perceiving that the ships which had passed La Mola were flying French colours, had rushed to Cala Llonga and opened fire against the three ships and two *pingües* which had just anchored very near the island of La Plana (later called the Quarantine Island). The result of this well-intentioned act of war was nil.

French supply ships went on arriving throughout the day until by evening there were thirteen craft anchored in the roads. The first landing of the disciplined French troops in Cala Llonga and Cala San Jorge was carried out in complete order, and a detachment climbed the hill, taking up a strong position by occupying San Antonio. When this bad news became known in Mahón, Captain Pedro Carreras was sent by night, wtih 200 men, to surround the farmhouse. The following morning, 2nd January, the noise of firing was heard from around the farmstead. But the besiegers sooned learned how badly prepared they were for a serious assault and urgently requested ammunition, «which was provided by the Bailiff of Mahón, Francisco Seguí». Again we find those two active doctors, Beltrán and Carbonell, coming forward with two boats to reinforce the San Antonio contingent; but in the face of the lively fire from the besieged French and the many losses suffered by the Mahonese, the attempt to take the enclosure had to be abandoned. Dr Carbonell returned to

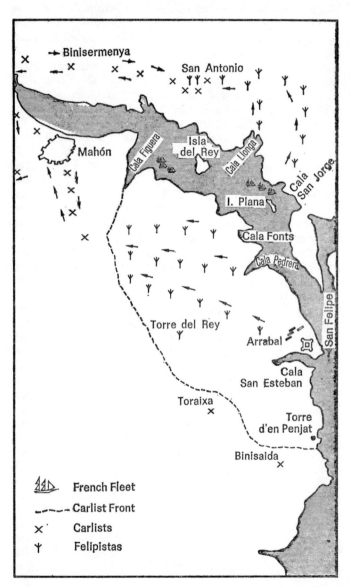

Binisermenya

San Antonio

Mahón

Cala Figuera

Isla del Rey

Cala Llonga

Cala San Jorge

I. Plana

Cala Fonts

Cala Pedrera

San Felipe

Torre del Rey

Arrabal

Cala San Esteban

Toraixa

Torre d'en Penjat

Binisaida

French Fleet	
- - - - -	Carlist Front
✕	Carlists
Ψ	Felipistas

Mahón, the Bailiff and Dr. Beltrán «remaining with our people who were besieging that point».

It is disheartening see with what good faith, but also with what lack of any military sense, these men defended their island. Friars, lawyers, doctors, notaries and gentlemen threw themselves into the fight, with swords more symbolic than effective, and with rudimentary firearms hardly adequate to go hunting with. Nor were their severe black clothes, with short breeches and starched collars, the most appropriate for such a campaign. The peasants fought beside them with equal ardour. The frugal country people, with their wide-brimmed hats and drab cloaks, were more accustomed to the slow trot of their donkeys than to the violence of war, and not even their strong island patriotism was enough to convert them into valiant men of arms.

Opposing them were experienced French soldiers, who had been given the close attention which Louis XIV devoted to his troops: they were strictly uniformed, with coats of fine cloth, stockings and breeches to match, and a black tricorn hat. Well equipped, with cartridge belts, muskets to the shoulder, bayonets fixed, they must have astonished the islanders, unaccustomed as they were to such a spectacular display of the martial art.

On 2nd January 1707, the second day of the enemy's assault, the situation was as follows: the French occupied the beach-heads and the farmhouse of San Antonio, besieged by the Mahonese; the slopes of the hill, right up to the top, where the farm was situated, was a sort of no-man's land, crossed as much by the French «blue coats» as by the dark Menorcan capes. On the other side of the port, the castle of San Felipe, in the hands of Dávila's *Botiflers,* continued unharmed in the face of the rudimentary Carlist blockade, and the Comte de Villars was already organising an offensive from that quarter. Troops and munitions were arriving continuously from the anchored ships.

Saura, on whom the whole responsibility for the struggle now rested (as Net still had not put in an appearance), tried desperately to attack the wedge of land occupied by the enemy, sending his scant troops from one point to another of the port, thus running the risk of de-manning his line of defence at Biniatap.

On the morning of that same day, La Jonquière — who seemed to be following in the footsteps of Alfonso the Liberal — gave orders for the mobilisation of eight or ten boats to carry out a last attempt to assault San Antonio and the hill of San Jorge, but the resistance put up by Andrés Sans — recently arrived with reinforcements at the beach-heads — caused them to re-embark rapidly. But this advantage of the Menorcans did not last long: by evening the naval guns had come into operation, sweeping the hills to cover the landing of a large contingent of men. Divided into two columns, the French infantry advanced in serried ranks along the heights of San Jorge and towards San Antonio, imposing harsh punishment on the Carlists, who had to retreat, abandoning the positions they had taken up between the sea and San Antonio. The whole of that terrain was now occupied by the French.

In heavy rain the Menorcans redeployed a few kilometers inland, behind San Antonio, choosing the Binisermenya farmhouse as the immediate point of defence. Captain Gonzalo de Bustamante, in command of this sector, asked Mahón for reinforcements, «so that the enemy may take no more land»; next morning, as a result of a combination of commands, 200 men arrived with Sans and Sanromán, «with the object of reconnoitering to see if that point needed a front line to prevent the advance of the enemy», as stated with some optimism in the report.

The importance of defending the opposite shore of the port had not escaped the attention of Captain Andrés Sans (one of the few professional soldiers serving in the anaemic Menorcan army), and he gave orders for the construction just to the north of Cala Figuera of «a fortification built of earth and bundles of brushwood, where the cannons from Ciudadela may be placed, together with two companies, a very important point for the defence of our people». But although Saura had taken these defensive measures, the French, with sound strategic sense, went further. Having occupied the coves and high lands on the north side of the port, they made a direct attack on the van of the enemy's front between Cala Figuera and San Felipe — the Biniatap cordon which surrounded the castle.

On the morning of the 5th, the Carlist leaders who were reinforcing Biniatap were taken by surprise, «on receiving the intelligence that the men were landing in Calas Pedrera and Fons, upon which they sounded the alarm, without even having taken time to call a Council of War».

In Mahón itself, the discomposure was great. The entire town having been mobilised («everyone who could be got hold of then left the town to provide greater reinforcement at the front lines»), an attempt was made to reorganise the men who had hurriedly arrived at the front with Captains Sanromán and Sans. The principal Councillor of Mahón, Bartolomé Seguí y Sintes, and others in authority, put themselves forward in the front ranks «to encourage the people». But, even disregarding the deficiencies of the Carlist army, its troops were too widely dispersed to provide any effective confrontation against the Bourbon attack.

The French ships anchored off Cala Figuera began a continuous cannonade on the Menorcan positions; the first charge of the infantry took place at eleven in the morning.

The Comte de Villars placed La Jonquière in command of an infantry battalion from his own ship's complement, two further French battalions, 200 of Dávila's veterans, a company of Spanish grenadiers and 150 volunteers: a total, according to French sources, of 1,330 men. La Jonquière and his officers, La Rochalard and Goyon, had orders to go out into the country with two siege cannons to skirt the enemy positions and take Mahón. However, they came up against two factors which slowed their advance: the roughness of the roads which, lined with dry-stone walls, served as parapets for the Menorcan soldiers, and the courage displayed by the Menorcans in their defence.

The battle which took place in the rough labyrinth of Menorcan *tanques* which divided up the countryside with their dry-stone walls, must indeed have been singular. No less so was the Carlist weaponry, for according to the description which has reached us of Saura's own weapon, it consisted of an enormous mediaeval sword, with the twelve apostles engraved on its blade, St. Peter occupying the place closest to the hilt. With this instrument Saura, despite his age, went out to fight the highly trained French troops, sinking his sword — to quote his own words — «up to St. Peter» in the chests of his enemies.

Cruel was the fighting throughout that morning between the Carlists and their enemies. «They defended themselves with great bravery until two in the afternoon, when the enemy paused for refreshments», a pause of which Dr. Carbonell took advantage to recover some lost ground and take possession of two French cannons (abandoned possibly because they were unusable on that terrain). But little by little spirits flagged, and by evening La Jonquière's army had broken through the front at Biniatap, the Menorcans retreating in open disarray pursued by the attackers right up to the Portal de Dalt (upper gateway) of Mahón. The efforts of Dr. Carbonell and Captain Seguí to reform their people were useless: «neither fair words nor threats» succeeded in detaining the men, who fled to the interior of the island beneath a cold winter drizzle.

Mahón was precipitately abandoned in the greatest confusion. Even Saura left the town without having time to save his clothes and silver and, «as it was now night, and the weather rainy», he had to spend the night in the Binijamó farmhouse, about a league from Alayor. The news that Mahón had to all intents and purposes fallen into the hands of the enemy was not confirmed until the 6th, upon which, Saura, giving up all hope, set out for Ciudadela.

The *Botiflers*, now masters of the field, put Mahón to blood and fire, murdering, burning houses and desecrating churches. The uncontrolled inhabitants of the Arrabal were the most active plunderers, whilst the Franco-Spanish soldiers murdered the Prior of the Oratory of the Virgen del Carmen, a heroic defender of his monastery. The conquerors reached Alayor, which also had to bear a cruel sacking.

In Ciudadela Saura attempted a final opposition, ordering all foodstuffs to be stored in the town and placing at Captain Sans' disposition all the brushwood bundles and other elements necessary for the defence of the city. On the 7th he sent the indefatigable Dr. Carbonell to Mallorca «to inform His Excellency the Count of Zavellá of the tragic events and to implore his aid». As invariably happened, the Menorcan messenger went unheeded.

Although Ciudadela could have sustained a long siege, protected as it was by eight stout bastions and seventy cannons mounted on their batteries, the fighting spirit of the capital began to deteriorate rapidly. Two anonimous persons «had contrived to call together 300 men who, when the French came in sight of the city, would proclaim as their King His Serene Highness the Duke of Anjou» (the name by which the Menorcans insisted in calling Philip V), and Net, who had not exactly distinguished himself for his zeal, appeared at the last moment, getting in the way of the defence operations. With the departure of Juan Miguel Saura — who, threatened with death, took refuge with his family in Mallorca, embarking secretly on the 9th at midnight — the Carlist party in Menorca was practically dismantled. All opposition ceased and it only remained to conclude a capitulation in the most honourable way possible.

The French knew that, although the greater part of the island could be subdued without difficulty, it would not be possible to besiege the capital if there was any opposition, protected as it was by bastions and cannons. But, as they wanted to get the campaign over as soon as possible, they accepted a capitulation which was, according to Villars, «very insolent».

The pacts were agreed on 11th January and signed in the Ferrerías camp. La Jonquière consented to the eight articles which had been drawn up, no doubt by Net.

«On the 13th,» wrote the Chevalier de La Rochalard, captain of a French battalion, «the army set off on its march to Ciudadela. The City Councillors came out to meet us, assuring us of their obedience. They were sent off in order that they might establish peace among the alarmed and seditious spirits of the populace, and at three in the afternoon, when the troops had arrived within a quarter of a league of the place, a delegation informed M. de La Jonquière that they would not receive more than 200 Spanish soldiers, for whom they would give hostages to ensure their safety; they feared that if all the troops entered the city, which would be against their privileges, we should fail to keep our promises. In the end they agreed that M. de La Jonquière should accompany 100 French soldiers and two companies of grenadiers. In that way 300 men entered the city that evening.»

In a letter to his Minister the Comte de Villars praised his officers highly and added, «I do not believe we have lost more than 60 men, between dead and wounded, the enemy having lost at least 400.» He concluded by extolling the person of Diego Leonardo Dávila, whom he considered to be «a very honourable man, very zealous in the service of his master, and I venture to say that this government could not be in better hands». In this he was completely mistaken.

VI

The motives behind the savage acts of revenge which Dávila imposed on the lesser Balearic island, when the uprising in the name of Charles III had been suppressed, appeared to be personal. Within a month of the conclusion of hostilities he declared the Councillors of the municipalities to be in default and replaced them by new officials loyal to Philip V, and a short time later the privileges, usages and customs of the Menorcans, for which they had fought with such abnegation, were suspended.

For many long months Menorca suffered under the terrorist government of the brigadier who, like one possessed, ravaged every part of the island in his search for victims. In April an officer wrote to the Bailiff of Mercadal: «I shall come to seek out and take prisoner all traitors to our King and Lord, Philip V, and those who have associated with them. Also the charcoal burners who ply their trade in the property known as Torralba

Nou, within the oak grove near the farm buildings, because they know where the traitors sleep... and if they do not confess where they are, my orders are that they shall be hanged.» Neither peasants nor priests were to be saved because, he goes on, «the peasants who work on the property of the Socós friars and also those who work at Biniquadrellet, Fonredonas, Biniguas, Torre de Jordi March, Albranca, Albranqueta and Son Carabassa, they must all come to see me.»

As the island's prisons were now full, a court-martial was instituted in the castle of San Felipe on 16th December 1707, presided over by Dávila himself and the temporary assessor, Dr. Rafael Guardia. Thirty-three Menorcans were sentenced to capital punishment and were hanged opposite the entrance to the fort; another six were condemned to the galleys, and 20 were exiled. Among the 18 Ciudadelans tried for having fought for the Archduke's cause was the Councillor representing the peasantry at the *General Universidad*, Domingo Marqués, together with Sergeant-Major Sebastián Roselló and his son Miguel. Among the seven sentenced in Mahón appears the name of the Augustinian priest, Fr. Juan Costavella. Alayor lost its notary, Juan Villalonga, the seventh from that town to mount the gallows. Other casualties of this court were doctors, soldiers, ordinary citizens, nobles, peasants, blacksmiths, cobblers and masons; every social class had its victims. The goods of those found guilty were confiscated, their houses demolished and salt strewn on their land, a biblical sign denoting eternal sterility. The government prohibited public Masses for the souls of those condemned, and refused to permit their names to be recorded in the parish lists of deceased persons.

On top of all they had lost and all they had given, the war cost the Carlists 15,333 Menorcan pounds.

The presence of La Jonquière, who stayed on in Menorca with 460 French soldiers, does not appear to have curbed in any way the fever of repression of the Bourbon Governor. Dávila's political purges were to last for about two years. The Menorcans waited hopelessly to be delivered from his yoke.

The English 1708-1756

I

Two great leaders, each with long experience of political, military and naval affairs in the Iberian peninsula and in the Mediterranean as a whole, were on board the English squadron which drew near to Menorca in the early days of September 1708.

Sir John Leake, Admiral and Commander-in-Chief of the British Mediterranean fleet, was a man of fifty: rubicund, robust, corpulent and a good drinker. It was said of him that he was «virtuous, humane, generous and a man of honour». Son of a sailor, he had begun his naval career when he was seventeen, achieving an uninterrupted record of service, both brilliant and daring, throughout his life. Always close to the Spanish coast during the War of the Spanish Succession, he took an active part in the Allied naval battles against the Franco-Spanish fleets and, accompanying Admiral Rooke, took part in the assault on Gibraltar in 1704. He covered the landings of the Archduke's troops in Cartagena, Alicante and Mallorca and, remaining closely attached to Charles in all his naval operations, was charged with accompanying the newly married Archduchess to Barcelona, where Charles had his court. In the spring of 1708 he transported a Carlist army to Sardinia, and having reduced that island he left the Count of Cifuentes there as Viceroy and proceeded to Menorca at the end of the summer.

He was supported in the Menorcan undertaking by Lieutenant-General James Stanhope, recently appointed Commander-in-Chief of the British expeditionary force in Spain and General-in-Chief of this operation. Grandson of the first Lord Chesterfield, this yound English General (he was thirty-five years old), dark and handsome, was an old Etonian and had done well at Oxford. Before he was twenty he had spent a long period in Madrid where he learnt the language and the character of the Spanish at the side of his father, who was English Ambassador there. Later on he was commissioned in the army and gained distinction in the Flanders and Italian campaigns. Elected a Member of Parliament in 1701, he returned to Spain where he served under the Earl of Peterborough in the War of Succession. This bold officer possessed an inventiveness and courage which earned him high praise from the Archduke in the capture of the fort of Montjuich and of Barcelona itself, and he became one of the most brilliant of the foreign soldiers in the Carlist army, being later appointed Ambassador to the court of Charles III. A gentleman, brave, liberal, sincere and clever — although given to anger in Parliamentary debates — Stanhope, according to Saint Simon, «never lost his sang-froid and seldom his courtesy; he was an ingenious and resourceful man».

It was unusual to find two such outstanding men as Stanhope and Leake in command of a military expedition which, although important, was nevertheless an assault on a small island defended by a weak garrison.

To counter the lagging Allied offensive in the Peninsula and the recovery of the Bourbons in the winter of 1708 in the shape of considerable teritorial gains, a good port where the English fleet could spend the winter had become indispensable. Because of this, Marlborough wrote to Stanhope on 15th June that year saying, «I conjure you, if it be possible, to take the port of Mahón.» The reasoning behind this was not, of course, quite so simple. London had devoted much attention to Menorca since the capture of Gibraltar in 1704, and as the war in Spain was really one more field of battle between France and England, a fleet anchored in Mahón would serve the double purpose of dominating the western Mediterranean and of keeping the nearby port of Toulon under vigilance. Another point which weighed in the argument was that to take Menorca would be a retaliation for the French intervention in the Menorcan uprising in support of Charles III.

But, although the covert reasons were these, Stanhope and Leake officially undertook their mission in the name of their Queen's ally, the Archduke Charles of Austria, who had entrusted them with the task of recovering Menorca for his cause.

II

The arbitrary manner in which the defence of the island was handled throughout Menorcan history is always hard to understand. The greater the danger, the less it would appear to have worried the military leaders. When the English fleet approached the Menorcan coast in September 1708, Governor Dávila had no more than 300 Spanish soldiers available in the whole of his territory; 200 defended the fort of San Felipe (to which must be added 460 French soldiers), 50 guarded the fort of San Antonio in Fornells, and 100 were detached to Ciudadela. In total, he could count on 850 professional men of arms. It is not clear whether this state of affairs had come about because the Governor was too involved with the mania for persecution or because there really was nothing he could do about it. Moreover, almost the entire population of the island was against him, such was their abhorrence at the punishments he had so harshly imposed on the supporters of the House of Austria, thus arousing sympathy for the allies of Charles III. Fearing possible reprisals, a certain number of Bourbon volunteers had offered to join his ranks on sighting the English sails, but even with this reinforcement Dávila had not the slightest chance of repelling an invasion, however weak it might be.

On 18th August Leake left Pula, near Cagliari, with his fleet, and arrived off Palma in the afternoon of the 25th. On the previous day Charles III had written to him from Barcelona: «After you have finished your operations in Italy I beg you to begin to reduce the Island of Menorca and Port Mahón, that the fleet may shelter in those seas and thus give greater security to my royal person.»

A few days later, the Admiral sent some ships to reconnoitre Menorcan waters and to find a suitable spot for a landing. Their captains lost no time, and near Fornells captured a French ship with a cargo of clothes and provisions for the garrison in San Felipe.

Meanwhile Stanhope had embarked in Barcelona on the *'Milford'*, and on route to Mallorca where he picked up a contingent of men and victuals he wrote to Leake: «I am to acquaint you that the number of regular troops with me, when all joined, will fall short of 2,000 men, which you must be sensible are few for such an enterprise... I shall beg of you that as many marines as can be spared from the fleet be put ashore to continue during the siege.»

On 7th September, reinforced by three Dutch warships, the fleet assembled to the south-east of Menorca, and Stanhope arrived on the 13th with his forces and the transports. Directed with caution by their leaders, who avoided exposing their ships to the fire of the 100 cannon on the fort of San Felipe, they anchored in the shelter of the Isla del Aire off the south coast of Menorca. This decision brought them several advantages: (a) in this region the coast was undefended and there were a number of deserted beaches which would ensure an easy landing; (b) though never very strong at this time of year, if the *Tramontana* should spring up the ships would be protected from it; and (c) Mahón was only a few leagues away, so the troops would only have to march a short distance to its gates. As well as being prudent, their decision seemed to be full of good sense. The only thing these soldiers did not take into account was the topography of the land; nor does the point chosen for a landing seem ideal. The sheltered cove of Alcaufar was surrounded by steep and stony terrain, its beach was difficult of access and that only by a steep path.

The Menorcans received the English with open arms. The restoration of their monarch was assured and the hated Dávila would be beaten. With this idea in mind they came forward in large numbers to help their allies to land troops and artillery.

The English no doubt relied on them because, although their arms were appreciable, they had almost no army, as we have seen. Stanhope, always resourceful, used 1,200 marines as effective troops and with these he carried out his landing in Cala Alcaufar on 14th September.

But it was not so easy to drag the 42 cannons and 15 mortars over the rugged slopes of that area. The English General, accustomed to the yoked oxen of the Peninsula, came up against an unforeseen obstacle. In Menorca the roads were not wide enough to permit this kind of transport and there were neither oxen nor carts. The painful transit of the English artillery, pushed and pulled by the peasants of the district, lasted twelve days. And, even so, only nine weapons of war could be emplaced on a battery facing San Felipe by the day of the offensive.

While Stanhope attended to this troublesome task, Leake had given orders to Sir Edward Whitaker to attack the fort of San Antonio in Fornells with two ships. This castle, of limited size, was equipped with only twelve cannons and was defended by no more than 50 Franco-Spanish soldiers. It was built on the western point of the narrow mouth of the beautiful harbour of Fornells in which the fishing village lay protected. It was important to reduce this fortification since it was the sole defensive point protecting the north coast of the island and, in case of necessity, was a good place for a landing from which to advance on Mahón.

Helped by a calm sea, the English ships of the line systematically bombarded San Antonio, and in turn came within the sights of the fort's artillery, which, with good accuracy, achieved numerous hits on the ships, causing eighteen casualties, among them two dead. The garrison defenced itself tenaciously but, despite losing only one man and four others wounded, soon considered itself defeated. The fort surrendered and the soldiers were taken as prisoners-of-war.

News of the surrender of San Antonio soon reached San Felipe, causing much discouragement among the government troops. Moreover, as the arrival of this news coincided with the placing of the English cannons on the battery opposite the castle walls, a defeatist attitude grew rapidly within.

At dawn on 28th September the English artillery opened fire. And it did not have to continue for long before panic spread among the besieged troops. The piece which Brigadier Wade commanded opened a breach in the dry-stone wall which surrounded the outer edge of the fortification, and the small English army advanced until it was able to regroup itself at the foot of the esplanade of the castle itself. By afternoon they had established their first battery. On the following morning the white flag appeared on the battlements of the fort. Shortly after, Dávila sent representatives to discuss the terms of peace.

The capitulation was signed at five in the afternoon on that same day, and on the 30th General Stanhope, with the soldiers and sailors under his command, entered the fort of San Felipe. An English regiment took possession peacefully of Ciudadela. The dead and wounded on the English side amounted to 40 men.

For the second time, Charles III was proclaimed King of Spain in the island of Menorca.

III

Considering it useless to prolong the fighting, and being pressed to make his entry into San Felipe, Stanhope acceded with good grace to the seven terms demanded by the defeated enemy in the capitulation agreement, which was signed in the afternoon of the 29th. The conditions accepted were indeed indulgent. Peasants, soldiers and officers who wanted to leave the island were given four months to sell their property; all Menorcans who had taken refuge in the castle were granted an amnesty; Allied ships would escort Spaniards to Valencia, Cartagena, Almería and Málaga, while French prisoners would be taken to Toulon and the Hières islands. The Bourbon troops came out of the castle with military honours; with flags unfurled, drum beating and arms loaded, six cannons and two mortars, thus they marched to the port of Mahón.

But if the English did not condemn them, history made it its business to do so. The great Menorcan historian, Rafael Oleo, is trenchant in his opinion: «The well-remembered Governor, Don Diego Leonardo Dávila, gave, with this action, public testimony to his great cowardice;

to send defenceless Menorcans to the gallows was not the same thing as to put up a defence (as was his duty) of that impregnable fort, with a garrison at his command of no less than 500 French and 200 Spanish soldiers.»

In similar cases, when a fort is surrendered, with evident display of cowardice, there is the inevitable suspicion of treachery and of a sell-out by its leaders. In his honour it must be stated that Dávila seems to have been too much of a fanatic to have succumbed to such weakness, which in any case could not have done him any good. As regards La Jonquière, his excellent qualities as an officer, demonstrated in the preceding campaign, would hardly be consistent with such baseness. The most logical explanation is that the English forces seemed to them far greater than they really were, and once Fornells had fallen they saw no possibility of bringing about an effective defence of the island with their scant military potential. But this naturally does not excuse them from not having put up a greater opposition.

In any case, when they reached their respective countries their compatriots judged them severely. The court-martial which was to try Dávila was particularly strict, but this patriot's urbane character bordered on the schizophrenic; rather than suffer final condemnation he threw himself from the window of his cell in Cartagena. His jailers chose to bury him where he had fallen, and there lay his remains for almost eighty years, when another Charles III, the Bourbon one, ordered them to be transferred to a sacred place.

The fate of La Jonquière was less dramatic, although his family connections with influential landowners in the Ardèche region did not save him from being stripped of his rank and taken as a common criminal to the lugubrious castle of Auxonne. From his prison he wrote numerous letters justifying his action and blaming Dávila for the dishonourable surrender of San Felipe.

Neither the one nor the other was the first victim — nor would they be the last — of the conquests and reconquests of Menorca throughout history.

The English lost no time in making themselves at home

in Menorca. Astute politicians, they cared little for the administrative set-up of the country, leaving Stanhope to confirm to the chief Councillor of the *Universidad* of Mahón, *Mosén* Bartolomé Seguí, the privileges, prerogatives, rights and immunities of old, granted to the Menorcans by the kings of Aragon and Castile. The document was drawn up on 17th October 1708, but was not ratified by Charles III in Barcelona for a year, the news reaching Menorca on 24th January 1710, which amply demonstrates how much Carlist maritime potential had diminished as a consequence of continuous defeats in the Peninsula; or perhaps it shows the disinterest of the monarch in the fate of the island, now that it was in the hands of his allies.

The island authorities, ignorant of all this and aware only that they had recovered all that was lost during the mandate of Diego Leonardo Dávila, once more proclaimed the Austrian pretender King of Spain, at the first meeting of the General Council which was held in Ciudadela on 20th November 1708.

Juan Miguel Saura returned to Ciudadela and was appointed Captain of Infantry, being honoured later with the title of Political Governor. The English also bore the cost of rebuilding his house, destroyed after his flight to Mallorca, and on the rubble a palace was built, which today is the premises of the *Caja de Pensiones* (Savings Bank) in Calle Obispo Vila. The indefatigable Dr. Carbonell also had his political appointments restored; the exiles returned and started negotiations for the liberation of those condemned to the galleys.

Once these problems had been resolved to the satisfaction of the islanders — thus winning for the liberators their complete confidence — the English devoted themselves to organising their own interests, supported at every step by the Hapsburg court in Barcelona. They began by improving considerably the island's defences. On the peninsula of La Mola (on the eastern side of the entry to the port of Mahón) a bastion was raised which was named the fort of Santa Ana in honour of the Queen of England, and right opposite San Felipe itself, on the other side of Cala San Esteban the small Marlborough fort was later built. San Felipe itself was also tremendously reinforced, to such an extent that four new barracks with room for eight battalions were built within the castle.

In an effort to make the inhabitants of the island militarily impotent the English demanded that the heavy artillery in Ciudadela be transferred to San Felipe, and Menorcans were prohibited the use of arms. This new usurpation by the English gave rise to much protest on the part of the authorities, who endeavoured to defend their people against rough usage by the English soldiery which formed the sole garrison for the protection of the island. Several further incidents, provoked by this force of semi-occupation, troubled the Menorcans, who observed with dismay how their redeemers were becoming occupiers. A weaver, Bartolomé Pons, was attacked by an English soldier, who in turn was killed by the brother of the victim; peasants and fishermen had to reduce the prices of their produce, considered exorbitant by the English forces; the *Universidades* and citizens had to pay for and put lodgings at the disposal of the troops; certain undercover interventions by the foreigners in ecclesiastical affairs exasperated the prelates; against the opinion of the Councillors, the Arrabal of San Felipe was allowed to be occupied by alarming numbers of «people of such bad character and depraved intentions that it is nothing but robbery, murder, violence and other atrocious crimes».

The Councillor representing the main branch of the Mahonese population, *Mosén* Bartolomé Seguí i Sintes, was sent to the court of Charles III in Barcelona for the purpose of respectfully reporting these problems to him, underlining the fact that the island had not sworn fidelity to him only to be dominated by the English. The reply to these complaints was rather ambiguous: «that this island will soon find consolation...».

The Menorcan authorities began to suspect from whence would come the promised consolation, although they were not aware of the contents of the letter which Stanhope had written to his Minister before returning to London in 1708: «England ought never to part with this island, which will give the law to the Mediterranean both in time of war and of peace;» a conclusion which his political superiors had not overlooked, their reply (by return of post) enjoining him «to much secrecy in the matter».

For these and other important services rendered by Stanhope to the Crown the title of Viscount Stanhope of Mahon was conferred on him in 1717, and he later became Earl Stanhope.

IV

With this constant tug-of-war between the Menorcan authorities and the English army the affairs of the island were maintained for some years.

Meanwhile, in April 1711, Joseph I, Emperor of Austria, died and his brother, the Archduke Charles, was unanimously elected to succeed him by the Electoral College of the Holy Roman Empire. He was crowned Emperor in Frankfurt on 22nd December, with the name of Charles VI. He left his wife as Regent in Barcelona, and Count Starhemberg in charge of his army in Spain.

Quite apart from the obligations imposed by this new crown, the truth was that the war was taking a turn which was frankly unfavourable to Allied arms in Spain. With the victories of Brihuega and Villaviciosa, Philip had assured himself of the throne of Spain. A whole series of events in Europe favoured the Bourbons, putting an end to the Archduke's dynastic claim. In England the Whigs had suffered a Parliamentary defeat, and the Tories initiated their peace policy, one which was shared by the aged Louis XIV. These secret peace negotiations coincided with Charles' accession to his new throne and provided the English with a solid basis on which to pursue their reconciliatory talks with France on realising that the union of the powers of Spain and Austria in one person would be even more serious than having a Bourbon king of Spain.

As far as Menorca was concerned, the matter was settled even before the signing of the Treaty of Utrecht in April 1713 between the European powers, and well before the Emperor Charles VI of Austria and Philip V of Spain reached an agreement on the points of discord between them, thus bringing to an end the Spanish civil war with the peace treaty signed in March 1714.

In the summer of 1712 agreement was reached between Louis XIV, Philip V and Queen Anne that, whatever the later conditions of peace should be, Gibraltar and Menorca would remain in English hands.

Rumours of all this reached Menorca, arousing unanimous protests in the *Universidades*; though they were Carlists, this did not make them Anglophiles. They tried to get annulment of the pact which so directly affected them but, far from achieving it, they did not even receive an official announcement of the future fate of the island from the Regent (i.e. the Empress, formerly the Archduchess).

In November of that same year (1712) the Duke of Argyll arrived in Menorca, with full powers from Her Britannic Majesty. He took possession of the island in a simple and efficient manner. The Duke's ship had hardly moored in the port of Mahón when the Austrian flag flying in the fort of San Felipe was lowered and replaced by that of Great Britain. On the morning of the 11th, the English plenipotentiary sent a courteous message to the General Councillors, informing them that «Menorca is now yielded to the Queen of Great Britain», and asked that a Councillor from each town on the island should meet him in order that he, as Governor, might inform them of the Queen's orders. The commissioners sent by Ciudadela to pay their respects to the Duke consisted of Juan de Bayarte and Bernardo Magín Olives. These alarmed gentlemen soon became convinced of the pacific intentions of the English: «It is Our Resolution,» read the Queen's words, «not only to preserve to you your Religious and Civil Rights, but to render you a rich and flourishing people by encouragement of your Trade and Navigation.» The Duke concluded: «I beg that you will be assured that as I have all imaginable inclination to serve you I shall not excuse any trouble nor endeavour possible to compass and carry into execution everything that may be conducive to the good of the island.»

When the pact between England and France was finally concluded in 1713, Article 11 stated:

«Moreover, the Catholic King doth in like manner for himself, his heirs and successors, yield to the crown of Great Britain, the whole island of Minorca, and doth transfer thereunto for ever, all right, and the most absolute dominion over the island, and in particular over the town, castle, harbour and fortifications of the bay of Minorca, commonly called Port Mahon, together with the other ports, places, and towns, situated in the aforesaid island. But it is provided, as in the above-written article, that no refuge or shelter shall be open to any ships of war of the Moors in Port Mahon, or in any other port of the said island of Minorca, whereby the Spanish coasts may be infested by their excursions: and the Moors and their ships shall only be allowed to enter the island aforesaid, on account of traffick, according to the agreement of treaties. The Queen of Great Britain promises also on her part, that if at any time it shall happen, that the island of Minorca, and the ports, towns, and places therein situated, be by any means hereafter alienated from the crown of her kingdoms, the preference shall be given to the crown of Spain, before any other nation whatever, of redeeming the possession and propriety of the aforesaid island. Her royal Majesty of Great Britain moreover engages, that she will take care, that all the inhabitants of the said island, both ecclesiastical and secular, shall safely and peaceably enjoy all their estates and honours, and the free use of the Roman Catholic religion shall be permitted: and measures shall be taken for preserving the aforesaid religion in that island, provided the same be consistent with the civil government and laws of Great Britain. Those likewise who are now in the service of his Catholic Majesty, shall enjoy their honours and estates, though they continue in the said service; and it shall be lawful for any person who is desirous to leave the said island, to sell his estate, and pass freely with the value thereof into Spain.»

From the start of the first official occupation of Menorca, the English did indeed make every endeavour to encourage the island to prosper and to achieve peaceful relations with its inhabitants. Thanks to the elements at their disposal and to the attention they devoted to its realization, they attained their first objective relatively easily, but it was a harder task to win over the discontented and resentful Menorcans. And, above all, during the forty-four years which followed, the most hostile and aggravating element which the English governors had to confront was the Church. The clergy saw the Protestant occupiers as a potential enemy, not only on account of doctrinal disagreements, but above all because of their fear at seeing supplanted the enormous power they wielded over the natives of the country. For somewhat similar reasons the nobility chose to remain isolated, refusing all contact with the foreigners. Ciudadela paid for her enmity with the transfer of the capital to Mahón, where it was in any case more logical to establish it, due first to its proximity to the fort of San Felipe, secondly because Mahón was the place of residence of the Governor, and thirdly because of the commercial and naval facilities offered by her magnificent harbour.

Attached to her past, Ciudadela sunk into decadence, while the more plebeian town of Mahón took advantage of everything that was offered. From an insignificant town of some 500 houses she was converted again into the fourishing port she had once been. The unhealthy marshlands at the head of the harbour were drained, giving way to active workshops and shipyards; the beaches became docks and wharves; Greek and Jewish merchants set up a large market at the side of the port; a naval hospital was built on the Isla del Rey. The town was extended and the ancient centre was rebuilt: by means of a great civic effort in town-planning the streets were straightened, widened and paved, and along them benches were placed to promote friendly meetings between the inhabitants. A great public clock was brought from London, and today it still strikes the hours in the tower above the Town Hall.

With regard to her first English Governor, Menorca had the good fortune to have an exceptional man. Energetic, honourable, intelligent, just, and of a paternal kindliness in all matters concerning the island, Richard Kane administered the country for more than twenty years. To provide better communications, the first task he undertook was the construction of a road, ten meters wide, which, skirting the towns of the interior, linked Mahón with Ciudadela. With praiseworthy practical sense he put the soldiers from the garrison to work on the project and these were exempt from military duties. The «Camí d'en Kane» was opened in 1720, not without first having to overcome the furious protests of those whose lands were expropriated. Later on, innumerable bridges and roads were built which connected distant farms and beaches — a network of communications with brought life to many isolated places and converted swamps into fields and gardens.

Resolved to improve the life of the island in all its aspects, Kane ordered the importation of cattle and sheep, new breeds of fowl, plant seeds and fruit trees (including the varieties of Menorcan apples and plums which still bear a derivation of his name, «quen»). He also gave a great deal of good advice on the advancement of agriculture.

A competent official, Kane, as Lieutenant-Governor and later Governor under Queen Anne, George I and George II, brought order to many civil problems: he introduced regulations for the sale of wine, meat, fish, game and cereals, and the hiring of beasts of burden; he introduced control in the felling of trees, imposed new laws covering weights and measures, unified the official seals of the *Universidades,* and created a Court of Vice-Admiralty which fulfilled the function of the «Bailiff-Consuls» created by Pedro of Catalonia and Aragon.

On the other hand the clergy rejected every form of interference in their affairs when Kane tried to introduce new ecclesiastical ordinances. Argument between the civil state and the Church went on for many years, with constant comings and goings between Rome, London and Menorca. The only result, more than justified, was the abolition of the Inquisition in the island a century earlier than in Spain. Throughout these disagreements, Menorcans remained faithful to their religion and only very few cases of apostasy are known, such as that of the three Poor Clare nuns who, secretly courted by three Protestant officers of the English garrison, abandoned their habits to marry them. The nuns' superiors prohibited the union, the English administration suported it: the couples emigrated to England.

Apart from these differences, there was also friction between the peasants and the soldiers of occupation. Some English soldiers were murdered near the Albufera, as a result of which incident the *Universidades* were severely fined. The time when the English endeavoured to coerce the peasants into a forced levy was called the «*any de ses pedrades*» (the year of the stonings), as the furious peasants repelled with showers of stones the soldiers who tried to take away youths to serve on their warships. The problems of billets and of drunken soldiers also created no few incidents. If we recall that even today, in rural Catalonia, «*agafar un gat*» means «to get blind drunk», and that the English «Johns» soon became «*jans*», we can well understand why, at the cry of «*un jan gat*», housewives would rush to bolt their doors to escape the attentions of the foreigners.

In general, although difficulties arose, and an odd governor would abuse his position, this long period of English occupation brought great benefit to Menorca. A printing press was imported from London, schools were opened to all social classes, prosperity spread to the country, new buildings were constructed, administrative order was achieved by means of monetary revaluation and of exact censuses of the inhabitants, cattle, farms and houses.

The great commercial revival and the possibility of cultural advancement converted the island into a flourishing nucleus under the protection of the political liberties of Britain. Nevertheless, stubborn in the defence of their ancestral customs, it was many years before Menorcans appreciated the improvements brought about by the new occupiers and recognised that through the tenacity and initiative of the English, Menorca had emerged from mediaeval obscurity into the Modern Age.

The French 1756-1763

I

Throughout the eighteenth century the policy followed by England, aimed at prosecuting a remorseless struggle against France to the point of crushing her navy and bringing about the loss of her colonies, was held in suspense for some years by the ephemeral peace of Aquisgrán in 1748. The French took advantage of the truce to develop the internal resources of the country, to bring prosperity to her colonies in the West Indies and Canada and, above all, to reform and reorganise her navy, mauled in recent decades by her enemies and abandoned in the time of the Regency, due to the pacifist policy of Fleury.

But if the peace of 1758 was no more than an armistice in Europe, in other parts of the world it was not even that, and in North America the rivalry of interests between the two countries exploded, intensified by France's new colonial prosperity and her renewed power on the seas. The problem of frontier demarcation in the Ohio valley highlighted the relations between the English and French colonies, and the impossibility of reaching agreement on the rights of the two Crowns gave rise to incidents of such magnitude that war became inevitable. In 1754 the Comte de Jumonville, a French lieutenant, was assassinated, together with his escort, opposite a fort occupied by the English, known as Necessité; a short time afterwards Admiral Boscowen was attacked in Newfoundland waters as a reprisal for the capture of two French ships carrying troops, and General Baddock was killed in the attempted invasion of Canada. It should be remembered also that France had to put up with the annoying pinpricks of the many corsairs who enjoyed the protection of the British Admiralty. In only a few months, during 1755, pirates captured 6,000 French sailors and 300 merchant ships, almost all of them engaged in trade with America.

On 18th May 1756, after many months of sporadic

fighting in America, France and England broke yet again the highly vulnerable European peace to begin what was to become the Seven Years War. On the very day on which the state of war was published, Marshall the Duc de Richelieu invaded the island of Menorca, a British possession for the past forty-four years. France officially declared war on England on 16th June.

At that time George II was on the throne of England and the country was run by the Parliamentary cabinet of Newcastle. It was one which can be described as only relatively efficient and was given to deliberate distortions of the truth in order to win the sympathies of the people. This listless ministry, more concerned with the nation's commercial progress than with the problem of events in America (the origin of the dispute between England and France) or with the danger which France, as a maritime power, presented, was so imprudent as to commit the grave error of neglecting to maintain her Mediterranean bases.

In the course of the years 1755 and 1756, alarming rumours were circulating in England to the effect that naval concentrations were forming in the French Atlantic ports, in preparation for a landing in Britain. These rumours spread to such an extent that the government feared for the security of the realm and assigned a considerable naval force to protect British ports, while other warships were ordered to escort merchantmen. In April 1756, 27 ships ploughed territorial waters and a further 17 were fitted out in various ports. In addition to this force, 21 frigates and corvettes kept guard over English waters. As it would seem that the Royal Navy had in that year a total of 83 warships, the proportion confined to home waters was enormous. There were only three ships of the line in the Mediterranean at that time. It was a situation which, because of the government's total lack of foresight, was to end in disaster.

Between August 1755 and April 1756 the repeated and precise intelligence reaching England, to the effect that a squadron composed of 23 warships was being fitted out in Brest and Rochefort and that troops, artillery and supplies were on their way from central France to the Channel ports, went unheeded. The objective of these preparations was not known but, barring the alarmist conjectures about an invasion, London assumed they were in support of operations in America. Just as it was also assumed that a second fleet of twelve vessels, feverishly armed in Toulon, would sail for the Atlantic: an assumption that was quite unfounded in view of the specific information sent in February by the British Consul in Genoa, Mr. Birtles, stating that this force, standing by to attack Menorca, would be ready by the spring.

Snug in his conviction of the naval supremacy of England, Newcastle lost all sense of the reality of the situation and not only underestimated the intentions of France but also neglected to protect British overseas possessions, showing a lack of imagination and a negligence rare in a British statesman; it resulted in the loss of Menorca and the fall of his government.

II

Louis XV was on the throne of the rich and frivolous France of the time, Madame de Pompadour reigned, and clever ministers tried to run the country. Noailles was Minister of State; Rouille, Comte de Jouy, Minister of Foreign Affairs; Argenson and Machault d'Arnouville were Ministers of War and the Navy respectively. Convinced that the continental war would become a naval war, first of all Rouille and then Machault made it their business to revive the navy. But despite their energetic projects, France in 1756 had only 63 warships and about 30 frigates. Lacking in economic resources, Machault employed an astute plan which succeeded in convincing the English that the ports of her enemies were bristling with ships prepared to attack her at any moment, and which gave such a stimulus to the shipyards that he was able to suggest to Louis XV that the navy was a potent arm, capable of avenging the offences inflicted by English pirates on the King.

The Royal Council, held in Choisy on 15th March 1756, approved a resolution which had been lightly put forward, to carry out an expedition projected months ago: the capture of the island of Menorca, in the Balearics, by means of a *coup de main* before England could have time to organise its defence and reassemble her Mediterranean fleet. The success of such an undertaking would bring benefit to the alliance with Spain and prejudice the interests of England in the Mediterranean, not to mention the shaking it would give to the pride of that nation.

It was resolved that the military concentration in Normandy and Britanny would continue the pretence of fitting out the navy to attack England, while the real expedition, under the name of the «army of the Mediterranean coasts», was preparing in Provence under the command of Marshal the Duc de Richelieu. Lieutenant-General the Marquis de La Galissonnière, naval chief of the fleet which was to protect the landing, had already been in Toulon since 2nd March preparing the ships, despite the serious difficulties he encountered in the execution of his orders, due to shortages of sails, ropes, artillery, etc. The negative attitude of the merchants in refusing to continue to supply goods until payment of past debts — contracted by an impoverished government — did not facilitate his task.

In the whole history of France it is hard to find two people so completely different than were the heads of this expedition. Both were over sixty and their lives had been dedicated to the service of their country, but even in this sole point of similarity there was a distinction. Richelieu lived in robust health until he was ninety-two, contriving that his every action contributed to his own glory; whilst La Galissonnière, worn out by his efforts to achieve glory for the Crown in everything he undertook, died soon after the conclusion of the Menorca expedition. Louis-François-Armand de Plessis, great-nephew of the famous Cardinal-Minister of Louis XIII, inherited his title of Duc de Richelieu in 1715, at the age of nineteen. A brilliant courtier, he had many easy successes in Court, on the battlefield, in business and, above all, in love: he was the very essence of seduction. Beside him the personality of Rolan-Michel Barrin, Marquis de la Galissonnière, who came from the lesser rural nobility of Britanny and was the son of one of the best naval men of the time of Louis XIV, faded into insignificance. Reserved and studious — perhaps because he was short of stature and slightly hunchbacked — he showed an absolute devotion to duty ever since he entered the navy as an adolescent. His vigorous honesty and moral strength made up for his physical disability, and his seriousness, firmness and integrity accentuated his natural affability and sweetness of nature, unusual in those who have some physical defect. Richelieu, on the other hand, was so outstandingly favoured by nature that by dint of his tact and skill his moral defects were ignored. Gifted with a rare vivacity of spirit, he made a talent out of impertinence, though his indiscretions became a danger. A pleasure-loving man, his prodigious amorous adventures became popular legends; brave and proud, he risked his life happily in battle. And if the Marquis de la Galissonnière became loved and respected by those who served under him, Richelieu — according to Argenson — ended up as one of the most hated and feared figures of his day.

The professional careers of these two men were influenced by their respective characters. Richelieu, from being a colonel of the King's Regiment in 1718, became Marshal of France in 1748. However much envious tongues said of him that his acts of bravery had the air of a military parade about them and that his prowess was like something in a comic opera, he had in fact taken part in innumerable battles. La Galissonnière, to whom the pleasure of court life meant little, did not get beyond the rank of captain until he was fifty, his naval actions being little known. Both men had been sent to represent France abroad. The sumptuous Duke brought some thorny negotiations in Vienna to a satisfactory conclusion, making subtle use of masterly intrigues; the sailor, appointed Governor of Canada almost against his will, conceived a vast plan of communications in the deserted regions of that colony, but all his zeal was not enough for an agreement to be reached over the frontiers between French and English possessions in North America.

The contradictions between these two lives show up on the intellectual side as well. Despite his brilliant reception in the Academie Française at the age of twenty-four, Richelieu was never able to write without spelling mistakes; La Galissonnière, in addition to his talents as a naval strategist, had acquired a wide knowledge of natural history and astronomy. And it was precisely because of this talent for strategy, coupled with the fame he enjoyed as a careful and competent man, that he was entrusted with the command of the fleet intended for the Menorca expedition. The King wrote to him on this subject on 22nd March: «This will confirm that my purpose is that you should concern yourself principally with the preservation of my fleet, and of the troops which I have destined for this enterprise.» The reason for the appointment of the Marshal is less clear, unless it be that the monarch's apprehensions about the exhibitionist tastes of his «cousin» would be dissipated with this paragraph of his letter to La Galissonnière.

Richelieu occupied the post of Governor of Guyana — where he must have been thoroughly bored — when he heard the news of the preparations which were taking place, and did not hesitate to offer to direct the operation. His attraction towards every new adventure in which his self-declared qualities as an army leader could shine was irresistible, and a weakness of which the court took full advantage, taking revenge on him for his glories, in a manner of speaking.

Louis XV was very fond of Richelieu. Indeed he admired him (as well as making use of him for his own amorous trysts), but he had treated him coldly ever since the Comte d'Argenson and, particularly, the Marquise de Pompadour had declared him their enemy. One of his contemporaries writes: «The fort of San Felipe, which protects Menorca, was always considered impregnable; it was decided to send the Marshal without any great preparations having been made for this dangerous expedition. Madame de Pompadour had an inner hatred for the general... She viewed his loss, should the attempted invasion turn out to be something beyond his power, with secret satisfaction. On the other hand, if he should win, the favourite would appropriate to herself the glory of having chosen him and of having overcome her personal animosity against him for the good of the State.»

Indeed, so superficial were the initial preparations that the general-staff could only get hold of an old map of the island and not a single new plan of the restored fort of San Felipe. The experts considered that with twenty-four cannons and fifteen mortar «there was more than enough to crush that little sentry-box of a fort».

Fortunately for Richelieu the expeditionary force turned out to be a great deal stronger than planned at the beginning. It was made up of an army of 12,000 soldiers, comprising 25 battalions. Command of the six brigades was divided between Lieutenant-General the Comte de Maillebois and the Marquis de Mesnil, who appointed as their brigadiers the Marquis de la Roquèpine, the Marquis de Pusignieux, M. de la Blinière, the Compte de Serre, the Marquis de Monti and M. de Talaru. There were five field-marshals on the general staff: the Comte de Lannion, the Marquis de Monteynard, the Prince de Beauvau, the Marquis de Laval-Montmorency and the Prince Louis-Eugène de Wurtemberg. In addition there were innumerable officers covering such key commands as quatermaster-general, war commissaries, engineers, artillery officers, etc.

The idle aristocracy, having no fields of battle at the moment with which to occupy their attention, took note, en masse, of the expedition and, as though it was a pleasure trip, nobody wanted to be left out of this latest amusement, nor of the opportunity, should it arise, of covering themselves with facile glory. These gentlemen, accustomed as they were to the most extraordinary luxury, became something of a problem when it came to boarding the ships, so numerous were their suites. The Duc de Richelieu especially, who was accompanied by his son the Duc de Fronsac, and his son-in-law the Comte d'Egmont-Pignatelli, could not do without the strictest protocol due to his rank.

For the transport of so much matériel, something like 200 merchant ships of every sort had to be hired. Forty-nine of these were occupied by troops; thirteen by artillery; eleven by general supplies; eight by horses; thirty-seven by provisions; forty-seven by cattle; five by sheep; six by water and forage. Whatever happened the force was assured of ample provisions.

La Galissonnière divided his fleet of twelve warships and five frigates into three divisions of four vessels each. The *'Foudroyant'* was the Admiral's flagship and headed the White squadron; Commander Glandevez, on board the *'Redoutable'*, led the Blue-and-White squadron; and the commander of the Blue squadron, the Marquis de la Clue, sailed in the *'Couronne'*. These ships were equipped with a total of 764 cannons, a further 130 being aboard the frigates *'Junon'*, *'Rose'*, *'Gracieuse'*, *'Topaz'* and *'Nymphe'*.

Despite the lavish nature of the preparations, it seems evident, to judge from Louis XV's instructions to Richelieu and La Galissonnière, that the attack on Menorca was considered mainly as a brief military digression. The King insisted several times that «the objective which must constantly be borne in mind is the preservation of the forces which His Majesty destines for this expedition». And in the very paragraph which deals with the conquest he makes the necessary arrangements for the return to Toulon, taking it for granted that the operation would be of short duration. For his part, the French historian E. Guillon later expressed the opinion that «the arrogant confidence of Richelieu and the talents of La Galissonnière were what achieved victory».

La Galissonnière's poor health did not influence either the efficiency or the speed of his organisation, and on 4th April the embarkation of troops began. On the 10th the fleet was equipped to set off on the voyage of 60 leagues which separated Menorca from the French coast.

With favourable winds this would mean a crossing of about thirty hours, but they had hardly got out of the Toulon roads when a strong sou'wester forced the ships to seek refuge in the Hières islands, whence they put to sea on the 12th, with a good north wind, soon to become a violent *Tramontana* which broke up the convoy. After rain, storms and serious dangers, the rugged north coast of Menorca was sighted on the afternoon of 17th April.

III

In April 1756 William Blakeney, the aged English Governor, had been *en poste* in Mahón for eight years. Son of a wealthy Irish squire of English descent, Blakeney had left his country life to join the army. He fought with Marlborough in the European campaigns but, lacking influence both in Parliament and at Court, he did not achieve the rank of colonel until he was sixty-five. He distinguished himself when he had to put down a revolt in Scotland, and as reward George II appointed him Lieutenant-Governor of Menorca, with the rank of Lieutenant-General. A jovial and kindly man, he soon won the sympathies of the Menorcans, even to the extent of being compared with Kane. Among the many improvements which were brought about in the flourishing island during his governorship, the census published in 1749 is particularly outstanding. Excluding the garrison, foreign residents and the clergy, the population was approaching 20,815, thus indicating a considerable increase since the arrival of the English. In addition, the naval hospital was repaired and Blakeney laid the first stone of the reconstructed Carmelite convent in the capital, today a municipal market where hams and garlic hang beneath its baroque mouldings.

But this good man, friendly, unbiased, an octogenarian, suffering from gout — and possibly also the palsy, to judge from his shaky signature — was not exactly the ideal general to withstand a siege of seventy days in the fort which defended the port of Mahón.

The fort of San Felipe at that time had reached its highest stage of development. The English had converted it from the state in which they found it in 1708 — mediaeval in appearance, square in plan, measuring some 90 meters across, surrounded by a wide moat and a curtain

173

wall which joined the four inner bastions — into a great fort with the reputation of being impregnable.

Hernández Sanz, in his admirable history of Menorca, describes the fort in the following manner: «The nucleus of the fort, comprising in itself a very respectable fortification, took the form of an irregular starred polygon, the perimeter of which was surrounded by a moat and an inner covered way.

«On the land side, that is to say in a broken line from Cala San Esteban to the port of Mahón, about two to three hundred yards from the covered way, there ran an entrenched passage known as the outer covered way (which separated the castle from the rest of the island), protecting in the following order the "South-West Lunette", the "Caroline Redoubt", the "Western Lunette", "Kane's" or the "New Lunette" and the "Queen's Redoubt", all of which were surrounded by moats.

«In a broken line following the ins and outs of the coast, a big wall was built at sea level up to the level of the glacis, a wall which supported, looking towards the port, the "Royal" and "Princess's Line" batteries and, looking towards the Cala, those known as the "Hospital" and "St. Stephen". These batteries were reinforced from the port side by the small advance redoubts known as "Anstruther" and "Argyll", and from the Cala side by the "South Lunette".

«This great mountain of a fort was complemented by that of "San Carlos" on the tongue of land separating the port from the Cala, by the "Marlborough" fort on the eastern bank of Cala San Esteban, and the "Filipet" on the north shore of the harbour.

«The castle was built on bed-rock; its underground works, like its moats (40 feet wide by 20 feet deep), must have been dug with picks — a colossal task which cost the English one million pounds sterling.

«The number of pieces of artillery mounted on the fort reached about 800, among which were 350 large calibre cannon and 22 mortars.

«But the really admirable part of this work was in its underground passages; mines which crossed in all direc-

174

tions and which allowed communication with the port and with Cala San Esteban, wells, hiding places, precipices, large stores for foodstuffs and ammunition, workshops, barracks, a shop and a hospital, all such a tangled labyrinth that it would have been difficult to go round it without an exact knowledge of its layout.»

Thus the harbour of Mahón was admirably defended but, once again, no account was taken of the vulnerability of the remaining ports. Neither in Ciudadela nor Fornells had forts of any consideration been built. San Felipe was indeed inadequate protection for the whole island.

The English garrison in Menorca amounted to 2,860 officers and men, of which, in December 1755, no less than 41 officers and a good number of soldiers were on leave. Alarmed by the news of the large concentration of troops in Toulon, and having observed that England seemed but little concerned about the Menorcan base, Blakeney and other commanders wrote repeatedly to London urgently demanding an increase in the garrison and requesting money for the necessary repairs to the forts. In their eagerness to maintain their Parliamentary majority, the Ministries of Pelham and Newcastle ignored the petitions from Mahón. But so numerous were the intelligence reports from the Mediterranean coasts that in the end the government decided to equip a force which would oppose that being prepared in Toulon. The ten warships fitted out under the command of Admiral Byng were fully rigged in the roads of St. Helen's on 6th April and reached Gibraltar on 2nd May. From the beginning this small fleet was manifestly inadequate and set out too late to impede any French naval action in the Mediterranean.

IV

On 8th April, Easter Sunday, the great French fleet sailed down the western coast of Menorca, piloted by the captain of a Mallorcan *jebeque* whom La Galissonnière had assigned to serve under him, he himself being unfamiliar with the waters of those parts. His objective was

175

the Isla del Aire, off which the English had anchored forty-eight years before; but the magnificent still morning forced a change of tactics which was extraordinarily favourable to the French landing. Being unable to get past Cape Bajoli, the fleet anchored in impressive half-moon formation off Ciudadela before nine in the morning.

As soon as he had been assured by a reconnaissance patrol that the garrison, composed of 300 English soldiers, had abandoned the city, and had observed that the population welcomed the invaders with lively demonstrations of sympathy — the Councillors coming on board to pay their compliments to the Marshal — Richelieu ordered the disembarkation of his troops. On Easter Monday, after High Mass, a solemn Te Deum was sung in the principal parish church of Ciudadela, presided over by the Duke. Thereupon the civil and ecclesiastical authorities of the island swore fidelity to the King of France.

Ciudadela, the principal seat of the aristocracy and clergy, was a particularly anglophobic centre. Its inhabitants welcomed the French invasion as a liberation and a revivification both of the Catholic religion and of the nobility.

Due to difficulties in the terrain, the French landings — at Cala Santandría and at Ciudadela itself — were arduous, but still more laborious was the transport of the artillery, when the French discovered — as had the English so many years before — that the island was ill-provided with oxen and carts. In fact the islanders hardly possessed more than a few mules, the weakly donkey being the beast of burden of the peasants. The oxen which had been brought to feed the invading army had to make up for this shortage, and local carpenters, under the guidance of French engineers, turned themselves to making carts as fast as they could.

Once he had ascertained that the road between Ciudadela and Mahón had been strewn with obstacles and the bridges blown up by the English in their flight towards San Felipe, Richelieu decided to send part of his armament by sea to Fornells, also deserted by its garrison. The retreat had not been effected without excesses and sackings on the part of the soldiers, and the destruction was especially bad in Mercadal.

Apart from the fort of San Felipe, the whole of the island — which, in the words of the Marshal, «was much bigger than I had thought» — fell into the hands of the French without a single shot being fired. As Blakeney reported: «The natives in general on this important occasion, have shown the highest disaffection to His Majesty's service.»

The army of 12,000 men, camped uncomfortably between dry-stone walls about a league from Ciudadela, set out to march, and on 22nd April Richelieu reached Alayor. The 35 kilometers of road were anything but a parade-ground walk, and the elegant and bewigged «*tacons-rouges*» from Versailles soon observed that the campaign would be more difficult than they had foreseen.

Into the bargain, the unseasonable heat was suffocating and caused many losses among the soldiers (mostly Bretons) employed in dragging the heavy armament. E. Guillon, a historian of this period, describes the scene thus: «For several days, over the whole island, along rough roads, through dust, under a burning sun, were to be seen these strange convoys, driven by our men and by some of the local population. Although not in this unknown place, but certainly in any other, our military prestige would have suffered.» Indeed, the white uniforms in which the French infantry were dressed were reduced to rags.

On the day of Richelieu's arrival in Alayor he received the following very British message from General Blakeney: «Not having received any communication that war has been declared between His Majesty the King of Great Britain and His Christian Majesty, I think it is my duty to ask you with what intention you have landed the troops under your command in this island. From the castle of San Felipe, the 22nd of April 1756.»

The reply, which contained a clear allusion to the English pirate raids, was sent without delay: «I have just received your letter of the 22nd about my arrival in the island of Menorca and my intentions here. I can assure

Your Excellency that they are exactly the same as those of His Britannic Majesty's fleets towards our French ships.»

On 23rd April, at four in the afternoon, Richelieu was in Mahón and his army camped outside the city on a hard and stony site. The difficulties multiplied. Not only did transport continue to be a serious problem but, according to the engineers' reckoning, four hundred days would be needed to surround San Felipe effectively. And although the lesser fort of San Felipet on the other side of the harbour opposite the main fort had been occupied, it had had to be abandoned because it was under enemy fire. The capture of the Arrabal was more effective, despite the fact that Blakeney had blown up four solid windmills there because their height obstructed the castle's defences.

Richelieu's worst enemy during this preliminary stage was the hardness of the ground, which caused a tremendous delay in installing the batteries. Digging the trenches became real slave labour, every handful of earth having to be moved in sacks. Under the constant hammering of the fort's artillery, French troops worked away feverishly by night for two months to emplace the siege batteries between the Arrabal and San Felipe, suffering heavy losses.

Having established that a surprise attack was out of the question and that the siege matériel available was insufficient to reduce the castle to ruins, the Marshal asked Toulon for reinforcements. But he insisted, above all, that La Galissonnière's fleet should maintain constant watch in Menorcan waters. His well-founded obsession was that the British fleet would arrive at any moment, an event which would seriously hamper his campaign.

With characteristic optimism and sang-froid Richelieu walked among his troops, encouraging them and emphasizing the need for speed. And it was no doubt at this period that a famous legend was born (although it is uncertain if the incident did in fact take place). The Duke, finding himself one day about noon in an isolated farmhouse and feeling hungry, asked for something to eat. The farmer gave him bread and the only other ingredients he had available, eggs and olive oil. The garlic omitted, the age-old Mediterranean «allioli» thus became the famous «Mahonaise» sauce.

V

In the fort of San Felipe, General William Blakeney knew that although he was well supplied with victuals and matériel he could not sustain a long siege unless he received reinforcements. His intentions, on deploying his forces in the castle — losing a number of opportunities to make a surprise attack on the enemy, hardly organised as yet — had been to strengthen the garrison as far as possible. But even with the support of the soldiers from the three war-ships and two frigates which Read-Admiral Edgecombe, anchored in the port, had landed before setting sail for Gibraltar when he heard the news of the French invasion, his military potential did not exceed 2,500 men. Moreover, the vast majority of these soldiers were men without much experience and commanded by inept officers. His only hope was therefore the arrival of the fleet commanded by Admiral Byng, recently appointed Commander-in-Chief of Mediterranean naval forces.

John Byng, at fifty-two, had behind him a solid naval career, achieved with the help of that brilliant seaman who was his father, Viscount Torrington. A meticulous man, with a thorough knowledge of his profession, he was nevertheless somewhat irresolute of character and prone to depressions, tending to create imaginary problems. These defects contributed to the tragedy with which his life ended.

Arriving in Gibraltar at the beginning of May 1756, Byng received the news that French troops had landed in Menorca. He wrote pessimistically to his Minister, Cleveland: «I am firmly of the opinion that the throwing men in the castle will only enable it to hold out but a little, and add to the number that must fall into the enemy's hands, for the garrison in time will be obliged to surrender.» In this frame of mind, with which Fowke and the Council of War held in Gibraltar were in agreement, Byng sailed for Menorca on 8th May, arriving off Cape Favaritx to the north of Mahón on the 19th. (The Council of War had decided that the danger, even the impossibility, of attempting a landing did not justify weakening the defence of the Rock to provide aid for Menorca.)

His fleet was composed of thirteen ships of the line, four frigates and one corvette; artillery consisted of 874 cannons. 4,000 soldiers destined to reinforce San Felipe sailed in her. Byng's flagship was the *'Ramillies'*, supported by the *'Lancarter'* with Rear-Admiral Edgecombe and the *'Buckingham'* with Temple-West.

La Galissonnière had been patrolling the south coast of the island for days with his fleet of twelve warships and five frigates, equipped with 764 cannons, in order to prevent the intervention of the English fleet. The vanguard was commanded by Glandevez on the *'Redoubtable'*; La Galissonnière took up a central position on the *'Foudroyante'*, and La Cue on the *'Couronne'* commanded the rear. It was not long before these powerful naval forces met.

On the 20th, around midday, the wind changed and began to blow from the south-west, clearing the mist which had been hanging about since the previous day. The English squadron manoeuvred so as to secure the «weather gage», i. e. to take up a position to windward of the French line, thus assuring itself of the initiative in battle. By two in the afternoon the squadrons were facing each other in almost parallel lines but on opposite courses.

The attack began under Byng's orders that each ship should tack until on the same course as the enemy, then steer down on its opposite adversary, approaching it obliquely. But instead of complying, the first ship of the English line, the *'Defiance'*, commanded by Captain Andrews, followed by the remaining three ships of Admiral Temple-West's division, continued on a course parallel to the French, at too great a distance from them, until commanded by Byng's red flag to attack. Their attack was so sudden that Glandevez's vanguard had to be regrouped, falling to the lee of La Galissonnière. Temple-West, seeing that his attack had put the enemy at too great a distance, did not hesitate to haul to wind in order to support Byng's centre group which, together with the rearguard, was under such intense fire from La Galissonnière that his line was badly damaged; indeed, serious disorder was created on the sixth ship, '*Intrepid*', who lost her foremast. The disorder kept the main nucleus of the British squadron temporarily out of action, so that Temple-West's vanguard had to bear the brunt of the battle.

For his part, La Galissonnière, no longer able to rely on the five ships making up Glandevez's vanguard which had fallen to leeward, kept his line closed with great firmness, maintaining a violent cannonade on the enemy and thus preventing Byng from forcing his rear to turn, cutting off their retreat to Mahón. La Galissonnière sums up the final state of the battle with these words: «They were forced to retreat rapidly without realising the bad state of the French vanguard, or at least without taking advantage of it.»

At six in the afternoon the wind separated the two squadrons. The British squadron remained for two days off Mahón carrying out repairs. On the third day the French squadron reappeared and Byng retreated to the open sea.

The French victory was complete.

The strict discipline which the French Admiral demanded from his fleet and the constant tactical exercises which he imposed on his officers led to the outcome that was to be expected: his ships kept in close battle order during the four hours of action, thus preventing the enemy from penetrating his line. Byng, on the other hand, was not able to follow up his early advantage of having secured the «weather gage», and the serious damage suffered by the '*Intrepid*' at the start of the action made him hesitate at a critical moment. It may well be said that, because he started the battle in a state of discouragement, or because his men were inexperienced, the English Admiral did not have the energy or the verve necessary to win. In his favour it must be acknowledged that if in this first encounter he had only lost the battle, in the second he would have run the risk of letting his ships fall into French hands.

To sum up, as both commanders had had to submit to circumstances outside those of naval strategy, they lost the opportunity of bringing about a real naval action. The responsibility of watching over the safety of the four thousand troops aboard Byng's ships hindered, without doubt, the manoeuvres of the heavy warships, always difficult to manage. And, obeying implicitly the orders of his monarch, La Galissonnière was forced to refrain from pursuing and inflicting heavy punishment on his adversary.

The British squadron, although badly mauled, does not appear to have suffered sufficient losses (45 dead and 162 wounded) or damage to justify the decision of the Council of War held on the '*Ramillies*', at which it was resolved that the fort of San Felipe could not be saved, that the squadron was in no state for a renewed confrontation with the enemy, and that it was more important to defend Gibraltar. Its return to Gibraltar cost the fall of Menorca.

La Galissonnière did not know until later that he had in fact fought against Byng's squadron and, expecting soon to be attacked by him, took up once more his position of sentinel off the port of Mahón. He had lost 38 of his men in the action and a further 184 wounded, but his ships were not badly damaged.

On learning of the victorious outcome of the naval battle of 20th May, the confused noise of which had been heard in the French camp from beyond the Isla del Aire, enthusiasm was delirious. Richelieu took advantage of the opportunity to infuse new fervour into his people, ordering the troops to march between salvos through the streets of Mahón; a solemn Te Deum was sung in the parish church of Santa María.

News of La Galissonnière's victory finally freed the Marshal from any doubts which, despite his natural optimism, he might have had about the outcome of the campaign. With the British fleet now out of reach, the danger of having to face an attack disappeared and the reinforcements requested from France could arrive from Marseille without fear of being molested. Even so, the problem of reducing «this strong place about which

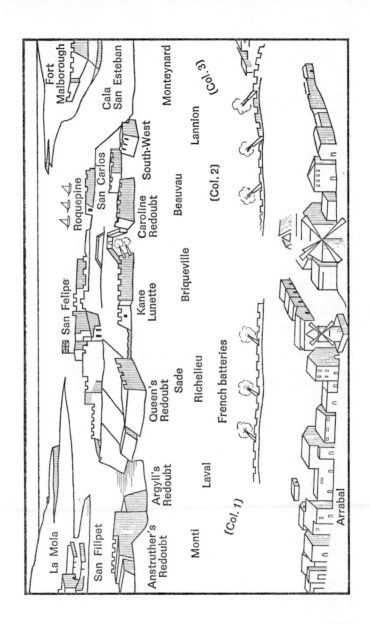

Fort Malborough

La Mola

San Filipet

Anstruther's Redoubt

Argyll's Redoubt

Queen's Redoubt

San Felipe

Roquepine

San Carlos

Cala San Esteban

Kane Lunette

Caroline Redoubt

South-West

Monti

Laval

Sade

Richelieu

Briqueville

Beauvau

Lannion

Monteynard

[Col. 1]

French batteries

[Col. 2]

[Col. 3]

Arrabal

183

we had no notion», as Richelieu himself wrote, turned out to be long and laborious. And not least among the many difficulties the Duke had to overcome were the criticisms of his general-staff, principally from the Marquis de Maillebois, an ally of Argenson, who had kept up throughout the campaign the back-bitings of Versailles. These intrigues did not seem to bother the Marshal who, with his usual enthusiasm, went on constant visits to the front while the siege operations progressed systematically. The summer heat became unbearable and the soldiers, worn out by the work on the trenches, began drinking to excess the cheap local wine. Fearing that discipline would get slack and that disease would become rampant, the General-in-Chief had published a standing order warning that any soldiers found drunk would be deprived of the honour of going to the front. Having won the sympathy of the troops, Richelieu imposed honour on them. The result was decisive.

From the beginning of June, all hope of help from Admiral Byng's fleet having been lost, discouragement became general among the defenders of San Felipe, to such an extent that they noticed almost with indifference the great activity displayed by the enemy emplacing new and more powerful batteries facing them. Blakeney, at eighty-four, had been bravely resisting the encirclement for more than two months. His cannon went on firing, but the fighting spirit of his people, who suffered more from disease and low morale than from privations, had disappeared.

Despite all this, on the 14th, in a last feeble attempt to spike the French batteries, the Governor ordered a sortie by a group of infantry, who soon fell into enemy hands.

Richelieu had succeeded in placing 62 heavy-calibre cannons, 21 mortars and 4 howitzers opposite the castle. The Queen's Redoubt had been given heavy punishment. His army were enjoying the best of conditions and were full of fighting spirit. The Commander-in-Chief called a Council of War and, to the surprise of everyone, announced to his officers his theatrical *coup de main*. The joint attack by his entire forces against the external defences of San

Felipe would take place on the following night by the light of the moon. Once more, luck was on the side of this picturesque personality.

The attacking force was divided into three columns composed of two brigades each. The left-hand column, commanded by the Comte de Laval, was directed against the Anstruther, Argyll, Kane and Queen's Redoubts. It was made up of 16 companies of grenadiers, two of the brigades being under the orders of the Marquises of Monti and Briqueville, the remaining companies being commanded by Colonel the Marquis de Sade. It was this column which was to bear the brunt of the combat. The centre column, commanded by the Prince de Beauvau, would attack the Eastern Redoubt and the Caroline Lunette. The right-hand column was commanded by the Comte de Lannion, the first of its two brigades being under his direct command and the other under that of the Marquis de Monteynard. Their objective was Fort Marlborough and the South-Western Lunette. The brave Marquis de Riquèpine, with 400 volunteers, 100 grenadiers and six naval *chalupas* commanded by Lieutenant Pignet-Guelton, was entrusted with the difficult operation of landing in silence on the rocks at the foot of the San Carlos fort, taking it by surprise and then advancing along the bank of Cala San Esteban until he could join forces with Lannion's column.

Richelieu, accompanied by Maillebois, du Mesnil and Prince de Wurtemberg, would establish his headquarters in the centre of the left-hand wing, the principal column of the attacking force, whence he would direct operations.

On the evening of Sunday the 27th the troops which were to take part in the assault mustered in the main street of the Arrabal with arms at the shoulder and cartridge cases filled. They were joined by 900 workmen, 6 engineers and 3 brigades of miners. At nine-thirty the fire of the batteries stopped. At ten a cannonade broke the silence of the night and four bombs were thrown from the signals tower by the invaders. It was the signal to begin the attack.

At the head of the left-hand column, Colonel Monti, under heavy enemy fire, ran in the open towards the

185

Anstruther and Argyll Redoubts. He and his men reached the covered way, crossed the moat and laid the first ladder against the walls of the fort itself. At the same time, Briqueville and de Sade resolutely attacked the Kane and Queen's Redoubts. The ladders proved too short but, in their determination to win, the soldiers stuck their bayonets into cracks in the walls and reached the parapet by climbing on the shoulders of their companions. After a bitter fight Monti occupied the Anstruther and Argyll Redoubts, losing a good number of grenadiers, victims of the mines laid by the retreating English. Protected by the covered way, he succeeded in making contact with the Queen's Redoubt and, in the underground tunnel, he surprised Lieutenant-Colonel Jeffries — Blakeney's right-hand man — whom he took prisoner together with the 15 men he led.

Briqueville's grenadiers, accompanied by those of de Sade, continued their attack on the Queen's Redoubt, but their keenness for the fight led them to go right into it instead of proceeding to the adjacent redoubt by the covered way and capturing the Kane Lunette. The Queen's Redoubt did fall into French hands, but this error of Briqueville's created a lacuna in the general plan of operations and the Kane Redoubt was not occupied.

Simultaneously with the first attack, Prince Beauvau, in charge of the assault on the centre, brought forward one of his brigades towards the Western Redoubt and the other towards the Caroline Lunette. But as they had to cover a longer field than the combatants of the left-hand sector, their advance became difficult under continuous musket and cannon fire. However, they took the covered way and reduced the redoubts, spiking 12 cannons and destroying their emplacements. But these positions were indefensible, being dominated by the Kane Redoubt — a point of resistance by the English — and so, after demolishing the pallisades and leaving the work in ruins, Beauvau was forced to evacuate his men in good order.

As for the third, or right-hand column, commanded by Lannion and Monteynard, its manoeuvre depended on the success of Roquèpine's attack from the sea on the San Carlos fort. After occupying it he was to signal the Breton companies of the right wing, instructing them to advance on the South-Western Lunette, the Cadogan and Amalia counter-forts and, after cutting communications with the castle, on the Marlborough fort. Flat on the ground, opposite their objective, the Royal and Breton brigades forced the enemy to maintain fire against them all night long, while awaiting the signal to attack.

The location of San Carlos, just at the entrance of Cala San Esteban, and of Marlborough on the opposite bank of that long cove, had helped to keep these forts safe from the fire of the French batteries and thus to remain intact. To assault them from the sea was as risky as it was desperate, because the general strategy of the battle was based on a synchronised convergent attack.

Contrary winds delayed the *chalupas* of Roquèpine's small contingent and when the first two boats could approach the shore the English, now on the alert, received them with furious fire. At the head of his marines Pignet-Guelton was the first to fall, riddled with five bullets; beside him also fell Captain Talouet and a good number of his grenadiers, as well as marines. Four boats were sunk, their crews swimming for safety. The remainder were forced to retreat. The operation had failed, but the constant fire from the right-hand French column had kept the defenders busy in this area, preventing them from counter-attacking the eastern redoubts, now in the hands of Laval's officers.

This violent fighting lasted throughout the night until, at one in the morning, little by little, the detonations of the cannons began to die down and musket fire ceased. Before dawn broke a profound silence reigned over the field of battle.

Four hundred French occupied the Queen's Redoubt and 200 the Anstruther and Argyll Redoubts. The Western and Caroline Lunettes were destroyed. The mine-layers had billeted themselves in the underground corridors of the fort. In their bold ascent of the walls the infantry had won the battle for France. Their losses were small: eight officers and 240 soldiers killed and 412 soldiers injured.

With his scant troops Blakeney — who, it is said, had not been to bed or changed his clothes during the ten weeks of the siege — was forced to redeploy in the centre of the castle in view of the impossibility of defending its external works under simultaneous assault from all sides. With no news of any military support, he soon realised the uselessness of trying to maintain this new position against an army of 12,000 men which surrounded the unfortunate castle of San Felipe. The losses suffered by the garrison amounted to 400 dead and wounded.

At seven in the morning the English General requested a period of twenty-four hours in which to draw up an honourable surrender. Less than twelve hours after the allotted time granted by the enemy, Major Boyd presented himself to Richelieu with a plan of capitulation containing twelve articles. The final document was approved and signed the following day, 29th June.

A few weeks later Admiral Hawke's fleet of 22 ships sighted the fleur-de-lis flying from the walls of the fort. The reinforcements so anxiously awaited turned and sailed back to Gibraltar.

After two long months of isolation defending the last British bastion in Menorca, the conquered troops emerged from the great gateway of the castle. The red jackets of the King's, the Welsh Fusiliers, the Cornwall and the Effingham regiments and a company of the Royal Artillery marched out with flags unfurled and drums beating, before Richelieu's general-staff. The ceremony took place in the tradition of the strictest courtesy of Versailles; it had been a hard fight, with none of the animosity of a political struggle. Mr. Williams, the Governor's Secretary, surrendered the keys of the fort, but when William Blakeney offered his sword the Duc de Richelieu refused to accept it, receiving his adversary with a brotherly embrace.

Thus commenced for Menorca seven years of aimiable French rule.

The British contingent of 4,000 men left Mahón in 32 transports on 10th July 1756, bound for Gibraltar; 171 wounded remained behing in hospital.

Proceded by his son, the Duc de Fronsac, and by his son-in-law, the Comte d'Egmont — the first emissaries sent urgently to France with despatches announcing the fall of Menorca — Richelieu embarked on the 'Foudroyant' on 7th July. Accompanied by his general-staff and his army, he had to suffer once more the violent storms which characterised that year. He arrived in Toulon on the 16th where he was received with delirious enthusiasm by the French people. The Duke crossed his country under triumphal arches and fireworks, welcomed in every village with brilliant receptions and solemn Te Deums. The impertinent welcome which Louis XV gave him in Compiègne and the frigidity of a jealous court did not detract in the least from his incredible popularity. The only official reward he received — framed with inappropriate dignity — was the famous phrase of the King on meeting the Duke: «Here is the Marshal. How did you find the figs in Menorca? They say they are very good,» which served to highlight not only his ingratitude but also his supine ignorance of the seasons and their fruits. On the other hand, the cunning Madame de Pompadour gave a small party in her country house in honour of «the Menorquin», the gentlemen's swords being decked which strings of bunting.

Rewards offered for military merit by the aristocratic officialdom were particularly splendid. Two *cordon bleus* were granted, seven nobles were promoted to the rank of field marshal, six to brigadier-general, and many others received pensions and decorations.

The Marquis de la Galissonnière, with his eternal ill-luck, died in Nemours before being able to accept his well-merited Marshal's baton.

The number of poems, odes and songs written in praise of the Menorcan campaign were worthy of the conquest of a continent. Voltaire, a friend of Richelieu's, dedicated a poem to him with the words: «To Marshal Richelieu, on the conquest of Menorca»; Audibert and Favers, among many other authors, gave free rein to their lyrical imagination in a fulsome appreciation of the military action, and even today there is a street in the centre of Paris called Port-Mahón, while a summer resort on the Normandy coast also bears that name.

In London the loss of the little Mediterranean island raised a tremendous outcry. The capital was draped in mourning. Newcastle's government fell, to be succeeded by that of William Pitt. To win over public opinion and to highlight the incompetence of the outgoing government, the new ministry demanded that heads should fall. The victims were Blakeney, Byng and the Governor of Gibraltar, Fowke. The first was accused of having defended San Felipe ineffectively, the second of having lost the battle off Port Mahón, and the third was court-martialled for disobeying orders and was expelled from the army. The aged Blakeney, towards whom the public showed more pity than animosity, was absolved, whilst Byng was condemned for the humiliation which the defeat of his fleet, an object of national pride, had brought on the nation.

The case against Admiral Byng, overwhelmed with calumnies, began in December 1756 on board the warship 'St. George' at anchor in Portsmouth harbour. Byng defended himself with energetic sang-froid, and his famous Political Testament, published after his death, justified the failure of the action by the lack of planning on the part of his superiors and the delay in sending the expedition. But neither his own highly relevant evidence nor the recommendation sent by Richelieu, nor the intervention of his family, nor even the letter from the court-martial recommending clemency, were able to save Byng from sentence of death, «for not having done everything in his power to capture and destroy the French ships». He was shot on 14th March 1757 by a firing squad of marines on the bridge of the 'Monarch'. According to the words of Martin in Voltaire's «Candide», this unjust political execution was necessary «pour encourager les autres».

In Menorca, the Comte de Lannion assumed the responsibilities of Lieutenant-Governor of the island and Lieutenant-General of the French forces of occupation, numbering 6,000 soldiers. Still a young man, Lannion possessed the rare quality of combining with his military experience that of a good administrator. A Breton by birth, he was used to respecting the franchises and customs of a local region, and those of Menorca were confirmed by Louis XV's royal edict ratifying the laws and customs observed by the English.

Lannion built signal towers, coastal batteries and military roads; he fortified Ciudadela and Fornells as well as donating a new printing press to the populace and charging his engineers with the task of producing accurate maps of the island. Like his successors, he discharged his responsibilties with skill and competence and, although Menorca did not become especially prosperous during the period of French rule (they were constantly preoccupied with the danger of an attack by the British), the sympathy which the inhabitants showed towards the troops — despite the trouble of having to lodge them in their houses — created a cordial atmosphere. Religious and country festivities brought the two peoples together, and the French language became popular among the islanders.

The honest French administration brought order to the large quantity of debts contracted by the *Universidades* and to the chaotic form of payment currently used throughout the island, by imposing the Spanish *duro* as the basic currency. Exchanges had formerly been carried out in English, Mallorcan and Portuguese money, frequently even in jewels and spices. Agriculture was now supervised and grain was imported during periods of shortage.

Nevertheless, the unhealthy state of the island caused the administration serious concern. Quarantine rules were strictly observed, drinking water supplies were analysed, and Mercadal, where many troops were in barracks, was evacuated because of its unhealthy marshes. Proof of the great care devoted by the French to matters of public hygiene is to be found in the long treatise written by the army doctor, François Posserat de la Chapelle, on the climate and diseases of Menorca, a work which had in fact been also done by his English predecessor, Doctor Cleghorn.

The unhealthy humidity and the freezing north winds which prevailed in the island favoured the spread of fevers, dysentry and pneumonia. Many soldiers succumbed to these afflictions, to which their leaders too were not immune.

The next Governor, the Marquis de Frémeur, died in Menorca in 1759 at the age of sixty-two. In memory of «this faithful and virtuous man» the King had a marble memorial stone engraved, which can still be seen in the parish church of Santa María in Mahón at the foot of the great organ. Another plaque in the same spot commemorates the well-loved Comte de Lannion, who succeeded Frémeur as Governor and who died of pneumonia on 2nd October 1762. The whole population attended the funeral which the authorities had organised in his honour.

Shortly before the death of Lannion the *Universidad* of Mahón had commissioned the painter, Giuseppe Chiesa, to do a portrait of the Count «for his eternal remembrance». On foot, with the castle of San Felipe in the background, the figure of the Governor stands out, clad in his green coat, on which are displayed his decorations and military crosses.

But the most lasting memorial to his rule, which Lannion bequeathed to the Menorcans was the construction of a new town, four miles south of Mahón; a well ordered and gay town of eighteen blocks was planned to be built on uncultivated land — the property was known as the Garriga de Binifadet — hitherto used for grazing. The new inhabitants built a well-proportioned church in neoclassical style opposite the municipal square. The French royal coat-of-arms was carved on the façade, together with those of Lannion and the *Intendente*, beneath which may be read the inscription: «Devi Ludovico sacrum dedicarvere galli. An. MDCCLXI» (This church is dedicated to St. Louis by the French). The church was finished in 1761 and, like the town itself, was dedicated to St. Louis, King of France (Louis IX). The name of the Comte de Lannion is still commemorated in the street which runs parallel to the main street of San Luis.

The nobility of Ciudadela were drawn out of the retreat they had imposed on themselves during the English domination by a bond of brotherhood with their Catholic occupiers and, influenced by the elegance of the French officers, at last changed their lugubrious breeches and black capes for the more colourful parisian styles. The ladies also profited from new customs imported from the court of Versailles, which did much to free them from the Moorish state of reclusion in which they had hitherto lived.

Considered as a whole, the French domination benefitted the Menorcans culturally, and although the departure of the foreign merchants and the burden of having to support such a numerous garrison did not help their economic development, the islanders tolerated with good grace their seven years of French occupation. Indeed, there was nothing else they could do about it.

I

Before their conquest of Menorca the question had already arisen as to the use the island could have for the French. That financial expert, Pâris-Duverney, wrote with great perspicacity: «One must not imagine, for it would be preposterous, that England would conduct the war with such ill luck as not to obtain in the peace treaty the return of Port Mahón. Consequently, whether we retain the island ourselves or whether we give it back to Spain, it will soon return to the English.»

Indeed, in Europe and in America, the Seven Years War, so disastrous for France, was drawing to a close. Allied to Austria, Russia, Saxony and, later, to Sweden and Spain against England and Frederick II of Prussia, France lost in this war not only considerable territory but also the prestige of being the worthy adversary of the nation which had become the principal European power. After the defeat suffered by Louis XV's soldiers in the battlefields of Europe, the militias of the American colonies and the mercenaries of the East India Company expelled the French from North America and from the East Indies. The British Empire was being built on the solid basis of a navy which was mistress of the seas.

In the peace treaty signed in Paris on 10th February 1763, the provinces of Mississippi, Nova Scotia, Cap Breton, the islands in the St. Lawrence estuary and the French possessions in Senegal were ceded to England. France also restored the lesser Balearic island to George III.

Articles 12 and 24 of the treaty read as follows: «The island of Menorca shall be restored to His Britannic Majesty, together with the fort of St. Philip's in the same state in which it was found by the arms of His Most Christian Majesty at the time of the conquest, and with the same artillery as was mounted at that time.» And added: «Three months after the exchange of ratifications of the present treaty the island of Menorca shall be restored by France or, if possible sooner.»

Not without sorrow the French administration set about ordering the complicated evacuation of her people from Menorca.

The Marquis de Pusignieux, who had arrived seven years previously with Richelieu's troops and had been promoted first to Lieutenant-General and then to Governor, was responsible for the evacuation of the eleven battalions making up the garrison of the island. The Medoc, Royal and Royal Italian regiments from Mahón; Royal Contois and Taladru from Alayor; the Vernandois from Ciudadela, and the 500 infantry and artillery of the fort of San Felipe, were soon ready to depart.

The work of that honest man Causan, *Intendente* of the troops, was not less arduous and, as well as organising the civilians and their dependants, he had to work out the accounts and settle the debts contracted by his government.

On 4th July 1763 the French force left the island on board two warships, the *'Tennant'* and *'Hector'* and the frigate *'Chimère'*.

The day before, Admiral Brest, commanding the English squadron of four warships and three frigates, arrived in Mahón and shortly afterwards Lieutenant-General Lord James Johnston took charge of the government of Menorca.

The new English domination, which was to last eighteen years, was not so successful as the first. The greed of the governors, especially the haughty Johnston and his wife Cecily — scandalously interested in getting the most they could for themselves out of the situation — was yet another contributory factor to Menorca's new problems. The English did not get on with the clergy, the island's political liberties created difficulties, epidemics were serious, droughts caused unemployment and emigration. Menorca went through some rather bad years.

The only really beneficial administration was the short governorship of General Moystyn. In 1771 he ordered the demolition of the ill-famed Arrabal which had caused so much trouble to one after another of the occupants of

San Felipe, and built a new military township overlooking Cala Fons on the shores of the harbour. To this great esplanade, surrounded by military barracks and pavilions, he gave the name of Georgetown, in honour of King George III. The Menorcans for their part called it «S'Arraval Nou», just as they also continued referring to the island where Alfonso the Liberal had landed four centuries earlier as «S'Illa del Rei», despite the fact that the island, on which solid buildings had now replaced the barracks that had made do for a hospital, was called by the English «Bloody Island».

At about the same time some people from Ferrerías founded another village on the land of Binicodrell. The man behind this project, Cristóbal Barber, donated a church — consecrated in 1775 — and the new town was named after his patron saint. San Cristóbal was the third town to be added in that century to the six already in existence — an addition undoubtedly necessary to house the 26,000 Menorcans who populated the island at that time.

During those years the effort to defend the vast empire which Great Britain had obtained with her naval power fell to the lot of that same Royal Navy. Scattered among the seven seas, her ships were ferociously harassed by the corsairs which France, like England before her, had armed against the traditional enemy.

Attacked in his turn by French pirates, Lieutenant-General the Hon. James Murray, at that time Governor of Menorca, took advantage of the new war, declared in 1778 between the two countries, to grant corsair patents to more than fifty Menorcan sailing ships. Without work and impoverished, peasants and artisans set out to construct boats with the timber from the fast disappearing forests of the island. Following the ancient tradition, the islanders soon showed their aptitude for this sort of work, and 3,000 men and 535 pieces of artillery were embarked in the frigates 'Minorca' and 'Porcupine' among others. They attacked the coasts of Spain, and so intrepid were they that they even reached the French ports. Such was the havoc caused by this corsair fleet (rapidly increased in size by Gibraltarians and Italians who operated from Mahón) and so cruel were the assaults of the «Mahonese pirates» that they were compared with the Algerians of old. Murray, unapprehensive, was the first of many to acquire riches with the booty captured from the Spanish and French.

But neither the profits of the Governor, nor of his corsairs, served to keep away the danger which threatened the small British possession in the Mediterranean.

The Spanish 1782-1798

I

The sense of insecurity which the colonial power of Britain caused the Spanish possessions in America — and which was responsible for the rather tardy entry of Charles III of Spain in the Seven Years War, a war which cost Spain the loss of Florida — was alleviated by the Declaration of Independence approved by the colonies in rebellion at their meeting in Philadephia on 4th July 1776.

The triumph of the rebels was due largely to the blockage of the American coasts by Franco-Spanish fleets, because both Spain and France, whose interests had been harmed by the Treaty of Paris in 1763, had participated for some time in the political emancipation of that new state, supplying resources to the rebels in the conflict between the Thirteen Colonies and the metropolis — a conflict which owed its origin to the burden of taxation which Britain attempted to impose on her colonies for the maintenance of her fleet, which she could ill afford after the economic shocks produced by the Seven Years War.

Taking advantage of the manifest weakness of England — a weakness for which she was to pay with a calamitous contest, during which at times she would be fighting alone — and with the excuse of harassments inflicted by her filibusters, Charles III declared war on England in 1779.

It was in this campaign that various prickly points in America were fought over, while in Europe the main points of dispute were the Spanish claims to rights over the two pieces of national territory which had been occupied by the British since the beginning of the century: Gibraltar and Menorca.

The first of these to be attacked was Gibraltar, in 1780, but the defeat which Admiral Rodney's fleet inflicted on that of Lángora made possible the relief of the Rock, under siege by the army of Sotomayor.

But if Gibraltar once more showed herself to be impregnable, Spanish arms succeeded in driving the English from Honduras and from the Gulf of Mexico in 1780-81, victories which encouraged Floridablanca, from the court of Madrid, to pour the maximum effort into the recovery of Menorca.

II

In the palace of the Marqués de Sollerich, in Palma de Mallorca, the first soundings were made regarding the taking of Menorca. It was necessary to assess the opinions of the clergy and nobility in Menorca — who, despite so many years of foreign occupation, were still able to direct the current of popular opinion — in order to be sure of a good reception to the Spanish expeditionary force. And no less necessary would be a discreet enquiry as to the English military potential and the state of the fortifications.

It is said that Sollerich's agent, on a secret quest, visited the neighbouring island, as a result of which he was able to assure the Minister of State that there was nothing to fear on that account.

The Menorcans, for whom the last few years had not been particularly pleasant, would in turn have received news of the economic and political change which was taking place in the Peninsula and which would influence them in favour of a change to Spanish rule, quite apart from any patriotic feelings.

In the second half of the eighteenth century, Charles III — a disciple in his own way of Enlightened Despotism — directed the policy of Spain towards a transfer of power from the nobility to the bourgoisie. Legislation permitting free trade with America, cultural and administrative reforms, the suppression of «vile professions», progress in public works, and scientific improvements in agriculture, etc., soon brought about a great economic upsurge. In Catalonia, manufacturing and commercial prosperity and Spain's new political horizons reconciled the people to the Bourbons and, once the interests of the Catalans could be identified with those of the Crown, the straightforward personality of Charles III won their sympathies.

Moreover, the overflowing coffers which the frugal Ferdinand VI had left helped to give a great boost to the army and navy. The Spanish navy, amounting to 79 potent ships of the line and many frigates, *jabeques* and landing craft, had become by that time the most powerful in Europe after the British.

Even so, Charles III did not venture to undertake the reconquest of Menorca without French aid. Recognising his obligations under the pact of mutual support between Bourbon crowns (the Family Pact), Louis offered his cooperation with good grace, his main object being to do battle with England in the Mediterranean.

The Count of Floridablanca — of whom Goya was to paint that admirable portrait in which the extraordinary blue eyes of the Minister are so well brought out — informed of the good disposition of the Menorcans and, above all, of the evident weakness of her occupiers, set in motion the military operation against Menorca. His selection of the General-in-Chief of the expedition fell on the shoulders of Louis de Berton des Balbes de Quiers, Duc de Crillon. On leave in Madrid since his arrival from the Portuguese front, where he had fought in the fall of Almeida twenty years previously, Crillon was nevertheless a good fighter. Since the age of fifteen he had participated with singular bravery in all the European campaigns of the time, from Parma to Lutzelberg, and his military prestige had merited him the rank of Field-Marshal and later that of Lieutenant-General in the French army. Offended by some insignificant detail of command, he transferred to the service of Spain, where he received under the terms of the Family Pact the same rank as he had held in France.

No doubt bored in the Madrid court, he had been pressing on the Minister of State for some time now his plans for the invasion of Menorca. And so to Menorca would come once more a general in his sixties (a respectable age at that time), which shows either the importance given to the conquest of the island or the lack of opportunity offered to youth in time of war.

Be that as it may, Crillon was eager to organise his army, which was well disciplined and equipped in view of the interest which the monarch had devoted to the project for some time. The General's main concern would be to carry out his preparations in the greatest possible secrecy, to avoid arousing the suspicions of the British garrison in Menorca. This was really an unnecessary precaution because, warned or not, there was nothing the English could do to increase their strength. Crillon signed his acceptance of the command with a formal promise to Charles III «that he would respond with his own head to give the place to the King in less than three months after opening trenches, with little loss of life and limited expenditure by the royal treasury».

By early summer of 1781, 7,802 soldiers were mustered in Andalusia, perfectly equipped, under the orders of the following Generals: the Marquises of Casa Cagigal, Avilés and Peñafiel, the Conde de Cifuentes and the Comte de Crillon (son of the Duke). The general-staff was composed of General Luis de las Casas, Lieutenant-General Horacio Borghese and Don Félix Gerónimo Buch. 264 large-bore cannons were embarked with the Generals in the fleet consisting of two warships of the line, two frigates and twenty-two smaller vessels, under the command of Brigadier Ventura Moreno. The ships of the line, frigates, *bombardas, brulotes, baladras* and numerous transports sailed from Cádiz on 23rd July and were escorted as far as the Mediterranean — where they were safe from the danger of attack by English forces in the Atlantic — by Admiral Córdoba's squadron.

On the 29th they anchored in Cartagena to pick up 19 more warships and 4 frigates, with 184 cannons, which had arrived from Brest with the French Admiral Guichen, and on route for Menorca they were joined by 1,200 Catalan and Valencian volunteers.

The expedition was not to be so luxurious as the cortège of the Duc de Richelieu, but all the same the Spanish aristocracy who comprised it did not lag behind as regards the antiquity of their lineage. Peñafiel was the 9th Duke of Osuna and his young wife (who no doubt was so enthralled by this adventure that she went with the Duke to Menorca) was the Countess-Duchess of Benavente, Duchess of Gandía and Béjar. The Lieutenant-General of the Spanish army and *Alférez mayor* of Castile, Don Juan de Silva y de Pacheco, was Count of Cifuentes, Marquis of Alconchel and a Grandee of Spain. He was later to become Governor of Menorca.

III

The Hon. James Murray, Governor of Menorca for the past seven years, was a man of about fifty, narrow-nosed and haughty. He had been widowed in 1779 but soon remarried, his second wife being Anne Witham, daughter of the British Consul-General in Mallorca. A veteran soldier, querulous and snobbish in manner, he was the son of the fourth Earl of Elibank and had served in the army since his youth, fighting in Flanders, Britanny and the East Indies, and was on the general-staff during the fall of Montreal to the British. He was appointed Governor of Quebec and promoted to the rank of General in 1762 on becoming Governor-General of Canada. For the rest, his life was strewn with law suits in support of or against his brother officers, but although he was greedy and a great grumbler he displayed, especially in Menorca, an exemplary loyalty and scrupulousness in the execution of his duty.

In recent years the problem of garrisoning Menorca had become so difficult that in 1779 Murray wrote to the Secretary of State complaining that «the two British regiments here look more like ghosts than soldiers. The invalids and drafted men are quite worn out, and in a siege would be useless.»

This time London was aware of the danger through which her Mediterranean possession was passing, and in February 1780, after sending aid to the blockade of Gibraltar, the government despatched an expedition to Mahón consisting of five warships and seven transports, all well equipped. A new load of munitions, victuals and troops landed in the port in April. England could do no more: all her available forces were fighting in America.

Gibraltar was soon besieged once more by Spanish forces, and Murray received orders to send battalions and provisions to its Governor, Elliot, at the expense of Menorca's security.

The historian of the British army, J. W. Fortescue, expresses his bruising opinion in these words: «It was perfectly clear that England could not provide the troops to hold both fortresses; and, since Fort St. Philip in Mahón, however strong, was extremely unhealthy, owing to the foul air in the subterranean defences, it would have been better to blow up the works and evacuate the island, even at the sacrifice of so good a harbour as Mahón.»

Murray, despite his grievous situation, laboured resolutely in the preparation of the defence of the island with all the means at his command. He armed the batteries in Ciudadela and Fornells, constructed a provisional parapet for four mortars on the point of La Mola and conditioned the fort of San Felipe for a long siege. The pirate frigate 'Minorca', together with two ships, 'General Murray' and 'Eagle', and ten transports were sunk at the mouth of the harbour, and strong chains closed the port of Mahón from one shore to the other.

Knowing that he would never receive reinforcements from England, the Governor was obliged to try to recruit soldiers from among the Menorcans, offering them all kinds of rewards. But both nobles and people declined so doubtful an honour. He must indeed have been desperate to have had recourse to the islanders, knowing as he did that they had never taken part in the invaders' business. (Moreover, he had little likelihood of inspiring the populace in view of his unpopularity since the affair of the pirates.) Nevertheless, there was one sector which did not relish the prospect of a change of government: the many merchants who owed their prosperity to the foreign dominations and the ultra-conservative who feared the suppression of their ancient political liberties. All in all the Menorcans, resigned to their fate, as ever, locked themselves in their homes to await the outcome of these new developments.

In these circumstances, dangerous enough in themselves, the very last bearable load was about to descend on Murray. He had hardly received any reinforcements, but his superiors were of the opinion that it was necessary to strenghten the administration of Menorca by appointing a Lieutenant-Governor. From the moment when General Sir William Draper — hero of the Philippines war — set foot in Menorca the antipathy between the two men was manifest, reaching the point of a complete rupture of relations between them; an enmity which made even more complicated the already difficult situation.

In the summer of 1781 Murray's army consisted of 2,016 regular troops distributed throughout the island. The 51st and 61st Light Infantry regiments and two Hannover-ian battalions formed the bulk of the troops, and 200 sailors recruited from pirates' ships were trained in the handling of the fort's cannons. Of this small contingent, 400 men were suffering from scurvy — a characteristic illness feared by all in the navy and in garrisons subject to long periods of siege — thus reducing the effective force to 1,816 able-bodied soldiers.

Having done all he could to protect the island, the Governor evacuated his family and awaited the inevitable invasion.

On the morning of 19th August the look-outs on the watch-towers sounded the alarm. A powerful fleet was approaching the Menorcan coast.

IV

From 6th August the 73 ships which made up the Hispano-French expedition sailed leisurely across a calm sea between Almería and the Balearics. On board the 'San Pascual' the Duc de Crillon finalised the details of the landing. His intention was to attack simultaneously from Cala del Degollador near Ciudadela, and from Alcaufar and Mesquida on the south and east coasts respectively.

Admiral Moreno's squadron which was escorting the convoy was in a state of alert; the four ships provided with landing bridges were at the front and the hospital ships 'Joven Juana' and 'San José' closed the rear. The attack was planned for the night of the 19th.

However, as so often happens in the history of Menorca, the sea played an unforeseen part in the battle. On the 18th a violent SSW wind sprang up, forcing Crillon to change his plans completely. The sea scattered many ships during the night and the 'San Pascual' found herself, at ten in the morning of the 19th, just off Mahón. Beaten by the waves, both Cala del Degollador and Alcaufar were unapproachable. Divided by the bad weather, the force of 5,000 men which Crillon had hoped to land was reduced to 3,600. Despite all this, the General-in-Chief made a rapid decision. He ordered Moreno to try to enter the first bay he could find protected from the wind, if possible Fornells, «which we will attack with sword in hand», to quote his own words.

The batteries of San Felipe let the 'San Pascual' and the remnants of the convoy pass by without harassment because, despite having had news of an imminent invasion, the English, inexplicably, were convinced that the ships sailing so close to Menorca's coast were part of a Russian squadron whose visit had been announced some time before. Moreno sailed on, hugging the east coast of the island. Protected from the strong summer wind which quite often blows from the southern quadrant, he reached Cala Mesquida during the morning, along with six ships under the command of Pedro Cañaveral which had joined the small convoy earlier, and together they prepared to land.

The landing was effected immediately on the pebbly beaches at the southern end of Cala Mesquida. Field-Marshal the Marqués de Casa Cagigal placed himself at the head of the first contingent, made up of grenadiers, light infantry and Catalan volunteers. Crillon, his general-staff around him, concentrated half an infantry battalion at the foot of some low hills and, after checking that the field was clear, began the advance towards Mahón. The ranks under Crillon marched in open formation on the capital, without meeting any resistance. They arrived there at nine in the evening, almost on the heels of the English soldiers who, only an hour before, had hurriedly retreated to San Felipe. The advance of the troops had been so rapid that they had outstripped their supplies and were forced to drop their knapsacks and bayonets and pass the night in the open, not far from the town. As in the past, the people of Mahón presented them with wine, bread and cheese.

Meanwhile, the *Universidad* had gathered to receive the Duc de Crillon at the foot of the Cuesta de los Frailes. Between embraces, expressions of courtesy, loyalty and obedience, the General-in-Chief was accompanied to the royal palace.

At last the bad weather came to an end, making it possible for General Las Casas to land in Alcaufar with the Saboya and Princesa regiments, protected by the four ships of Captain Quevedo. The main landing of troops and matériel took place at Cala Mesquida. The Marqués de Avilés, at the head of 200 dragoons, took the road to Ciudadela and, like Mahón, the town immediately opened its gates. With equal ease Peñafiel's 500 soldiers became masters of the fort of San Antonio in Fornells, where the English garrison and the patients in the hospital were taken prisoner. Firty-three stores filled with food and arms fell into the hands of Colonel Caro's detachment.

Master of the towns and ports, once the English, Greek and Jewish civilians had been dislodged and he had been assured of the inhabitants' peaceful intentions, the Duc de Crillon prepared to coordinate the Menorcan campaign.

As was invariably the case in all military operations against the island, the first difficulty to present itself was the opening up of roads for the transport of heavy artillery trains from the coast to the front line. (In the case of the Spanish, the delay seems to have been even more exasperating than usual, with the result that the troops had to live many days in the open before camps could be established.) Munitions and supplies having been placed on the hill overlooking Cala Figuera to the south of Mahón, and the churches of Carmen, San José and San Francisco adapted for use as military hospitals, Crillon proceeded to examine the terrain which, once more, would form the front line threatening the fort of San Felipe.

Brigadier-Engineer Balestá draw up a great plan of campaign the moment the siege began. Like previous historians we will base our appraisal of the siege on this chart.

The Franco-Spanish general did not repeat the mistake of *Mosén* Saura in the War of the Spanish Succession, and restricted his front to a concentrated line surrounding the castle. It was shaped like an irregular star, starting in Font Nova on the shore of the harbour, passing in front of the castle by Torre Nova and Binimaimó and ending at Torre Veya. A strong nucleus of artillery based on Binisaida threatened the Marlborough fort from the rear.

Availing themselves of the *tanques* in the area, a dry-stone wall was built first of all, some three or four feet thick and topped with sacks of earth covered with branches, for the purpose of protecting the construction and hiding the emplacement of the batteries. The soldiers detailed off for this job worked hard at it by night and kept guard by day; in a month the curtain wall, parallel to the artillery lines, was complete.

Once the bastion was ready, facing San Felipe from the north-east, five powerful batteries were sited, bearing the names of the various regiments: that of Burgos, with nine 24-pounders and four mortars; Saboya, with twelve 24-pounders and four mortars; América, with eight 24-pounders and four mortars; Ehler, with ten 24-pounders; and Murcia, with eight 16-pounders. Seven more mortars were mounted on the heights of Toraixer, covering the first line of fire.

A further four batteries covered the remaining façades of the fortress from various points. On the opposite shore of the harbour, above La Mola, six 24-pounders and four mortars controlled Cala San Esteban, and twelve 24-pounders and four mortars bombarded the south-east towers from the small fortress of San Filipet. On the hill of Binisaida nineteen cannons were aimed towards the sea. In all, 116 pieces of artillery, manned by 931 gunners, surrounded the fort of San Felipe.

To guard the batteries, camps were erected beside them. Two companies of Milan, Naples and Buch grenadiers camped on Binisaida; the Marqués de Avilés established his cavalry, consisting of the King's, Villaviciosa and Sagunto dragoons, in Toraixer. The First Light Infantry of Catalonia, under the command of Brigadier Antonio Plácido, occupied the lands of Trebaluger; Colonel Ventura Caro installed three squadrons of Almansa dragoons and four hundred Catalan volunteers in the Georgetown barracks.

While these preparations were slowly progressing outside the castle, Murray organised a daring sortie against the batteries on San Filipet and La Mola. His soldiers destroyed one of them and many prisoners were taken. The Governor referred to them later on in his famous letter to the Spanish General-in-Chief: «If you have any humanity, send cloaths for your pitiful prisoners in my possession.» Conditions of life in the castle must indeed have been harsh.

During the first months of the siege, with Cala San Esteban in the hands of the English, the blockade of the port was not wholly effective, as it allowed small boats to slip through by night and help the fortress with fresh food. (This was the main shortage in that besieged rock on which not even a cabbage would grow.) Taking advantage of this negligence on Crillon's part, a group of Corsican volunteers, captained by the nephew of the famous patriot Pascal Paoli, joined Murray in the defence of the fort. Even including these, there were barely 2,000 soldiers in his garrison. As a reprisal for this infiltration, the Hispano-French forces tried to set fire to the enemy ships anchored in the creek, but with little success.

The summer passed between preparations and skirmishes, and on 25th October the French regiments, under the command of General Falckenhayn, supported by the Marquis de Bouzols, arrived at Fornells from Toulon; a strong force of Swiss and German mercenaries landed with them. A few days later the Britanny, Lyonnois, Royal

Suedois and Bouillon regiments, captained by the Comte de Spare, arrived in Mahón and set up camps on the hill of San Antonio, near La Mola, and in the Cala San Jorge. The mercenaries pitched their tents on the lands of Binisermenya.

In all, the Hispano-French expeditionary force numbered 15,279 combatants: 10,559 soldiers and 574 Spanish officers, and 3,886 soldiers and 260 foreign officers.

The problems of feeding, lodging and controlling such a large body of men must have been serious. No less oppresive was the situation of the islanders in having to put up with this army — in the main a bunch of adventurous soldiers — which represented an increase of fifty per cent in the population of the island.

Crillon soon learned that even with this show of strength the helpless fort was so solid as to be proof against all cannon fire. Aware no doubt of Murray's weakness for money, he endeavoured to get him to surrender with the famous offer of a bribe of one million pounds sterling. Murray sent a disdainful reply to this insult: «When your brave ancestor was desired by his Sovereign to kill the Duke of Guise he returned the answer which you should have done when the King of Spain charged you to assassinate the character of a man whose birth is as illustrious as your own or that of the Duke of Guise;» to which Crillon gallantly replied: «Your letter puts each one of us in his place and confirms the high opinion I have always had of you.»

The siege continued relentlessly until the end of December. Fire from Crillon's batteries constantly rattled against the walls of the fort, and Murray's cannons answered with equal persistence. Losses on both sides were considerable. On 26th December a soldier of a Swiss regiment, Charles Garain, a native of the Vaud canton, was hit in the right leg while repairing a battery. He was urgently evacuated to the hospital of the Carmen convent, where he roundly refused to be stripped of his clothes in preparation for the necessary amputation. He died a few hours later and to the surprise of all — and the interest of future historians — «he» turned out to be a twenty-four year-old girl. The nuns shrouded her appropriately in Carmelite habit and the Mahón public filed curiously past her remains for hours.

But not all the victims were so romantic. The situation in San Felipe was barely supportable. During the months of the complete blockade of the port the garrison fed itself on bread, rice, salted meat and smoked bacon: a diet devoid of vitamins which increased the incidence of scurvy to epidemic proportions, and the pestilential air of the underground passages and the casements where the soldiers fought helped to spread the disease.

As well as the troops and their officers, seventeen surgeons and doctors and three chaplains, there were a hundred and fifty women and twenty-one children living shut up in the fort.

In his description of the siege the singular style of the historian of the British army, J. W. Fortescue, cannot be bettered: «Still, the garrison, though never strong enough in numbers for the extent of the fortifications, persisted manfully in resisting. The men concealed their ailments rather than go into hospital. Day after day they fell in for duty, mere shadows of soldiers, stood at their posts for the allotted time until the relief came around, and marched back uncomplaining to the guard-room, to wait the hour which should summon them again to their work; nor was it until the roll was called that the sergeants, striving to rouse the men who failed to answer, discovered that a sterner sergeant had been there before them, and that the soldiers were dead.»

The chiefs of the Hispano-French forces were well aware of the horrific conditions in the fort, and Fortescue goes on in the following paragraph: «The officers of both nations vied with each other in giving succour to the captured garrison, Crillon in particular showing a generosity and gentleness well worthy of chivalrous Spain.» On one occasion Crillon sent medicines and green vegetables to the invalids, deprived of everything since the time when a bomb blew up five medical and food stores, causing a blaze which lasted seventy hours. On another occasion, learning of the penury of the officers' wives who did not have time to enter the castle before the arrival of the invaders, he sent orderlies from his own forces. In gratitude — and no doubt fearing to lose her — Murray made him a present of his magnificent mare.

But such courtesy did not change the course of the struggle. Crillon went on attacking, and Murray — thwarted in every move by General Draper — tried to silence the batteries by fruitless and costly sorties. The works of the castle had suffered terrible damage and every enemy battery destroyed was soon replaced by another.

On 5th January 1782, Crillon summoned his officers and ordered a general offensive for the morning of the following day, the feast of the Epiphany.

The General-in-Chief had sited his headquarters on top of the Talayot of Trepucó — a megalithic monument to the south of Mahón — defended by a thick stone wall and flanked by batteries. During the night the walls which hid the batteries from the enemy's sight were knocked down. The troops were drawn up in battle formation and the gunners took up their positions.

Before dawn a cannonade and three discharges of musket fire from the different sections unleashed a simultaneous attack against the fort of San Felipe.

For twenty-nine days the uninterrupted fire of all the enemy's cannons and mortars assailed the fortifications of the castle with an infernal clamour. Every hour between seventy and eighty bombs exploded, bursting open and destroying the external works and pulverising the interior. The defences destroyed and the merlons swept away, the fort's cannons were unusable. Stores of ammunition were running low and hardly any soldiers were left to carry them. Each captain of the guard had no more than ten soldiers.

After four weeks' bombardment, the garrison of San Felipe was reduced to 750 able-bodied men; 124 had died, there were 149 wounded, and hundreds of invalids occupied the straw mattresses of the hospital.

The fort was in ruins.

At first light in the morning of 4th February the white

flag was raised alongside the English flag on the West bastion.

Murray drew up a capitulation of ten articles, which the Hannoverian Captain Lins took to Trepucó at ten o'clock; they were received by the Comte de Crillon, son of the General-in-Chief, who amended some of the conditions before accompanying the officer back to the fort. He returned at five in the afternoon with Mr. Down, the Governor's secretary, the nine final articles having been finalised and approved by both sides.

In the first article, Crillon stipulated: «The garrison will be prisoners of war, but, in consideration of the steadfastness and bravery displayed by General Murray and the troops under his command, in their magnificent defence, they will be permitted to come out with arms at the shoulder, beating the march, match-cords lit and flags unfurled until, having marched through the Army, they will surrender their arms and flags.»

In the remaining articles it was agreed that the English troops would be repatriated in Spanish vessels, to be paid for by Britain; permission was granted for greens and other foodstuffs necessary for the convalescence of the sick and wounded to be purchased in the markets of the island; the sick would be allowed to travel home by land from Marseille; the victorious army would not ill-treat or insult the English soldiers, etc.

That same night two of the companies of grenadiers took possession of Fort Marlborough and next morning, 5th February, at ten o'clock, Spanish forces drew up in battle order on the right of the principal exit from the castle, with the French and Germans on the left. The Duc de Crillon, accompanied by Lieutenant-General Buch, Baron de Falckenhayn and the Conde de Cifuentes, was received by General Sir William Draper and escorted to Murray.

The English flag having been replaced by that of Spain, the enfeebled and exhausted garrison of San Felipe — composed of 600 soldiers, 200 sailors and 120 gunners — marched with full military honours between the ranks of the 15,000 Spanish, French and German soldiers. The

English soldiers placed their arms on the glacis of the New Road; the officers kept their swords, declaring according to tradition «that they would surrender only to God, for their conquerors could feel no pride at having taken a hospital». Lieutenant-General James Murray marched between the Duc de Crillon and Baron Falckenhayn. Behind him came General Sir William Draper, protesting at the surrender of the fort.

So complete was his disagreement with the Governor that «as he could not sit next to a traitor» he refused the invitation to dinner, courteously given by the Duke in his residence, in honour of his gallant adversaries.

V

The disarmed English troops were taken to Alayor to await their passage to England. General Murray left for Leghorn in a Venetian boat on 20th March to join his wife, and General Draper left for Marseille.

On 23rd March the occupation of Menorca was solemnized by the representatives of the Spanish monarchy, and the Conde de Cifuentes became Governor of the island.

A few days later the Duc de Crillon sailed for Barcelona in the packet-boat 'San Luis', arriving there by night on the 28th. On 7th April he was received with full pomp by Charles III in the Royal Palace of Aranjuez. The King appointed him Captain-General of the Spanish armies and honoured him with the title of Duke of Mahón and Grandee of Spain, First Class, for his services and his brilliant performance in the capture of Menorca. The Marqués de Sollerich was also rewarded with a Grandeeship for his collaboration in the conquest of the island.

The whole country celebrated the recovery of the lesser Balearic island. Writers and painters immortalised the feat of arms. A heroic play by Calvet de Rolland, bearing the bizarre tittle of «La Prise du Fort Saint Philipe, ou le Triomphe de L'honneur et de la Vertu», was printed in Avignon, and the farce «Las Mahonesas», by the poet Ramón de la Cruz, became fashionable in Spain. Three paintings by Maella of scenes inspired by the capture of San Felipe were hung in the upper corridor of the Casita del Príncipe in the Ecorial, and the Italian artist Chiesa (resident in Mahón), a delightful illustrator of every-day life in the Menorca of that time, painted a water-colour of the exit of the conquered army.

In England, on the other hand, although news of the fall of Menorca was not greeted with the same outcry as in 1756, General Murray had to submit to a court-martial in which Draper presented twenty-nine charges against him. The court, presided over by Sir George Howard and made up of eighteen generals and an auditor, was held in the headquarters of the Horse Guards at the end of 1782. Murray was completely absolved of all charges against him in January 1783. These covered a wide range of alleged faults, from the embezzlement of provisions and public funds to extorsion, rapacity and cruelty. «Old Minorca» — as Murray was nicknamed among his contemporaries — had the satisfaction of seeing the case signed and sealed by the King, with the following words of praise: «His Majesty is graciously pleased with the zeal, bravery and firmness which General Murray has conducted in the defence of the Fort of Saint Philip, as well as of his former and approved services.»

VI

«It must be agreed that only with a Governor like Cifuentes could the island have adapted itself to the new regime,» asserts the Menorcan historian Hernández Sanz. Indeed the laws and franchises, the usages and customs which Crillon had promised to respect, were soon sub-stituted by the administration of the Peninsula.* The islanders saw with displeasure the imposition of a severe customs system which controlled the import of merchan-dise; the sale of tobacco and gunpowder was supervised; tributes and taxes made their reappearance after an ex-

* Historians have now brought to light documents that contra-dict this assertion.

emption lasting more than half a century; the registration of boats took away the liberty of the owners, fishermen and sailors. There were two further matters which Menorcans considered ignominious and which annoyed them to an extraordinary degree. Proud at having remained faithful and devout Catholics through so many vicissitudes during the English occupations, they now had to bear the arrival of missionaries who dealt with the country as though its evangelisation was an indispensable necessity; the Court of the Inquisition was reimposed. And to add insult to injury, Catalan, the only language spoken, learnt in the schools and used in official documents issued by the *Universidades* since 1287, was replaced by Castilian. At the height of the foreign occupations Menorcans had achieved a flowering of their vernacular tongue, beyond the literature of the other Catalan-speaking provinces, decadent since Bourbon centralisation, and many of the illustrious writers who belonged to the *Societat Maonesa de Cultura* (founded during the second English domination) had to adapt themselves to the new language in their writings.

It was only the well-deserved popularity enjoyed by the honourable, active and kind Conde de Cifuentes that managed to pacify the inhabitants, who were exasperated also by the one-in-twenty levy which the Spanish government attempted to impose on them for military service, which, in accordance with mediaeval privileges, they had always been excused from performing outside the island. The Governor did what he could for the good of Menorca and during his mandate industry and commerce were promoted; Georgetown grew and was rebaptised «*La Real Villa de San Carlos*» — the Villacarlos of today — in honour of Charles III of Spain. A large arsenal was built in the port of Mahón, the shore of which was beautified by the romantic Paseo de la Alameda, so often reproduced in drawings of the time. Moreover, Cifuentes won the full and unconditional esteem of the people in choosing Mahón as his place of residence when he was appointed Captain-General of the Balearics.

But neither Cifuentes nor any other authority could refuse to comply with the governmental order to destroy the fort of San Felipe. The verse attributed to Andrea Doria, written almost three centuries earlier, was forgotten, though still as true as when it as written:

> *«Junio, julio,*
> *Agosto y Mahón,*
> *Los mejores puertos*
> *Del Mediterráneo son.»* *

Also forgotten was that the reason which had impelled England to spend one million pounds on the fortification of the castle was specifically for the defence of that port. They forgot too that if the island had been coveted by foreign powers for so many years, it was not for its defensive potential but for its geopolitical position. The ministers of Charles III made the highly original deduction that the mere act of making it disappear would make Menorca safe from the warlike incursions of her enemies. And so the powers that be decided to destroy it.

The demolition order was given on 16th February 1782, only ten days after Murray's surrender: «The King being aware that all the fortifications of the Castle are now useless... considers it appropriate that, starting from this moment, all the fortifications of the Castle itself and its dependencies should be demolished and razed, including in this order the blocking up and destruction of all the mines of its galleries, branches and fougades.» Six months later, the Lieutenant-Colonel of artillery, Juan Guillelmí, reported to the Conde de Cifuentes that the Castle of San Antonio in Fornells and the colossal star-shaped fort of San Felipe, one of the greatest in Europe, had been competently and economically demolished.

The only defensive elements which remained in Menorca were the battery of La Mola, four batteries mounted on the rubble of San Felipe, another three, weak and temporary, in Fornells, and the imperfect fortification represented by the walled precinct of Ciudadela, protected by

---

* «June, July, / August and Mahón, / Are the best ports / In the Mediterranean.»

the San Nicolás tower. To guard against a possible landing on the island, the garrison comprised only the infantry regiment of América, a battalion of Swiss mercenaries, 80 dragoons and some gunners.

It is not to be wondered at, therefore, that Cifuentes himself regretted that the Menorcans should again be terrified at the necessity of having to depend on nothing more than their own resources to assure their survival: «As they see themselves with few troops and no defence fortifications, no one can convince them they are secure.»

The last English occupation 1798-1802

I

By the end of the eighteenth century the tremendous political upheaval brought about in Europe by the French Revolution and the execution of Louis XVI having diminished, Spain again allied herself to France, governed at that time by the more moderate Directorate.

The traditional friendship between the two countries, based always on their common interest in combatting powerful England, was consolidated in 1796 by a defensive and offensive treaty under which Charles IV (managed by his insatiable and toothless wife and her supremely cunning and opportunist favourite, Manuel Godoy) stipulated that, «as England is the only power from which Spain has received direct injuries, the present alliance shall only have effect against her in the present war».

The struggle would inevitably be maritime and colonial, the sea being in fact the Hispano-British frontier and England's naval power constituting the eternal danger to Spain.

The first operation of the Spanish fleet was to protect Napoleon Bonaparte in his advance in the Italian peninsula. Later the war went to the Atlantic, where Jervis defeated Córdoba off Cape St. Vincent, a defeat soon to be countered by Mazzaredo's victory over Nelson in the blockade of Cádiz. The Canary Islands also found themselves threatened, but the British Commodore had to retreat on losing his arm. On the American continent, although the English were driven off in Puerto Rico, nothing could prevent the island of Trinidad falling into their power. However, for years the real battlefield would again be centred in the Mediterranean.

After the first few months of 1798 Napoleon was already master of Holland, Switzerland, the Cisalpine and the Roman republics. England, impotent in the face of these spectacular conquests, due to the fact that she almost entirely lacked an army, put into operation her only means of curbing the French advances. A maritime offensive, with the aim of blockading Napoleonic troops in foreign lands, was to be set in motion by mustering the fleet and sending it to the Mediterranean.

The English fleet did not arrive in time to prevent Malta being captured in June of 1798. A few days later Bonaparte landed his expeditionary force in Alexandria, and in July he concluded the conquest of Egypt. For his part, Nelson, in his tireless pursuit of the enemy, wiped out the French fleet in the bay of Aboukir, a victory which once more conferred on England her irrefutable dominion of the Mediterranean.

Pitt's government, aware that this victory would have to be consolidated by a naval base where British ships could shelter, had recourse as ever to the safe port of Mahón. At all events a renewed occupation of Menorca had figured for some months in its strategic plans.

Portugal, threatened by a Franco-Spanish invasion, sought military protection from England, who sent her a few infantry regiments, reinforced by various battalions of French monarchist emigrées. This heterogeneous army — more inclined to knightly adventures than to strict military discipline — was placed under the command of Sir Charles Stuart, recently appointed Lieutenant-General at forty-five years of age after serving his country brilliantly in the American war. He had the reputation of being a man of exceptional gifts for strategy, and Nelson, on receiving news of a possible Menorcan campaign, wrote: «I believe Charles Stuart to be the best general that you have... No one can manage Frenchmen as well as him and the British will go to hell for him... The more I reflect on the services expected of the troops the more important I think it for him to be at their head.»

As a result of this pressure, and in the strictest secrecy, Stuart set in motion from Portugal the preparations for an attack on Menorca in September of 1798.

II

The festivities for the coronation of Charles IV of Spain in January 1798 had been celebrated in Mahón with some ill humour and, as in other times, the coming years were not to be very prosperous for the Menorcans. The endemic evils of the island again made their appearance; poor harvests, storms, plagues of rats, epidemics and — due to their having to supply the Spanish fleet and to receive a wave of French political refuges — a sudden rise in the prices of basic commodities, all made life difficult for the islanders. Problems reached such a pitch that by the nineties the death rate almost exceeded the birth rate. And the situation became even worse when Spain declared war on England in the autumn of 1796 and Menorca had to deal with the constant danger of her helplessness in the face of an invasion.

At the beginning of the war the Governor, Anuncivay, requested — in vain — from the Spanish government reinforcements and military supplies as a result of the alarming rumours which were going round the island of an imminent enemy landing.

Later on, in 1797, Spain's Secretary for War sent the Governor the oficial news that the English were preparing an attack. This threat was considered so serious that the military and civil forces held a meeting to deal with the defence of Menorca. The results of their efforts were frankly depressing. To quote the words of the Governor: «We must not count on the peasantry with the exception of a few individuals who, borne up by their love of the Sovereign, may perhaps offer themselves... After protecting the Ciudadela batteries with 120 men, that of Fornells with 100 and those at the mouth of the port with however many it may be possible to detail to that duty, the main body of the defence force will be placed in the centre of the island... The best support point for the retreat is Ciudadela, although the weakness of her walls does not hold out any promise for a long siege.»

In May 1797, on the death of Anuncivay, Brigadier Juan Nepomuceno Quesada assumed the position of Governor. A veteran of the American campaigns, he had been taken prisoner on a number of occasions and a long stay on the Mosquito coast, to the east of Honduras, had undermined his health with repeated attacks of malaria. Despite this, he undertook the reorganisation of the military forces of the island with energy, trying to find solutions to the thousand difficulties resulting from the lamentable state into which the army and its armoury had been allowed to fall, uncared for as they were by the court of Madrid.

Quesada found that the Menorcan garrison consisted of only 1,777 infantry soldiers from the Valencia regiments and the San Gall mercenaries, 80 dragoons and a handful of gunners. Left for the main part without campaign rations or adequate billets, their losses due to illness were considerable and the slack discipline of the men caused much pillaging throughout the country and fights among themselves. On the other hand, any collaboration between the work force of the arsenal and the workmen employed in the repair of the batteries was ruled out, because they had none of them received any pay for months. As far as the peasantry and the naval recruits were concerned, they had refused to take up arms, and there were many cases of desertion among the seamen.

The state of the island's defences was no more hopeful. The lack of care suffered by the few batteries had produced a considerable deterioration of the armaments. Through lack of funds and the requisite materials the frames of the artillery had gone six years without being painted, and many cannons, open and exposed to the elements, had become unusable; a good number of them were in need of urgent repair, and those considered satisfactory were so old that they could not stand for long the temperatures reached on intensive firing. And as a result of even greater incompetence, a large part of the armament was intended for use by the navy and was adaptable only with difficulty for land operations.

The report which Quesada was to send to the Secretary for War on 9th January 1798, on the state of Menorca's defences, warned that if reinforcements were not received it would be impossible for him to put up any opposition to a landing due to the lack of troops, divided necessarily into small groups throughout the island, since the demolition of the fort of San Felipe had rendered impossible a concentration of such forces. The Spanish Colonel of artillery, José Cotrina Ferrer, in his treatise entitled «El desastre de 1798» («The disaster of 1798») passes harsh judgement on the government for this failure to respond to the justified demands of the Menorcan Governor: «The Government, then, left the Governor with nothing but his own forces, as though they were denying every sort of help to a shipwrecked sailor in danger of drowning.»

Despite this, Quesada did not cease his tireless approaches to the authorities to seek aid. He was impelled also by the risk of depredations by the English corsairs (who had captured the Barcelona-Palma packet boat) and by the frequent passage of British convoys sighted from Monte Toro. The absolute dearth of funds and the threat of epidemics were among others of his worries. But neither the Captain-General of Catalonia nor the Minister for War, still less the Minister of Finance, whose ministry was completely bankrupt due to the deplorable financial state of the country, could do anything to help the island. In fact the government appeared indifferent to the danger of losing Menorca once again.

In the spring the Governor tried to impose some order on the defences of the island. He succeeded with difficulty in repairing the roads which led to the coastal batteries; he had great openings made in the dry-stone walls of the *tanques* to facilitate the passage of artillery: he concentrated his troops in Villacarlos, Alayor, Ciudadela and Mahón; he mounted and dismounted cannons in the most vulnerable points of the south coast, convinced that the enemy landing would be made at Cala Galdana, Cala Alcaufar or Cala Mesquida, since the north coast was considered dangerous and impracticable.

The ancient regiment of San Gall was disbanded in May and its chief, Field-Marshal Cristóbal de Rutiman, mustered a new mercenary corps, not without causing scandals and brawls among his soldiers. In July another battalion of men, recruited in various Swiss cantons, landed in Menorca under the command of Colonel Carlos Yann. These Swiss volunteers, grouped into four companies of musketeers and one of grenadiers, reached a total, like those of Rutiman, of 1,500 men. Their lack of military experience, added to their completely undisciplined conduct and absence of the slightest spirit of loyalty towards the Spanish sovereign, disillusioned the hard-pressed Quesada who had hoped for some relief of his tribulations with their arrival. Moreover, the chronic suffering of the ailing Yann, who was prostrate in Ciudadela with an attack of gout, left the command of these dubious reinforcements in the hands of his captain, Josef Bartmetler.

During the summer Quesada continued to receive negative responses — or, even worse, unkept promises — to his requests to obtain the garrison strength of 5,000 to 6,000 men considered indispensable. After a Council of War, held at the end of October, he confirmed that, despite the new recruits, he could only count on 3,671 soldiers: 1,371 Spanish and 2,300 disorderly mercenaries. According to an estimate by José Cotrina, this force was reduced, in round figures, to 2,600 able-bodied men. This assumes that losses due to illness or other causes had reached — at such a serious juncture — a figure of over 30 per cent, a proportion which can only be explained by lack of care of the soldiers and the incompetence of their leaders.

The state of defence of the artillery continued to be disastrous. A little more than 100 cannons — mostly short-range — defended the island. The south and east coasts, comprising Cala Alcaufar, Punta Prima, the port of Mahón, Cala Mesquida and El Grau, were covered by 58 pieces; 12 were emplaced on the north coast, including the port of Fornells; and nine more batteries, with a total of 30 cannons, were divided between Santandría, Cala Blanca, Ciudadela and the surrounding country. Communications between the batteries and the watch-towers were maintained by the 80 cavalry dragoons who, under the command of Lieutenant-Colonel Antonio Manrique, kept the coast under surveillance.

And to complicate matters even further, on top of the

problems of lack of troops and supplies and serious economic difficulties, Quesada had to bear the disappointment of the passive indifference of the Menorcans. No money arrived to pay for the upkeep of the livestock, nor for the manufacture of gun-cartridges, and canvas bags made good the lack of cartridge cases. Part of the campaign rations for the soldiers, that is cheese, had disappeared from the market in Mahón, and in Ciudadela the insolvent authorities conserved stocks by prohibiting sales. And once again in the history of Menorca, the inhabitants, indifferent to the nationality of their rulers, took no part in the military events of the island. The Governor, even with the use of the greatest threats, did not succed in getting the towns to contribute a guide to conduct the regiments through the tangled network of roads, and the Menorcans' disinterest reached such an extreme that not a single peasant volunteer came forward when a proclamation was made, calling on all inhabitants in case «someone, moved by his faithfulness or love of his Sovereign, might wish to take up arms in his defence».

Throughout the month of October suspect ships which had been cruising off Menorcan coasts became more numerous, but until the 'Santo Cristo del Grau' reached Mahón on 6th November no one had clearly envisaged the reality of an immediate invasion. Lieutenant Antonio Pardo landed with a despatch for Brigadier Quesada, notifying him that the English expedition, made up of seven warships, one corvette, one frigate, two sloops and eight private ships, with victuals and war supplies, had set sail from Gibraltar two weeks earlier on an easterly course.

Quesada had already given orders to detach Rutiman's regiment to San Luis, Fornells and Villacarlos; those under Yann would cover Ciudadela, Mercadal and Ferrerías; that of Valencia would remain in Alayor and Mahón, feebly reinforced by those under detention and the useless men from the garrison. Campaign rations consisting of a pound of biscuits, half a pound of cheese and another half pound of brandy for each man had been distributed; ammunition was given to each soldier: 20 cartridges and a further 30 for the front-line soldiers. The medical department, consisting of only four surgeons to cover six groups of troops, was supplemented by local people, from whom stretcher-bearers and assistants were also recruited. The mouth of the port of Mahón was sealed by a chain 700 feet long. Sailors and dragoons in the convent on Monte Toro ensured the exact transmission of signals announcing the dreaded invasion.

And although the Governor's superiors hoped with illusionary optimism that «bravery, spirit and love of the King would be sufficient to instil respect and fear into the enemies of the Crown», the truth was that Menorca was once again at the mercy of its own efforts, and the inevitable story of a landing by foreign forces was to be repeated.

III

On 7th November 1798, at six o'clock in the morning, the look-out at Monte Toro signalled the presence of a squadron approaching from the south, having passed between the Balearic archipelago and the Peninsula. The warning given by the dragoons on Monte Toro was repeated by Santa Águeda and La Mola: 25 enemy sails were making for the north coast of Menorca, probably for Fornells or one of the many natural anchoring points nearby. At seven o'clock Brigadier Quesada ordered the chief of the Mercadal artillery to send 3,000 cartridges and 20 quintals of powder, and specified that «munitions and victuals for the troops must be taken to Cala Molí».

The landing had already taken place at this cove and at the ancient Arab port of Addaya.

José Cotrina believes that «the choice of this point to commence the invasion shows that the English had exact knowledge of the deficiencies in the defence of that place». On the other hand, the English historian Fortescue is of the opinion that, as the reconnaissance corvette sent by Stuart had returned without obtaining any information of importance and as the ostentatiousness of his presence showed that his arrival could not have taken the Spanish

225

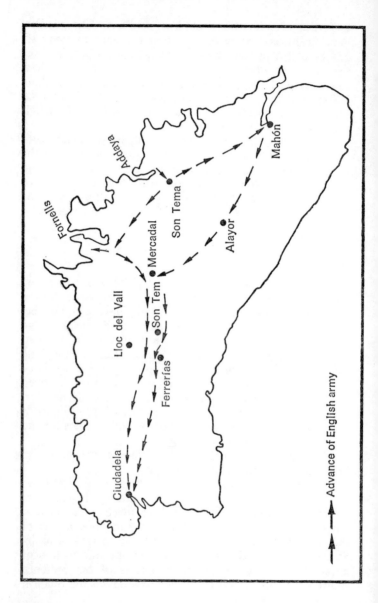

Addaya

Fornells

Mahón

Son Tema

Alayor

Mercadal

Lloc del Vall

Son Tem

Ferrerías

Ciudadela

Advance of English army

by surprise, the General decided to run the risk of a chance landing (without taking into account, apparently, the danger of the wind changing to a strong autumnal *Tramontana*).

However this may be, 800 English soldiers landed, to be followed immediately by the remaining forces, covered by the fire of Commander Duckworth's frigates anchored opposite Cala Addaya.

Meanwhile Quesada's army began to move and, transferring his general-staff to Mercadal, the Brigadier sent Marshal Rutiman to defend the landing point of the English with 350 of his men, 650 from the Valencia regiment which had arrived from Mahón and 350 of Yann's soldiers detached in Mercadal and Ferrerías. But it was not long before the indolence of the Swiss mercenaries became manifest, with fatal effect, and before making contact with the English 440 men out of the 1,320 who had started to march against the invaders had fled. Despite all this the 800 who remained succeeded in containing the English and were still in defensive positions in Son Tema on the hills overlooking the cove at 4.30 in the afternoon. General Stuart, within gunshot range of them, hesitated for lack of information about the terrain and the intentions of the Spaniards; the 100 deserters who had just joined his ranks could only tell him that the strength of Quesada's army was about 4,000 men.

Quesada, in Mercadal, was still awaiting details of the operation but, having observed a few hours earlier that the troops marching towards the front had been provided with double rations of biscuits and cheese and forty rounds of ammunition per head, was surprised to receive a despatch from Rutiman advising him that «the troops have nothing to eat and almost no ammunition». However, his answer was: «At the present moment, 8.30 in the evening, I have just received the despatch which you ordered your Aide, Don Pedro Hallegg, to bring to me, from which I learn the position of the troops of Valencia, Rutiman, etc., occupying the heights of Son Tema, facing the enemy and in defensive positions, it would be best if they maintain those positions preventing the enemy from penetrating to the centre of the island and Mahón, for this I am sending you the victuals and ammunition you ask for with a reinforcement of the dispersed troops which have re-mustered, and as soon as I am joined by those from Ciudadela which I hope will arrive soon, I shall proceed to help those positions, but if you absolutely cannot hold them, what you must try to do to your utmost limit is defend the terrain inch by inch and see that your retreat has the objective of taking up the most advantageous position, close to the roads which lead from that high land to Aleor (sic), and let me know the result.»

This picturesque letter, given the gravity of the moment, produced an unforeseen and cowardly reaction on the part of Rutiman. Before the reinforcements sent by Lieutenant-Colonel Gramaren had arrived from San Luis, the marshal, his captains, subalterns and grenadiers undertook a retreat, without any orders whatsoever, until they were stopped, at ten o'clock at night, by the guard which Quesada had sent to the Royal Road to try to muster the dispersed troops. Against the Brigadier's charges, Rutiman justified his desertion of the front, alleging that he had not been able to hold the position due to the violence of the enemy's fire, «their great number» and the deaths of his men for lack of food. Quesada, fearing no doubt that he would weaken even further his already compromised situation, did not impose any exemplary punishment on the mercenary, and the confusion created by this useless retreat became even greater when excessive rations of brandy were distributed to the Swiss soldiers who had fled from Addaya. One can easily imagine the scene. The troops of the ailing Colonel Yann, who had left Ciudadela at six o'clock that evening, arrived after midnight, worn out, to be mixed with Rutiman's drunken soldiers, grouped along the sides of the road on that cold and windy November night. In the darkness the orders and counter-orders, the rumours and despatches, all became confused in the noisy disorder of the troops. Quesada, badly supported and having lost confidence in his army, was resolved to return before dawn to the abandoned front with the new reinforcements arrived from Ciudadela. But a despatch from the military governor of Ciudadela, Colonel Juan Chicheri, cooled his ardour and completely changed his plans. Chicheri wrote at six o'clock on the evening of the 7th: «Throughout the day there have been two frigates almost constantly in sight, presumably enemies, and if these, with a few other ships which are said to be near, should try to effect a landing on these coasts (which I think they could not readily do in this strong wind) we should be entirely without troops to oppose them, because the hundred men remaining to me are hardly sufficient to cover the posts of this place; all of which I bring to your notice, for your intelligence and information.»

This was certainly bad news. Ciudadela was intended to be the last bastion and now that it was threatened from the sea, Quesada saw his line of retreat cut off and, even worse, the whole of his army, now in Mercadal, exposed to annihilation by convergent forces, if the enemy also succeeded in landing on the west coast. The holding of Ciudadela had figured in the foreground of all plans for the defence of the island since 1782, and although the scant defence works had but little strength and therefore did not offer an effective resistance to the invader, it had superiority over Mahón, of greater strategic importance because of its port but now an indefensible open city since the demolition of San Felipe.

After conferring with his officers the Brigadier resolved to retreat to Ciudadela in the hope of seeing some reinforcement arrive there from abroad in the meantime. The troops had hardly had time to rest before they were on the march again, at four o'clock in the morning, carrying their victuals and ammunition; and they were back in Menorca's former capital at 12.30 on the 8th.

Apart from having succeeded in crossing the greater part of the island in thirty hours, the result of this first day of combat was as follows: the shameless flight of Rutiman, the retreat of the whole army to behind the weak walls of Ciudadela, the desertion of 128 soldiers from Yann's battalion and of more than 300 (soon to become 900) from Rutiman's, the arrival in Mahón on the night of the 7th of three or four wounded men, and the fall of Fornells.

After the retreat of the Spaniards, as darkness fell, Sir Charles Stuart found that the bad roads would slow down any attempt to pursue them to the hilly and steep regions of the island where they could easily defend themselves. But the English General, aware that the two strongly populated places were at each end of the island, decided to occupy a high place in the centre and thus cut the lines of communication between them. On the 8th he detached 600 men, under the command of Colonel Thomas Graham, to take Mercadal. Luck was on his side, Quesada having just evacuated the place, and the colonel took prisoner some officers and laggard soldiers, and several stores fell into his hands. Next day Stuart followed him with the bulk of the army, reinforced by the 250 sailors charged with dragging the campaign cannons to that point. On that same day Stuart received the news of the helpless situation of Mahón and sent Colonel Edward Paget there with 350 men of the 28th regiment.

In Mahón, after the Monte Toro signals announcing the invasion had been observed, the major part of the troops marched to oppose the landing, and later, when the look-out signalled the retreat from Son Tema, the guards from the Principal regiment, together with those from the arsenal and the dockyard, followed by cannons, ammunition and provisions, set off on the road with the object of reinforcing Ciudadela. Mahón therefore remained undefended to such an extent that the Bailiff, Antonio Andreu, organised patrols of residents to safeguard the streets of the town, ordered the closing of taverns at the sound of the Angelus, and arranged for the inhabitants to leave lanterns alight in their windows all night. Despite all this, when the criminals imprisoned on the Lazareto broke out, they and the rabble of the town sacked and looted the private warehouses and the arsenal, taking away their booty in a Mallorcan *laud* and another from Ibiza.

On the 9th two English frigates and five large transports appeared off the port, very close to land, from which the King's Lieutenant, Juan Milesimo, deduced that an English landing in Mahón was imminent. For some unknown reason he them transferred his forces to the old site of the fort of San Felipe, now in ruins. Paget did indeed arrive, when darkness had already fallen, but by land, probably along the Alameda on the waterside; but before actually entering the town he was received opposite the convent and church of San Francisco by the Councillors of Mahón, with a large retinue, offering him the keys of the town. Colonel Paget, for his part, demanded three Hurrash, which the Councillors duly shouted, with appropriate response from the people. Paget, a young and handsome man, brave and courteous, allowed the ministers — prisoners-of-war — freedom to walk the streets and to continue living in their own homes. He waited till the following morning to see the King's Lieutenant and present him with an invitation to capitulate. The Spanish flag was replaced by the English flag and the chain removed from the mouth of the port. For the third and last time British forces were in occupation of Menorca. Their conquest was celebrated with illuminations and music, imposed perhaps by the English, since later on the Councillors raised the question of how and by whom these expenses were to be paid.

Back in Ciudadela, Quesada held a Council of War and by unanimous agreement it was decided that no greater force than that strictly necessary for its protection would remain in the town; the army was to be deployed in the most advantageous places for attacking the enemy and «would not retreat except in the case of obvious inferiority». So a headquarters was set up near Ciudadela in the «Hostal des Moll», and a rudimentary fort was established at a distance of one and a half gunshots from the town.

Quesada's situation was hardly promising. The English occupied half the island and her ships were blockading it; Ciudadela offered scant possibilities of being able to sustain a siege; almost 1,000 deserters had joined the invaders; and on top of all this the Brigadier's blunder based on the false information supplied by Rutiman, was that his army, reduced to little more than 2,000 men, would have to face a force of 3,000 English troops. A final misfortune put paid to the already enfeebled powers of command which remained to Quesada. On the morning of the 10th, having received the news that Stuart's army was mobilised, he came out of Ciudadela to go to the front when, as José Cotrina related, «he had the bad luck to fall from the bridge over the moat and injured his right arm, and had to stay in bed because, overcome by a fever, he could not move that hand.»

Despite this accident, he did not give up his command (had he done so he would no doubt have saved himself from many responsibilities) and appointed Pedro Quadrado, a captain in the Almansa dragoons, as his temporary Major-General. But his morale must have been very low because he wrote on that same day to the Captain-General of the Balearic Islands: «All is now too late; I have been attacked since seven o'clock this morning and I am here with the troops, a most miserable place in all respects, where I shall receive the enemy as best I can, because the absolute lack of everything I requested from you and from the Kingdom of Catalonia, added to the present indefensibility of the island, the lack of troops and of funds to attend to the many things which should be done, puts me in the hard position of getting out of it in the most honorable way possible.»

The inevitable attack drew near. The English landed victuals, amunition and matériel from the six transports anchored off Fornells. From there they were transported to Mercadal by the animals comandeered in the villages. On the 11th at midday the advance troops of Stuart's army, under the command of Colonel Moncrieff, were close to Ferrerías; they dominated the heights of Son Tem to the left, and to the right they were placed between the Lloch del Vall and the old road. Paget left 150 men in Mahón and joined Moncrieff with the remaining 200. Contrary to what Quesada thought, the English General in fact suffered from a marked deficiency of troops and had to augment his war potential with the marines from the fleet. Even so, the strength of his army hardly reached 4,000. To cover this deficit he improvised a tactic designed to make his enemies believe they were facing a much larger force than was in fact the case. Feigning two dense columns, Moncrieff advanced with his men along the old road while Stuart filed along the Kane Road with the bulk of the army, reinforced by 90 marines and six light ships' cannons until, on the 13th, he was emplaced opposite the line of fire set up by Quesada.

Face to face in this inevitable confrontation with a reputedly powerful enemy, the Brigadier summoned his officers and the retreat of the army behind the weak walls of Ciudadela was agreed upon.

The inhabitants of the town, on seeing themselves fatally threatened and without the least defensive equipment to protect their lives and property, began to abandon the town to take refuge in the countryside. Even the Poor Clares obtained permission from the Prelate to leave their cloisters and transfer to the estates of Torre del Ram and Torre d'en Lozano. As the only means available to counteract so alarming a contingency, the Councillors and the Bishop of Menorca presented a petition to the Governor, setting out the danger to which the people would be exposed should Ciudadela be bombarded. The petition, signed by the General Councillors of the island, Barón de Lluriach, Martín Cursach, Lorenzo Sastre and Juan Vives, read as follows: «British forces being now in this Island and carrying out military operations around the walls of this city, it is manifestly obvious that they have chosen this place as their headquarters and final meeting point. This has placed the authors of this letter and all their people in the greatest consternation, contemplating the dangers they must inevitably suffer when besieged in a Place surrounded in part by weak walls, the rest being wholly uncovered, in a Place, in short, which His Majesty's august father considered nothing as a fort, as may be seen from the accompanying document. Indeed, in the case of bombardment it is notorious that, as there is nowhere to take refuge from the mortal trouble which such an event would cause, there would be no further service to render to His Majesty than that of being buried beneath the Ruins with the troops and the peasantry. In this communication the writers hope that Your Lordship, in his zeal and mercy, will exercise his liveliest efforts to avoid exposing the lives of all the aforementioned people who with such generosity and affection have contributed to the greater service of His Majesty in all that his forces have been able to achieve.»

On the same day Bishop Vila «reminds Your Lordship that considering the situation of this Place and the weakness of its walls, and also the scarcity of victuals and ammunition necessary for a vigorous defence, an honourable capitulation will be inevitable».

His sluggish army weakened by the disloyalty of the mercenaries (more than 400 had already swelled the ranks of the English), without the support of strong fortifications or of the populace and its leaders, and seeing the English army encamped within two cannon shots of the city, Quesada realised that he was forced to capitulate. But despite this, when on the 14th the English Lieutenant-Colonel of artillery, John Duncan, went to Ciudadela with the first suggestion of a surrender, it was rejected by the Governor, who also replied in the negative to the second approach put forward by Major-General St. Clair.

According to Fortescue, this hesitation was due to the fact that, at the last moment, the Spanish were in some doubt as to the reality of the numerical superiority of their enemies. «Accordingly», he writes, «during the night Stuart solemnly threw up two batteries within eight hundred yards of the town and as solemnly armed them with three light twelve-pounders and as many light howitzers; these weapons, which were really horse-artillery guns, being all that he had been able to bring with him. Then, when day broke he formed the main body of his troops with great parade before the enemy's batteries, connecting them cunningly by piquets with the two detachments upon each flank so as to present an imposing line, partly, as he said, real and partly imaginary, four miles in length.»

At first light on the morning of the 15th there was a symbolic exchange of cannon fire between the besieged and their besiegers, and, based on the resolution of the

Council of War summoned by Governor Quesada, it was decided to accept an honourable capitulation, always providing it conformed to the military spirit. The Council made very clear that, «having regard to the small stock of victuals... the weakness of the walls... the impossibility of receiving aid, the lack of roofing material and of timber to construct defences, the scant population, their expressions of alarm, the fears of an uprising and the small number of troops relative to those of the enemy... it is thought proper, as surrender would appear to be inevitable when foodstuffs run out, and as it would be of service to the King to conserve these troops so that they may be used elsewhere, to see if it is feasible to obtain the maximum possible advantage, providing we are not taken prisoners of war.»

Negotiations terminated on the morning of the 16th. At one o'clock in the afternoon the English entered Ciudadela and took possession of the place. In the capitulation signed by Quesada, the English General and Commodore Duckworth, it was stipulated that the Spanish officers would have the right to retain their kit, the soldiers their arms and the dragoons their horses and saddles. Yann's battalion and a detachment of dragoons would be embarked for Mallorca, and Quesada with the staff of the Ministries for War and the Navy together with the remaining troops would leave for the Peninsula in the British ship 'Calcutta'.

In his despatch dated 19th November to General Troncoso, Captain-General of the Balearics, the Brigadier offered his excuses and apologies in the following heartfelt words: «The state of confusion into which I have been cast by this unfortunate event, which I am persuaded would not have taken place if I had had the necessary troops to prevent the landing, as I have clearly pointed out in my earlier letters, I leave for Your Excellency's consideration; after all, there is nothing to be done about it but my heart is wounded with the thought that, under my command the King has lost this his sovereign territory, this being the first misfortune I have had in the whole of my lengthy military career.» The British victory, on the other hand, was reported to George III by Stuart in the following terms: «I have the honour to announce that the forces of Your Majesty are in possession of the Island of Minorca, without the loss of a single man.»

IV

Several years later, Juan Nepomuceno de Quesada and his general-staff were judged by a court-martial «for the indecorous surrender of the Island of Menorca in November of 1798». On 10th June 1802, Charles IV of Spain decreed, «that if the above-mentioned Governor Quesada is still alive he should be punished by loss of office and demotion, for his lack of activity and military vigour in the critical situation which called for the best exercise of these qualities, and for not having placed himself at the head of his troops to seek out the invaders.» Before receiving such a dishonourable punishment, Quesada, weakened by illness and by the anguish of his military failure, had died, adding to the number of those who paid with their lives for their innocent involvement in the history of Menorca. The penalties imposed on the other officers who took part in this episode were less severe and, although it was decreed that Rutiman's regiment should be disbanded, and some of its officers were summarily sentenced, its commanding officer was absolved. It was considered that Colonels Yann, Juan Chicheri and Antonio Manrique, among others, «have purged their faults in the detention already suffered». Lieutenant-Colonel Pedro Quadrado and Lieutenant Arebol, captain of the port of Fornells, were exonerated from all charges against them.

During this new incorporation of Menorca into the British Crown, General Stuart held the post of Governor for a year. According to the Menorcan historian Hernández Sanz, he was «an honourable and active man who, like another Kane, devoted himself from the outset to striving to obtain everything conductive to the improvement and well-being of Menorca». Backed up by the population and with the cooperation of the able Menorcan jurist, Nicolás Orfila, he decreed new laws and organised the town councils, but what contributed most to the prosperity of Mahón were the constant visits of the powerful English fleet, which, under the command of Admiral Lord Nelson, kept Napoleon's Mediterranean armies at bay.

The four years of this final domination can be considered as the most harmonious of all the six long decades of English occupation. As the historical vicissitudes of Menorca drew to a close, the Menorcans as a whole displayed a lively sympathy for their invaders and, either as a reaction against the sixteen years of incompetent Spanish rule, or because of the greater facilities they were granted, the result was that British influence was markedly fruitful during this period and left for posterity indelible signs of its rule.

Not only did numerous words of English origin become incorporated into Menorcan speech but architectural styles, culinary dishes, children's games, dances, etc., were imported from England. The «*boinders*» (bow windows) and the typical sash windows still decorate many Menorcan homes and, especially in the neighbourhood of Mahón, large houses with red fronts in the colourful Georgian style may be seen; and some ancient mansion may have its façade decorated in this way while the body of the building is whitewashed with the traditional Mediterranean lime. The most sumptuous of these is the farmhouse of San Antonio, which the English called «The Golden Farm» or «Nelson's House» because of the myth which grew up to the effect that the great Admiral himself resided there when he called at Mahón in the '*Foudroyant*' in October 1799 accompanied, it is said, by his mistress, Lady Hamilton. (In the interests of historical accuracy it should be added that this myth is not supported by the facts, which are that Nelson himself — *not* accompanied by Lady Hamilton — did come to Mahón for a period of four days in 1799, during which time he never left his ship.)

A great deal of period furniture was imported from Britain in Queen Anne, Chippendale and Sheraton styles, which were later reproduced by Menorcan carpenters. The word «mahogany» became *móguini,* and many of the names of carpenters' tools (for example, *escrú, tornescrú, pènals* and *rul*) were taken from the English screw, screwdriver, panels and rule.

Nor did the invaders forget to implant their culinary tastes, and the traditional English puddings became many forms of *greixera dolça* and the beef tea *brou de xenc.* The meat juice or *grevi* and the *mantega anglesa* enrich many Menorcan recipes, and the savoury *piquels* are gherkins and capers in sauce. *Xel* is a flat-sided shell-fish, the festive punch becomes *punx,* and gin, distilled in accordance with old British formulae, the national *aguardiente.*

Children still play *mèrvels* (marbles), tickling and pranks are *joques* (jokes), and they still chase each other shouting *faitim* (fight him). «Fools' Day», which in Spain is the 28th of December, is still celebrated in Menorca, as in England, on the 1st of April, while the *ball des còssil* (dance of the Scots) was probably brought from Scotland by the grenadiers.

But although *stop, plis, in, out, peni* and so on remained in Menorca, the close-knit inhabitants of the island did not go so far as to marry the foreigners. The Sauras, Olives, Olivars, Squellas, Martorells and Quadrados, who were the bailiffs, deputies and councillors of the fourteenth century, remained part of the island's aristocracy, and the Carreras, Orfilas, Sintes, Seguís, Huguets, Rotgers and Pons, to name but a few of those whom we have met in the course of Menorca's history, are still her landowners, notaries, lawyers, doctors, businessmen and artisans.

V

It became obvious by mid 1801 that a treaty between France and England would be timely. France needed to strengthen her army and her fleet, to prepare for a decisive attack against England, the main obstacle to her plans for total hegemony in Europe. On the other hand, in England, which was bearing single-handed the burden of an enormously expensive war, a pacifist trend caused the downfall of Pitt's war government, which was replaced by the conciliatory ministry of the first Viscount Sidmouth: As a consequence, a preliminary peace treaty between the two countries was agreed in London in October 1801, under which the First Consul, Napoleon Bonaparte, recognised the conquest by the English of the Spanish island of Trinidad but gave special importance to restoring Menorca to Spain. For obvious reasons, both strategic and patriotic, cession of the distant and almost uninhabited island off the coast of Venezuela as compared with recovery of the lesser Balearic island, was of outstanding advantage to Charles IV of Spain.

In Menorca, peace rumours were confirmed in the autumn by the arrival of a ship which brought despatches to this effect. Admiral Warren, commander of the English squadron anchored in Mahón, was notified, and on 8th November Sir Henry Cleophane, Governor and Major-General of the British forces in Menorca, received orders to stop the reconstruction works on the demolished castle of San Felipe. From that moment on, the English war supplies stored in Mahón were gradually shipped to Malta.

Under the treaty signed in Amiens on 25th March 1802, France promised to give up Egypt and the kingdom of Naples. Article 11 specified that «English forces shall evacuate Porto Ferraio and in general all ports and islands which they occupy in the Mediterranean or the Adriatic». As a subtle measure, Menorca was included but not specifically mentioned, and subsequent events appear to indicate that England was proposing to remain in that island (as indeed she did in Malta).

The Captain-General of Mallorca, Juan Miguel de Vives, reached Ciudadela on 14th June on a small private *jabeque,* preceded by 600 men of the 2nd Batallion of the Soria regiment who were embarked in merchant ships, also modest in size. He himself was received with full military honours by Colonel Moncrieff, Lieutenant-Governor of the island, and his general-staff by the Bailiff of Mahón and the Ciudadela authorities. Having delivered the keys of the city and after a short exchange of speeches, the Spanish flag was raised and greeted by an 18-gun salute by the cannons of the English grenadiers. Two days later General Vives moved on to Mahón with his troops and on that same day, 16th June, the handing over of San Felipe was solemnised, thus completing the formalities for the transfer of the island to Spanish sovereignty. Thereupon the Spanish, with full pomp and circumstance, bade farewell to General Sir Henry Cleophane, his officers and troops as they embarked in the *'Caesar'* to set sail, with all the British warships anchored in Mahón, for Malta.

Next day Vives presided over a Te Deum of thanksgiving in the parish church of Santa María in Mahón, and in the presence of the civil and ecclesiastical authorities and the people Charles IV was proclaimed for the second time legitimate sovereign of the island of Menorca. The arrival of the new government was celebrated by the Menorcans with the usual fireworks and festivities.

There is one remarkable incident which confirms the supposition that the English endeavoured to postpone the transfer of the island, no doubt hoping to receive last minute orders against it. Hernández Sanz describes the incident as follows: «On the 18th an English ship arrived in full sail, with secret despatches for Cleophane, not knowing that he had already effected the transfer of the island. England had agreed to give up the Mediterranean islands of Elba, Malta and Menorca, with the object of obtaining at all costs the evacuation of Egypt, but on learning that France had abandoned that country before ratification of the Treaty of Amiens, they immediately gave orders to the troops on the islands not on any account to evacuate them. The orders arrived too late, thanks to the energetic action of the Count of Spain, Vives's assistant.» Thus Menorca was returned to Spain despite the fact that England endeavoured to retain the island.

The change of government does not appear to have been very popular with the Menorcans, as the distinguished historian Pedro Riudavets recalls half a century later: «As regards our island, it soon found itself completely bogged down in the complicated Spanish administration reestablished here,» and «Menorca again became completely forgotten by the government.» We do not doubt the patriotism of the islanders to Spain, but it must have been a hard blow to them to exchange, in the words of the chronicler, «the liberal and protective government of the English for the absolute and restrictive Spanish rule», referring to what he calls «the decadent Spain of Charles IV, who only held the title of King insofar as he had been defrauded by the favourite who had dishonoured it».

From then on, with ups and downs in her economy and internal affairs, the island has been incorporated in the historic destiny of Spain, but if the conquests and reconquests have left the traces of their passing, Menorca has always kept her independence of spirit and that most personal and detached temperament which so characterizes her.

Alcaide: the governor of a castle or fort.

Alfaqui: a doctor of, or one wise in, the law.

Almogávares: a kind of light militia chiefly employed in mediaeval Catalonia to make frequent incursions against the Moors.

Almojarife: literally a royal tax-gatherer or customs-house keeper; in this context the head man or governor.

Almoravide: regions of Moslem Spain, named after their conquerors.

Alhóndiga: a public granary.

Bajá: a Turkish title; Pasha.

Bey: a Turkish governor.

Barranco: a deep valley or gorge, typical of the limestone topography of Menorca.

Balandra: a small single-masted vessel or sloop.

Bombarda: bomb-ketch, a ship fitted out to throw bombs and shells.

Brisa: literally a breeze; a large-bellied vessel used for transporting troops.

Brulote: a fire-ship, a vessel loaded with combustible materials.

Cadi: a magistrate in Moorish times.

Cala: a small cove or creek.

Caid: a lord of high official.

Caliphate: the rule of the Caliphs, successors of Mohamed.

Cektina: a small Turkish sailing vessel.

Chalupa: a shallop or launch, a small naval vessel.

Dinar: an ancient Spanish copper coin.

Dromo: a type of galley.

Ducat: an ancient Spanish coin.

Duro: a silver coin, worth ten *reales* silver or twenty *reales* velon.

Emir: a title of dignity among the Turks; prince or lord.

Escudo: literally a shield; crown, a coin of different value in different countries; in ancient Spain a gold coin worth two doubloons or forty *reales,* and a silver coin worth ten *reales.*

Falucho: a small boat with oars and one lateen sail.

Florin: a silver coin, no longer used in Spain.

Fusta: a small vessel with lateen sails.

Galeaza: a type of armed galley.

Germanías: members of a political faction in Valencia and the Balearics in the time of Charles V.

Guangüil: a small fishing boat formerly used in the Balearics.

Infante: a title given to all sons and some nephews of the kings of Spain.

Jabeque: a type of fishing vessel formerly used in Mallorca.

Jeque: a governor or chief among the Moors.

Kabyle: a tribe of Barbary living in the Atlas region.

Leño: literally the trunk of a felled tree; a type of galley; used in poetic sense to mean any type of boat.

Libra: a pound, ancient currency value.

Micer: an ancient title of respect in Aragón.

Moana: a small Turkish sailing vessel.

Mosén: a title given to nobles of second rank and the clergy in the kingdom of Aragon.

Pingüe: a pink, or vessel with a very narrow stern.

Real: a Spanish coin; *real de ocho*: doubloon, piece of eight.

Syndic: a parliamentarian, elected from among men of distinction and given powers of attorney.

Sueldo: an Aragonese coin worth half a real. Also 60 *sueldos* purchased 1 oz. of gold in the thirteenth century. Thus, to give some idea of its equivalent purchasing power in terms of modern currency, the *sueldo* would be worth ten dollars at a time when 1 oz. of gold was priced at 600 dollars.

Taifa: faction or party among the Moors.

Tanca (pl. *tanques*): a field or parcel of land usually enclosed by a dry stone wall. From the Catalan *tancar,* to enclose.

Tarida: a vessel formerly used in the Mediterranean for carrying implements of war.

Tartana: tartan, a small coasting vessel.
Tercio: regiment of infantry.
Visir: the Turkish prime minister.
Wadi: literally a valley; in this context an administrative territory.

Bibliography

ACHARD, Paul: *La vie extraordinaire des Frères Barbe-rousse.* Editions de France, Paris, 1939.

ARMSTRONG, John: *The History of the Island of Minorca.* London, 1752.

BALLESTER, Pedro: *De Re Cibaria.* Ed. Sintes, Barcelona, 1973.

BAULIES, Jordi: *L'illa de Menorca.* Ed. Barcino, Barcelona, 1965.

BENEJAN SAURA, Juan: *Història de Menorca.* Imp. Fábregas, Ciudadela, 1897.

BOFARULL Y BROCA, Antonio de: *Historia crítica de Cataluña.* Ed. Juan Aleu, Barcelona, 1876.

BOSCH FERRER, Rafael: *Contribución al estudio histórico del sitio y saqueo de Mahón por Barbarroja en 1535.* Imp. Moll, Ciudadela, 1934.

CAPMANY, Antoni de: *L'antiga marina de Barcelona.* Ed. Barcino, Barcelona, 1937. («Memorias históricas», Madrid, 1779.)

CARRERO BLANCO, Luis: *Les Baléars pendant la Guerre d'Amérique au XVIII siècle.* Ecole de Guerre Navale, 1933.

CHEVALIER, E.: *Histoire de la marine française.* Paris, 1902.

Chrònica e comentaris del rei En Jaume I. Ed. Aguiló, Barcelona, 1905.

CISTERNE, Raoul de: *La campagne de Minorque.* Calmann Lévy, Paris, 1899.

COTRINA FERRER, José: *El desastre de 1798.* Imp. Balear, Mahón, 1936.

Crònica de Jaume I. Ed. Barcino, Barcelona, 1961.

DELÁS, Ramón de: *The stories of the Golden Farm.* (English language version by Bruce Laurie). Delás, Barcelona, 1979.

DESCLOT, Bernat: *Crònica.* Ed. Barcino, Barcelona, 1949.

FORTESCUE, J. W.: *A History of the British Army*. Mac-Millan & Co., New York, 1906.

FORT I COGUL, Eufemià: *La mort i l'enterrament de Pere el Gran*. Ed. Rafael Dalmau, Barcelona, 1966.

— *Roger de Llúria*. Ed. Rafael Dalmau, Barcelona, 1966.

GOSSE, Philip: *Histoire de la Piraterie*. Ed. Payot, Paris, 1952.

GUILLON, E.: *Port-Mahon*. Ernest Leroux, Paris, 1894.

HERNÁNDEZ SANZ, Francisco: *Compendio de geografía e historia de la isla de Menorca*. Imp. Fábregas y Sintes, Mahón, 1908.

LAFUENTE VANRELL, Lorenzo: *Geografía e historia de Menorca*. Imp. Castillo, Barcelona, 1907.

LEAKE, Stephen Martin: *The life of Sir John Leake*. Navy Research Society, 1820.

LOZOYA, Marqués de: *Historia de España*. Salvat Editores, Barcelona, 1969.

MARTÍ CAMPS, Fernando: *History of Menorca — A brief summary*. (English language version by Bruce Laurie.) Lucia Mora, Alayor, 1979.

— *Iniciació a la història de Menorca*. Ed. Moll, Palma de Mallorca, 1973.

— *Ciutadella de Menorca*. Ed. F. Martí, Barcelona, 1971.

MARTÍNEZ FERRANDO, J. E., SOBREQUÉS, S., BAGUÉ, Enric: *Els descendents de Pere el Gran*. Ed. Vicens-Vives, Barcelona, 1954.

McGUFFIE, T. H.: *The Defence of Minorca 1756*. Journal of the United Service Institution, 1951.

MONLAÜ, Jean: *Les Etats barbaresques*. Presses Universitaires de France, 1964.

MUNTANER, Ramón: *Crónica*. Alianza Editorial, Madrid, 1970.

— *Crònica*. Col·lecció Popular Barcino, Barcelona, 1951.

— *Chronicle*. English translation by Lady Goodenough, London, 1920.

OLEO CUADRADO, Rafael: *Historia de la isla de Menorca*. Imp. Fábregas, Ciudadela, 1874-1876.

PARPAL Y MARQUÉS, Cosme: *La construcción del castillo de San Felipe en el puerto de Mahón*. Ed. Sintes Rotger, Mahón, 1920.

— *La Conquista de Menorca.* Ed. Rafael Dalmau, Barcelona, 1964.

— *La invasión turca de 1558 en Ciudadela de Menorca.* Imp. Casa Provincial de Caridad, Barcelona, 1903.

PONS, Guillermo: *Historia de Menorca.* Ed. Menorca, Mahón, 1971.

PRIEUR, Albert P.: *Les Barberousses.* Arc en Ciel, Paris, 1943.

RAMIS Y RAMIS, Juan: *Varones ilustres de Menorca.* Imp. Serra, Mahón, 1817.

— *Relación de la real proclamación de S. M. el señor rey Don Carlos IV.* Imp. Fábregas, Mahón, 1789.

— *Alonsiada.* Imp. Serra, Mahón, 1818.

RAMIS Y RAMIS, Antonio: *Noticias relativas a la isla de Menorca.* Mahón, 1826.

RICHARD, H. W.: *Papers relating to the loss of Minorca.* The Navy Records Society, 1923.

RIERA ALEMANY, José: *Combate naval de Mahón.* «Revista de Menorca», 1943.

RIUDAVETS TUDURÍ, Pedro: *Fragmentos de la historia de Menorca.* Imp. Fábregas, Mahón, 1882.

— *Historia de la isla de Menorca.* Imp. Fábregas, Mahón, 1885-1888.

RONCIÈRE, Charles de la: *Histoire de la marine française.* Plon, Paris.

RUSSEL, J.: *Nelson and the Hamiltons.* Penguin, London, 1976.

SAINT SIMON, Duc de: *Memoires.* Plèiade, Paris, 1969.

SERRA BELABRE, María Luisa: *Distribución de la tierra después de la conquista de la isla de Menorca.* Casa Cultura, Imp. Sintes, Mahón, 1967.

SOLDEVILA, Fernando: *Vida de Jaume I el Conqueridor.* Ed. Aedos, Barcelona, 1958.

— *Vida de Pere el Gran.* Ed. Aedos, Barcelona, 1963.

— *Pere II el Gran.* Ed. Barcino, 1953.

— *L'almirall Ramon Marquet.* Ed. Barcino, Barcelona, 1953.

— *Els almogàvers.* Ed. Barcino, Barcelona, 1952.

— *Història de Catalunya.* Ed. Alpha, Barcelona, 1963.

— *Historia de España.* Ed. Ariel, Barcelona, 1954.

TARTAVULL ESTRADA, Bartolomé: *Reconquista de Menorca por las armas católicas en 1782.* «Revista de la Historia Militar», Madrid, 1958.

TASIS, Rafael: *La vida de Ramón Muntaner.* Ed. Rafael Dalmau, Barcelona, 1964.

VICTORY, Antonio: *Gobierno de Sir Richard Kane en Menorca.* Imp. Sintes, Mahón, 1924.

VILA, Gabriel: *Mossèn Bartolomé Argimbau.* Ciudadela, 1905.

Memoire of the life and actions of General William Blakeney. London and Dublin, 1756.

Dictionary of National Biography. London, 1889.

Journal of the Society for Army Historical Research, Vol. XXVIII.

Les occupations militaires de l'isle de Minorque. «Revue Historique de l'Armée», 1957.

Bibliographie Universelle. Madame Desplaces, Paris.